# THE ARGENTINE FIGHT FOR
# THE FALKLANDS

# PEN & SWORD MILITARY CLASSICS

W e hope you enjoy your Pen and Sword Military Classic. The series is designed to give readers quality military history at affordable prices. Below is a list of the titles that are planned for 2003. Pen and Sword Classics are available from all good bookshops. If you would like to keep in touch with further developments in the series, including information on the Classics Club, then please contact Pen and Sword at the address below.

## 2003 List

## PEN AND SWORD BOOKS LTD

*47 Church Street • Barnsley • South Yorkshire • S70 2AS*

**Tel: 01226 734555 • 734222**

E-mail: enquiries@pen-and-sword.co.uk • **Website:** www.pen-and-sword.co.uk

# MARTIN MIDDLEBROOK

# THE ARGENTINE FIGHT FOR THE
# FALKLANDS

PEN & SWORD MILITARY CLASSICS

First published as *The Fight for the 'Malvinas': The Argentine Forces in the Falklands War*
in 1989 by Viking

Published in 2003, in this format, by
**PEN & SWORD MILITARY CLASSICS**
*an imprint of*
Pen & Sword Books Limited
47 Church Street
Barnsley
S. Yorkshire
S70 2AS

Cover illustration:
*Argentine Prisoners of War.*
Courtesy of the Ministry of Defence.

ISBN 0 85052 978 6

A CIP record for this book is
available from the British Library

Printed in England by
CPI UK

# Contents

# List of Photographs

1. Mass on board the landing ship *Cabo San Antonio*, Sunday, 28 March 1982.
2. Raising the Argentine flag at Stanley.
3. Rear-Admiral Büsser, General García and Rear-Admiral Allara in Stanley on 2 April.
4. Argentine officer with captured Royal Marine officers on 2 April.
5. Captured Royal Marines and sailors.
6. Argentine Amphibious Commandos at Government House.
7. An Amtrac patrols the streets of Stanley, 2 April.
8. Argentine trucks, Amtracs and infantry, Stanley, 4 April.
9. Lieutenant-Commander Pedro Giachino.
10. Funeral service at Puerto Belgrano for Pedro Giachino.
11. Argentine president General Leopoldo Galtieri.
12. Excited soldiers off to the war.
13. Jubilant Argentines.
14. First view of the 'Malvinas' by troop transport aircraft.
15. A confident army unit just after landing at Stanley airfield.
16. Argentine Air Force officers map reading at their base on the Falklands, 14 April.
17. Argentine troops at an encampment.
18. The aircraft-carrier *Veinticinco de Mayo*.
19. Neptune aircraft which guided in the Super Étendards which attacked HMS *Sheffield* on 4 May.
20. The standard Argentine naval attack aircraft, the Skyhawk A-4Q.
21. Tracker recce aircraft which discovered the location of the British task force (see map on page 85).

The author and publishers are grateful to the following for permission to reproduce photographs:

Editorial Atlantido, 10, 13, 14, 15, 25, 38, 45
Rear-Admiral Büsser, 1-6
Argentine Navy, 9
Topham Picture Library, 7, 8, 11, 12, 16, 17, 24, 26-7, 36
Brigadier-General Jofre, 33
Captain Alimonda, 18-21, 34-5, 39, 40, 44
Captain Bonzo, 22-3
Ministry of Defence, 28, 32, 37, 41-3, 46-9
Captain Dell'Elicine, 29-31

# List of Maps

*Maps by D.M.D. Ltd., Oxford from preliminary drawings by Mary Middlebrook*

# Introduction

I had to wait five years to write this book.

When the Falklands War of 1982 ended, I was anxious to cover that episode of history in the same way as I had written all my earlier books – as impartially as possible and describing the experiences of both sides. But the Argentine Government refused the visa application I made, and my first Falklands book, *Operation Corporate*, which was revised and reissued as a Penguin paperback in 1987 under the new title of *Task Force*, contained no more than a few fragments of Argentine material. I researched and interviewed among the British units involved in the war and also travelled to the Falklands to interview the islanders and study the battlefields, but I always regarded that book as incomplete, and it remained my ambition to visit Argentina and interview the commanders and the men who fought in the Falklands. That ambition was fulfilled in 1987 when I was granted a visa, the first to be granted to a British military writer. This book is the result.

When I arrived in Buenos Aires it became clear that I was being handled as a specific operation, mainly by the Argentine Navy, which made every effort to grant my interview requests. I was even flown to the main naval base at Puerto Belgrano where a team of two interpreters assisted in what were the most intense three days of interviewing I have ever done, one day being spent with the naval air arm, another with the marines and the third with ships' officers and crew members. I was free to ask any question I wanted to, and the answers were freely given; they were also honestly given – after nearly twenty years of interviewing, I could tell that. No initial attempt was made to convert me to the Argentine view of the sovereignty of the Falkland Islands until a carefully arranged meeting right at the end of my visit pressed me on the subject. I stressed that I was a military historian, not a political one, and stated that my book would confine itself to the military story and would take a neutral line on the sovereignty issue despite my personal views which did not coincide with theirs.

The Army also provided considerable help, with a retired senior officer who had served in the Falklands, Brigadier-General Oscar Jofre, taking over the task of finding the men I wanted to meet. Again, as long as these men were available, they usually appeared for interview. Brigadier-General Jofre managed to find officers from every major unit involved in the Falklands fighting. I was also free to make appointments with any retired officers or released conscripts I could find. The Argentine Air Force gave no help, despite repeated requests. No reason was given for this refusal, which was both frustrating and disappointing. But of all the Argentine armed services, this loss of coverage is the least important. Many books have been published about the 1982 air operations, and I did at least have the benefit of the interviews with the naval pilots. I was also fortunate in being given the English translation of many personal contributions which an Argentine Air Force pilot had collected from his fellow pilots for his own book and this has filled that gap.

I was fortunate in being able to meet most of the men involved in the major events of the war: the admirals who planned and carried out the original landing in the Falklands and the capture of South Georgia and the later naval operations which resulted in the loss of the *Belgrano*; the captain and several officers and petty officers of the *Belgrano*; the naval pilots who hit the *Sheffield* with an Exocet and sank the *Ardent*; the commander of the army unit which fought the first land battle at Goose Green; the general responsible for the defence of Stanley; and many officers and ordinary soldiers who fought in the final battles on the hills around Stanley. I carried out sixty-two interviews in all. I did not meet Galtieri and the other members of the junta; they were all in military detention. I did not meet Brigadier-General Menéndez but I have had his personal memoirs translated and I had a useful meeting with his chief-of-staff.

I was treated at all times with considerable politeness and helpfulness. There was much professional interest in details of the British units against which the Argentines had been directly opposed during the war. Several men asked to be put in touch with their opposite British company or platoon commanders. 'When will we be able to meet?' I was sometimes asked. Very few had any regrets about the war. Most were proud to have fought in 1982, and the impression was received that many would be willing to fight again. Those men who were still serving could easily be identified in a crowd; the blue-and-white Malvinas campaign ribbon is the only one worn on the everyday uniforms of Argentine servicemen. The greatest problem was the unwillingness of so many Argentines to accept the truth of wartime incidents when units made mistaken or exaggerated claims of damage inflicted on British forces or when the junta deliberately lied about those actions. Post-war Argentine books seemed determined to perpetuate the mistakes and exaggerations rather than to establish the truth. A combination of national pride, unwillingness to accept the scale of the 1982 defeat and perhaps an unfamiliarity in examining recent military history – of which British writers have had far too much opportunity – seems to have prevented most of the Argentine writers from searching for the truth, however embarrassing that truth may turn out to be. The difficulty of dealing with wartime myths was my greatest problem, both when interviewing in Argentina and in the subsequent writing of this book.

I would like to mention two small points which arise over the difficulties of language. I tried, in this English version, not to use any of the Spanish-language ranks used by Argentine servicemen. Naval and army ranks were not difficult to translate into easily understandable equivalents, but some air force ranks were difficult. For example, a *vicecomodoro* looks incongruous when translated as 'wing commander', and I have decided to leave some ranks in their original form. There was also the difficulty over the word 'Malvinas', the name which all Argentines use for the Falklands whether they are speaking in Spanish or English. I will be using the term 'Falklands' in the ordinary text of the book but, when quoting directly the accounts of Argentine contributors, I will use their own term, 'Malvinas', to preserve the sentiment they hold so strongly. I cannot stress too much the deep and almost universal belief of the Argentine people that the Falklands should be theirs; this will help to explain the background to the military story which I am about to tell.

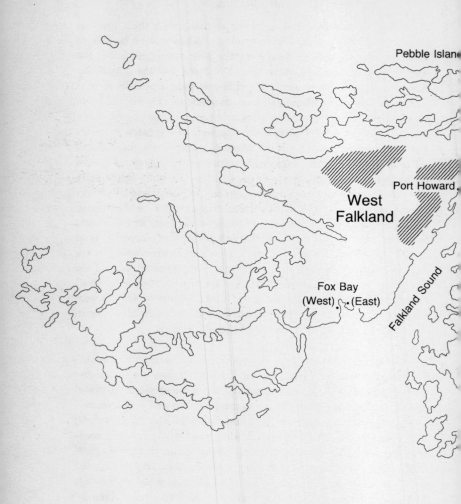

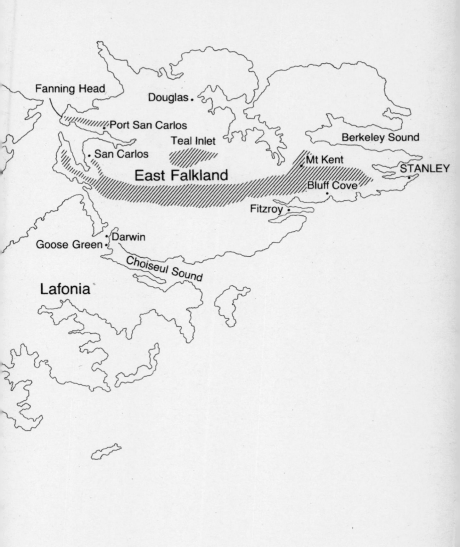

Fanning Head

Douglas .

Port San Carlos

Teal Inlet

. San Carlos

**East Falkland**

Berkeley Sound

Mt Kent

**STANLEY**

Bluff Cove

Fitzroy .

Goose Green . . Darwin

Choiseul Sound

**Lafonia**

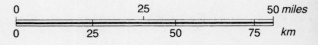

| 0 | | 25 | | 50 *miles* |
|---|---|---|---|---|
| 0 | 25 | 50 | 75 | *km* |

# 1 · The Year of the Malvinas

On Tuesday 15 December 1981, Admiral Jorge Anaya flew from Buenos Aires to the main Argentine naval base at Puerto Belgrano, 280 miles away to the south-west. He went there to perform the official installation of Vice-Admiral Juan Lombardo as the new Chief of Naval Operations; it was a routine change of post. After the ceremony, Anaya surprised Lombardo by quietly telling him to prepare a plan to occupy the Falkland Islands: to 'take them but not necessarily to keep them' are the words Lombardo remembers. The conversation was a brief one, and after stressing the need for absolute secrecy Anaya returned to Buenos Aires.

Anaya was the Commander-in-Chief of the Argentine Navy and a member of the military junta which had ruled Argentina since 1976. His visit to Puerto Belgrano took place only a few days after General Leopoldo Galtieri became President, replacing General Roberto Viola, whose health was deteriorating. It has been suggested that Admiral Anaya, longest serving member of the junta, made the recovery of the Falklands a condition of his support for Galtieri as President. Certainly, the character and attitude of Anaya would be crucial in what was to come. Fellow officers describe him as a 'solitary, severe, self-disciplined person, quite unlike the normal naval officer'. He was an old school friend of Galtieri, that bond being the basis of a friendship between naval and army officer not often seen in Argentina. Anaya had been Naval Attaché in London in the early 1970s during a period of weak leadership in British politics. He knew little of Margaret Thatcher. He was an ardent 'Malvinist', but the suggestion that he made the recovery of the islands a condition of his support for the new President is not supported by senior Argentine admirals. They believe that when Galtieri became President he asked

Anaya and Brigadier Lami Dozo, the Air Force member of the junta, what future plans the old junta had been developing and what suggestions they could make for the new presidency. Policies were discussed for various sectors of government; the head of the list for foreign policy was the resolution of the 'Malvinas problem'. The vital role for Admiral Anaya was that the use of his Navy would be essential if the islands were to be occupied and held. If Anaya was not whole-heartedly behind the endeavour, then little could be achieved. But Anaya was enthusiastic, and his orders to Admiral Lombardo in the last days of 1981 set in train that tragic sequence of events.

It must be stressed, however, that the plan to use armed force was no more than a back-up to a forcefully renewed diplomatic initiative. January 1983 would see the 150th anniversary of the removal of an Argentine governor and settlement from the Falklands by the Royal Navy and the establishment of the British settlement. The junta determined that the islands would be recovered by one means or another before that anniversary; 1982 was to be 'the year of the Malvinas'. A renewed round of negotiations with the British was due to start in February; these and the harnessing of world opinion would be vigorously pressed. But, if the diplomatic offensive failed, then the junta wanted a plan ready in case conditions developed which might seem favourable for military action. Rear-Admiral Gualter Allara, the Commander-in-Chief Fleet, who would soon become involved in the planning, sums up the situation at the turn of the year:

> It was only a contingency plan. The mood was dictated by the absolute lack of progress in negotiations. It was believed, particularly in the Navy, that a time would come when conditions would arise which would require something more active than negotiations. There had been plans in the past – some only academic, such as in our War College – but at that time, at the end of five years of fruitless negotiations, we had become very frustrated. The political belief was that it would be necessary to put some dynamism into those negotiations. For that reason a plan to recover the Malvinas was put in hand. But I must stress again that it was all of an absolutely tentative nature at that stage.

Vice-Admiral Lombardo soon decided that he needed some clarification of his orders. One point that emerges from his description of the next moves is that Admiral Anaya, at least at this time, was not necessarily determined upon the *retention* of the Falklands, probably hoping that the taking of the islands followed by a voluntary withdrawal would be sufficient to force a conclusion to the diplomatic negotiations:

Soon after receiving my first order, I flew to Buenos Aires to meet Admiral Anaya again and ask for clarification. I set out my questions in a handwritten document to make sure that they were 'on the record', but no copies were made. I asked these questions:

Was the operation to be purely naval, or joint with other services?

Was the intention to take and keep the islands, or take them and then hand them over to someone else, and, if so, would this be an Argentine force or a world force, that is the United Nations?

Could he guarantee that the secret nature of the planning be maintained?

These were the answers I was given:

It was to be a joint operation, but no one else had yet been informed. I didn't know at that time whether Galtieri and Lami Dozo were aware of Admiral Anaya's orders to me, but it was confirmed a few days later that they were.

I was to plan a take-over; but not to prepare the defence of the islands afterwards.

About secrecy, he said that I would only be working with three other admirals – Allara, Büsser of the Marines and García Bol of the Naval Air Arm; these were all near to me at Puerto Belgrano.

I started talks with those three, and they all asked the same or similar questions. So I went back to Buenos Aires to insist that, if the operation was to be joint, co-operation with the other services would be essential. Anaya agreed that General García of the Army was in mind but had not yet been informed. He repeated that it was a Navy task – to take over the Malvinas;

what followed was for the junta to decide. They did not think that there would be a military reaction by the British.

The second main problem was the need to maintain secrecy, because if the British discovered our plans they could cause our entire naval operations to fail just by placing one nuclear-propelled submarine in the area. In 1977, when Anaya was Commander-in-Chief Fleet and I was in command of submarines, we were buying some German submarines. Anaya asked me if those new submarines could be used in the anti-submarine role against British nuclear submarines. I was sure that he was thinking of the Malvinas even then. He even showed me a note he had written to the Commander-in-Chief of the Navy at that time, saying that something should be done about the Malvinas.

The other armed services soon became involved. Their work was overseen by a Comisión de Trabajo – a Working Party – which held its first meeting at Army Headquarters in the Liberatador Building in Buenos Aires in mid-January 1982. The three members were Vice-Admiral Lombardo, General Osvaldo García of the Army and Brigadier-General Siegfriedo Plessl of the Air Force. The Air Force would play only a very small role at this stage, and its representative will not figure in this story again, but General García is an important figure. He was the commander of V Corps, with headquarters in Bahía Blanca not far from the naval base at Puerto Belgrano. His corps area covered the whole of the southern part of Argentina; the only army units to be included in the early plans would be from his command, and all naval and air preparations would also take place in that area. This concentration of activity in the south, remote from the capital of Buenos Aires and the more populated north, would be a valuable aid to the maintenance of secrecy.

The three officers each appointed small working parties to carry forward the planning process. Admiral Anaya's initial plan to take the islands but not necessarily to stay or to defend them was abandoned at an early stage, and a period of permanent garrisoning by Argentinian troops was envisaged while the full civil process of what the Argentinians viewed as the reintegration of the islands into the homeland after the 150-year gap took place. A date of 15 September

was given for the completion of the planning. No move was envisaged
before that date for these reasons: Most of the year would be devoted
to allowing the diplomatic offensive to proceed. The worst of the
midwinter weather would be over by September. HMS *Endurance*,
the Antarctic patrol vessel, would have been withdrawn under planned British naval cuts. The training of the army conscripts, who
were taken in early each year for their period of service, would be
well advanced. It was still expected that the British would make no
military response to a landing, but, if they did, the re-equipment of
the Naval Air Arm's main strike unit with fourteen French-built
Super Étendard aircraft and fifteen Exocet anti-ship missiles was
expected to be complete by September.

The planning went ahead, steadily but without urgency. The
main landings would be carried out by the Navy and its marines. A
small army contingent would be carried with the landing force, and a
full regiment of infantry would take over as soon as the small British
Royal Marine force had been overcome. The Argentine Air Force
would only be asked to provide some transport aircraft. Much of the
early planning involved Rear-Admiral Carlos Büsser, the Commander of Marines; he was also a keen 'Malvinist'. He received his
orders on 29 January and, by 2 February, had set up a five-strong
'Landing Force Cell' in a small office at Puerto Belgrano. A second
naval planning unit was soon established under Vice-Admiral Lombardo, with just two other officers to produce the ship-support plan.
One officer from Naval Intelligence worked in both cells.

The 2nd Marine Infantry Battalion was chosen to form the main
landing force and this unit started carrying out amphibious exercises
on a stretch of coast on the Valdés peninsula in Patagonia where
there was a beach which resembled the planned landing beach on
the coast near the Falklands town of Stanley [1] and a network of
tracks similar to those linking the beach with the airport at Stanley
and with the town. There was, however, no town at the exercise
area; that might have resembled the Falklands too much and given
away the game. The 2nd Marines practised their landing several
times in February and March, but only three officers from the

---

[1] There is some confusion over the names Stanley and Port Stanley. The postal authorities use
'Port Stanley', but the official title is merely 'Stanley', which will be used in this book. The
Argentines always called it Puerto Argentino.

battalion knew that they were rehearsing a possible landing in the Falklands.

The basic landing plan was ready by the third week in February and was presented to the junta on 9 March. The junta accepted it and forwarded it to Admiral Suárez del Cerro, the Chief of the joint Armed Forces Headquarters, whose duty it was to incorporate this military plan into the overall 'national plan' which was moving forward into 1982 with the recovery of the Falklands as one of its main objectives. Vice-Admiral Büsser concludes: 'We were told to be prepared to continue the planning right up to the last three months of the year. I have to stress that it was a truly national plan, not just a military one, with the main emphasis always on recovering the islands by negotiations.'

## 2 · Crisis in South Georgia

In October 1978, Constantino Davidoff, an Argentine businessman, asked the Edinburgh-based firm of Christian Salvesen whether it would sell the scrap material in four abandoned whaling stations in South Georgia – three at Leith, Husvik and Stromness, which were all grouped together in Stromness Bay but came under the general name of Leith, and a fourth at Grytviken which was twenty miles distant. An agreement was signed in September 1979 under which Sr Davidoff could dismantle and take away the buildings and equipment at the three stations at Leith, but not the one at Grytviken. Davidoff agreed to pay just over £100,000 and to remove the material before the end of March 1982. Ironically, the stations at Husvik and Grytviken had been Argentine owned until their recent purchase by Salvesen's. But Davidoff found it difficult to complete his arrangements in this remote part of the world and had to ask for an extension. His working expedition was not ready to leave Buenos Aires until 11 March 1982, and Salvesen's agreed that his dismantling party could remain at Leith for the remainder of that southern winter but under several conditions: that he provide his party with all necessary supplies and power, that he would not make use of Salvesen's facilities at Grytviken and that the party comply with the British regulations while in South Georgia.

The British Government claimed sovereignty over South Georgia and had maintained a presence there since 1909. South Georgia was classed as a 'Dependency' of the Falkland Islands; its local regulations were handled by a magistrate who was a member of the British Antarctic Survey station at Grytviken. Argentina also claimed South Georgia as its territory and found the British regulations irksome.

When Sr Davidoff visited South Georgia in December 1981 to

carry out a reconnaissance of the scrap material he had purchased, he failed to report at Grytviken. When he returned to Buenos Aires to prepare his main expedition, the British Embassy there stressed that the regulations must be complied with on a future visit.

Davidoff's working party which left Buenos Aires on 11 March 1982 sailed in the *Bahía Buen Suceso*; this was a transport ship of 5,000 tons, able to carry eighty passengers as well as cargo. It was owned by the Argentine Navy and was used as a naval transport when so required, but much of its time was spent on commercial charter work, its usual 'beat' being the long coastal run down to the extreme south of Argentina; the ship also made one voyage each summer taking tourists to visit the Argentine scientific bases in Antarctica. When the ship was hired out to Davidoff and sailed from Buenos Aires, its captain and crew were all members of the Argentine mercantile marines; there were no Argentine Navy personnel on board. The ship carried Davidoff's equipment and the forty-one civilian workers of his party; it also carried some general cargo for delivery to the Argentine port of Ushuaia on its return voyage. Ushuaia, in Tierra del Fuego, is the southernmost town in the world.

Sr Davidoff was not on board the *Bahía Buen Suceso* when it sailed from Buenos Aires; one of his engineers would be in charge of the dismantling crew. Davidoff had reported the sailing of the expedition to the British Embassy in Buenos Aires but had not had time to obtain a landing permit, agreeing instead that a representative of his party would report at the British Antarctic Survey base at Grytviken, which was twenty miles away from Leith. The Embassy made no objection to this arrangement. The ship's master, Captain Osvaldo Niella, continues the story:

It was a normal voyage with exceptionally fine weather except for fog in the last twenty-four hours or so. We arrived off Stromness Bay in the night of the 16th of March but waited for dawn because of the fog before going into the bay and on to Leith. Then we had to repair the old whaling pier carefully before we could anchor. It took the workers two days to do this and then another two days to unload all their equipment. There was no one else there.

Davidoff's senior engineer did not go around the coast to obtain his landing permit from the British at Grytviken during this period. One of the British scientists, out on a field survey, came within sight of Leith on the 19th, the third day of the Argentine presence, saw an Argentine flag flying and heard shots being fired, both items being contrary to local British regulations. I asked Captain Niella about this:

> Yes, the workers fixed up a flagpole, only an improvised one three or four metres high, and put up an Argentine flag. It was nothing to do with me. The men seemed very pleased to be there. They would be making good money; also, one feels a bit more patriotic when one is away from home, particularly when one has arrived in a place which you feel belongs to your country. They were working hard during the day and had a bit of a party at night, with some drink and tango music under that flagpole.
>
> As for the rifle firing – yes, that was probably members of my crew. They often used to go ashore sport shooting when we were at Ushuaia, and this was an even more remote place. I don't think anyone thought about the British regulations.

The British magistrate at Grytviken reported the Argentine infringements by radio to Rex Hunt, the British Governor in the Falklands. Hunt replied, on the 20th, telling the scientists that they were to contact the Argentine party by radio, insisting that the flag should be lowered and that someone must come to Grytviken and obtain a landing permit. The flag was lowered, but no one came to Grytviken. Next day, with all Davidoff's equipment ashore, together with sufficient food and supplies for the winter, the *Bahía Buen Suceso* departed. Contrary to some accounts, she did not take any of the scrap-metal workers with her; they were all left at Leith. The ship set course for Ushuaia, her captain and crew unaware of the intense diplomatic activity caused by the visit.

The matter ceased to be a local one on 20 March, the day before the *Bahía Buen Suceso* sailed from Leith. Governor Hunt signalled London, reporting the incidents and the continuing failure of the Argentines to complete the required formalities at Grytviken, and also saying, incorrectly, that Argentine military personnel were ashore, as well as stating his belief that the Argentine Navy was using the scrap-metal party to establish a presence on South Georgia. The British Government, through the Foreign and Commonwealth Office, sent a formal protest to the Argentine Government, asking that the *Bahía Buen Suceso* return and remove the entire Argentine party; if this was not done, 'the British Government would have to take whatever action seemed necessary'. That same day, H M S *Endurance*, with twenty-two Royal Marines on board, sailed from Stanley, its departure being observed by Argentine airline officials there and reported to Argentina. That demand from London and the sailing of the *Endurance* escalated the affair to a completely new level; either the British would have to climb down or the Argentines would have to submit to the British demands. It was a crucial day.

The following day, 21 March, the Argentine Government informed London that it assumed that all of the Argentine workmen had left when the *Bahía Buen Suceso* sailed that morning. The temperature cooled, and *Endurance* turned back towards the Falklands. But, on the 22nd, the British on South Georgia reported that the workers were still present and that no immigration document had yet been completed. On 23 March, Lord Carrington, the British Foreign Secretary, sent an even stronger message to Buenos Aires. If the *Bahía Buen Suceso* was not ordered back to remove the working party at Leith, the Royal Marine party would do so forcibly on the *Endurance*. *Endurance* was ordered to change course again and made for South Georgia. She reached Grytviken on 24 March and was ordered to stand by.

Far from acceding to the British demands, however, the Argentines were responding with a military move of their own. The naval vessel *Bahía Paraíso*, part of the Argentine Navy's Antarctic Squadron, had been carrying out a routine training exercise near the South Orkney Islands. The Carrington ultimatum of 23 March was more than the junta could stomach. *Bahía Paraíso* was ordered to the Falklands. *Endurance* put her twenty-two Royal Marines ashore at Grytviken on 24 March. The *Bahía Paraíso* could only scrape together a smaller party – fourteen men; the ship arrived off Leith late on the 25th and put this party of armed Argentines ashore the following day.

(There have been some British misconceptions over the size of the

Argentine party put ashore at Leith, the group often being described as 'a large party of marines' with the figure of 100 being quoted. The fourteen men were actually a mixed party of sailors and marines, the marines being members of the Buzos Tácticos underwater demolition team unit. The rank of the commander, Alfredo Astiz, is also erroneously reported as 'lieutenant-commander' or 'captain'; he was actually a *teniente de navío*, equivalent only to a British naval lieutenant.)

The events at South Georgia can be left at this stage, with two armed parties of men ashore at points twenty miles apart. Grave decisions were being taken elsewhere, and much larger forces would soon be on the move. One of the strongest feelings I brought back from my visit to Argentina was that the British mishandled the incident. Captain Niella of the *Bahía Buen Suceso* may have been cleverly misleading me, but I have been interviewing people like him for nearly twenty years and I believe his description of events was a sincere one.

He painted a scene of a purely commercial voyage, without the presence of Sr Davidoff who should have briefed his foreman more carefully. The affair of the flag appeared to be no more than a piece of light-hearted relaxation; it was lowered when requested. The firing of shots did take place and, admittedly, was repeated after the first British protest. (The deer being shot had originally been introduced to the island for sport-shooting purposes.) The sticking point was the British insistence that someone go round to Grytviken and obtain a landing permit. That entailed a forty-mile round journey by sea. The *Bahía Buen Suceso* was only present for four days, days during which everyone was working hard. There was a storm during that period. The Davidoff party was left with only two L C V P landing craft after the *Bahía Buen Suceso* sailed, which was before the strongest of the British demands was made. Getting a piece of paper at Grytviken may not have seemed the most important thing at that time.

Captain Niella was, admittedly, vague in answering my questions about the radio messages, mentioning the later loss of his papers when his ship was damaged in the Falklands fighting and stressing the fact that everyone was very busy at the time and that there was a storm and poor radio reception. 'For me,' he stressed, 'it was just an innocent voyage, like many others I did.'

Captain Niella and the other Argentines on South Georgia could have been unwitting pawns in an Argentine effort to dent the British established sovereignty in this area. But the provoking of a crisis so early in the year conflicted with the timetable of the Argentine 'national plan' being developed. I cannot be certain that the crisis was not deliberately engineered but I do not think it was. I think it was a normal commercial expedition, which, through a combination of practical difficulties and Argentine irritation with British regulations, was met by a British over-reaction. It is easy to be wise in retrospect, but did the reluctance of a busy Argentine foreman to travel forty miles to obtain a piece of paper really constitute such a threat to British sovereignty? The British Antarctic Survey team had obvious means of mobility, because they were keeping Leith under observation. Could not one of the team have quietly taken the document down to Leith and asked for a signature? It was unlikely to have been refused.

## 3 · The First Steps to War

The dispatch of the *Bahía Paraíso* and her small landing party to South Georgia showed that the junta was not prepared to see Argentine workmen forcibly removed from Leith by British Royal Marines. The decision to send the *Bahía Paraíso* was taken on 23 March, the day of what the Argentines call the 'Carrington ultimatum'. Not only were the junta members not prepared to be humiliated over South Georgia, they would actually use the crisis as an excuse to occupy the Falklands and hope that world opinion would approve their action. No better opportunity to regain the Falklands might occur. The carefully planned long-term diplomatic offensive would be abandoned and the world be presented with a *fait accompli* instead. That same day, 23 March, the two groups which had been planning the long-term military operation were asked how quickly an immediate plan could be produced. Rear-Admiral Büsser, who would be the commander of the landing force, says:

> In the evening of the 23rd, we were asked how quickly we could bring the plan together. All the people involved were near to each other. Admirals Lombardo and Allara and myself were all at Puerto Belgrano; General García was at V Corps Headquarters at Bahía Blanca, only 37 kilometres away.
>
> I immediately ordered an increase in my staff, and we worked all through that night and very hard in the next two days. We gave an answer to the junta on the 25th; I think Admiral Lombardo went to Buenos Aires and told them that the decision was that it would be possible to land on the Malvinas on the 1st of April. The South Georgia operation was planned for the same day. We had to be ready to sail on the 28th.

The step-by-step escalation towards war proceeded. The junta accepted Admiral Lombardo's timetable and immediately ordered that active preparations go ahead for both a landing in the Falklands and the dispatch of a reinforcement for the small party from the *Bahía Paraíso* which arrived off South Georgia that day. The Falklands plan provided for the capture of Stanley, with its airport and Royal Marine barracks, and of the next largest settlement in the Falklands, Goose Green. The fourteen-strong party from the *Bahía Paraíso* was ordered to go ashore at Leith immediately, to give protection to the Argentine workers there; and a frigate, the *Guerrico*, was to be dispatched to reinforce Lieutenant Astiz with further marines and to capture Grytviken, where the only permanent British presence in South Georgia was located.

(It is a misconception that two other ships, the Argentinian frigates *Drummond* and *Gránville*, sailed south to intervene in South Georgia, but this is not correct. Admiral Anaya did send a signal, ordering these two ships south, but Vice-Admiral Lombardo objected, saying that he needed them for the main Falklands operation. The British picked up the original signal and assumed that *Drummond* and *Gránville* were heading towards South Georgia, but the two ships were never detached from the main Argentine naval force. These ships, together with the *Guerrico*, are classed as 'corvettes' in the Argentine Navy, but they would be called frigates in most other navies, and it will be more useful to refer to them as such here.)

The operations being planned would be almost entirely carried out by the Argentine Navy. This was partly dictated by the amphibious nature of the operations, just as the later dispatch of the British task force would be commanded and controlled by the Royal Navy, with the core of the British fighting units being provided by the Royal Marines. But, in the case of the Argentine operations now developing, there was also the exceptional enthusiasm of their naval commanders for the repossession of the Falklands and the removal of that contested British sovereignty in the South Atlantic which came between Argentina and her ambitions in Antarctica.

The plans were made. Figure 1 shows the organization table for the operations. But the plan was developed beyond the initial phase. The marine landing force in the Falklands was to be withdrawn as soon as it secured its various objectives – hopefully within hours of

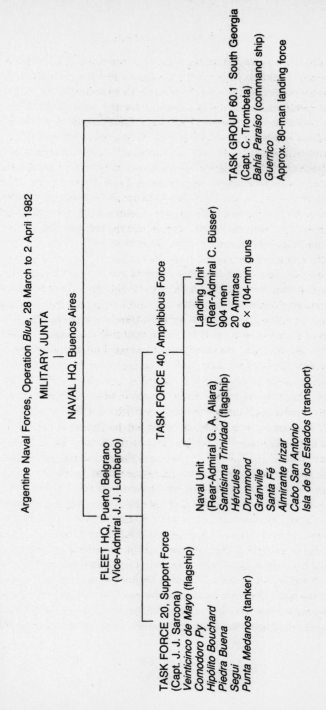

Argentine Naval Forces, Operation *Blue*, 28 March to 2 April 1982

MILITARY JUNTA

NAVAL HQ, Buenos Aires

FLEET HQ, Puerto Belgrano
(Vice-Admiral J. J. Lombardo)

**TASK FORCE 20, Support Force**
(Capt. J. J. Sarcona)
*Veinticinco de Mayo* (flagship)
*Comodoro Py*
*Hipólito Bouchard*
*Piedra Buena*
*Segui*
*Punta Medanos* (tanker)

**TASK FORCE 40, Amphibious Force**

Naval Unit
(Rear-Admiral G. A. Allara)
*Santísima Trinidad* (flagship)
*Hércules*
*Drummond*
*Granville*
*Santa Fé*
*Almirante Irizar*
*Cabo San Antonio*
*Isla de los Estados* (transport)

Landing Unit
(Rear-Admiral C. Büsser)
904 men
20 Amtracs
6 × 104-mm guns

**TASK GROUP 60.1  South Georgia**
(Capt. C. Trombeta)
*Bahia Paraíso* (command ship)
*Guerrico*
Approx. 80-man landing force

landing – and was to be replaced by an infantry regiment and an engineer company of the Army brought into Stanley Airport by air. That aspect of the plan finally answered the question Vice-Admiral Lombardo had asked the previous December when Admiral Anaya first ordered him to start thinking of a Falklands operation. This landing, if it went ahead, was to be no symbolic affair followed by a dignified withdrawal as part of a diplomatic offensive. It was to be a full-scale occupation. It was hoped that the British would not respond, but if the British did decide to come down to the South Atlantic with a military force, then the Argentinians would have either to withdraw ignominiously or to fight it out. The Argentine Army as well as the Navy would be deeply committed and the Air Force partially so, with transport aircraft immediately and maybe combat units later if the British did respond.

But the decision to dispatch the fleet was not yet confirmed and, when it was, there would be the opportunity for a recall if there was a change of mind. Vice-Admiral Lombardo remembers that 'right up to the last days of March, we were asked three or four times what was the latest date it could all be cancelled. We had been in dispute with Chile for ten years and had often sailed on operations like this but then been withdrawn.'

The Argentine ships and units involved had little more than two days to make their preparations. Those days of Friday 26 and Saturday 27 March were quiet ones diplomatically, with the centre of attention still on South Georgia. The helicopters of HMS *Endurance* were watching the *Bahía Paraíso*, but the hoped-for signal that the ship had removed the remaining Argentines at Leith did not reach London. Lord Carrington and his advisers were coming to the conclusion that *Endurance* should go in and remove the Argentines forcibly. The British did not realize that a fourteen-strong armed party was now ashore with the scrap-metal workers.

Just about every serviceable warship in the Argentine Navy would sail on the operation being prepared. The aircraft carrier *Veinticinco de Mayo* would be the flagship of Task Force 20, which would give distant support to the landing operation. It is difficult to escape the conclusion that Task Force 20 sailed mainly for purposes of prestige and display; there was little operational requirement for these ships.

The only British ship likely to be encountered was the *Endurance* with two 20-mm Bofors guns and two light Wasp helicopters. The next nearest British units were the small garrison and one ship at Belize in Central America and a group of warships exercising in the Atlantic off Morocco. A senior Argentine army officer, who served in the Falklands and became a prisoner of war, made this comment to me:

> That large amphibious operation was not necessary. Three transport aircraft full of troops could have done it easily, but they sent the whole Fleet. The whole thing was a crazy expedition by demented people. It was stupid to offend a big country like Britain and to do it without the support of world opinion. They went with that big display of ships and forces – all of it unnecessary.

The actual landing force was designated Task Force 40. Its ships were under Rear-Admiral Gualter Allara, a short, cheerful officer, who had been Naval Attaché in London the previous year. His ships were two Type 42 destroyers, two frigates, a submarine, a polar vessel, a transport and the most important ship of all, the amphibious landing ship *Cabo San Antonio*. The most modern ships of the Argentine Navy were in this force. The two Type 42 destroyers were of British design; *Hércules* had been built in Britain and the *Santísima Trinidad* under licence in Argentina. The Argentine Government still owed a London bank £3.8 million for the Type 42 contract; the debt was quietly settled soon after the war!

The role of the warships in this group was to provide protection for the vulnerable *Cabo San Antonio* and supporting gunfire for the landing force if required, but most of the ships also carried helicopters and small parties of men who would take part in the landing. Task Force 40 was actually two ships short of the strength envisaged in the original Falklands plan, because the transport *Bahía Buen Suceso* and the polar vessel *Bahía Paraíso* were both involved in the South Georgia incident. Their absence resulted in the landing force being short of room for four Puma helicopters and in men being packed more densely into other ships, particularly the *Cabo San Antonio*.

The busiest people were the men in the marine and other landing units who had to pack and move from their various land locations to their allocated ships. It says much for the efficiency of the Argentine Marine Corps that these moves were completed within the required period. Active preparations had started when the small group of officers who had been carrying out the previous planning for a Falklands operation had gathered to hold a routine meeting at the headquarters of the 2nd Marine Infantry Battalion at Puerto Belgrano. This is a joint description by several of those present:

> It was mid-morning on the 25th. Rear-Admiral Büsser burst into the meeting and said, 'Bullshit (*mierda*). You can throw all that rubbish away; we are going into serious business. We must be ready to sail in seventy-two hours.' He told us that the junta's decision was not necessarily to land, but to sail to the target area alongside the diplomatic moves in progress.
>
> We, in the planning team, didn't sleep in that period. The outline plan was ready but not the logistics, and we had to do everything in a way that would make the men in the units concerned think that it was a routine training operation. Then there was the communications plan, the boarding plan and the last touches to the landing plan. It was all done in one room still, but we had to increase the planning group to twenty officers. We got it all done in the end. As marine officers we were very proud to be a force 'in readiness'. There might have been a little more expertise if we had had until the original September deadline, but only minimal.

Carlos Büsser, senior officer in the Argentine Marine Corps and chief planner of the actual landing operation, would have the honour of leading it. The core of the force would be a battalion of his marine infantry. The 1st and 2nd Battalions were located at Puerto Belgrano and were specifically trained to work with the Fleet. The choice fell upon the 2nd Battalion, probably because it had taken part in a joint exercise with United States Marines in Patagonia only five months earlier. This was the first time there had been any co-operation with the Americans since President Carter's long 'civil rights' embargo during the 1970s. The 2nd Marine Infantry Battalion had been trained and equipped to perfection for that prestigious exercise and so was selected for the Falklands operation. The 1st Battalion's consolation was to provide Büsser's Operations Officer as well as the reserve company for the Falklands operation and the platoon which would be sent on the *Guerrico* to overcome the Royal Marine detachment in South Georgia. The following list gives details of all the marine units which would be embarked for the Falklands:

> Headquarters and Communications Unit – 42 men
> 2nd Marine Infantry Battalion – 387 men
> Amphibious Vehicles Battalion – 20 Amtracs, 5 wheeled
>    LARC transport vehicles – 101 men
> Amphibious Commando Company – 92 men
> Buzos Tácticos (beach reconnaissance) – 12 men
> Marine Field Artillery Battalion (detachment) – 6 × 105-mm
>    guns – 41 men
> Force Reserve – 65 men of 1st Marine Infantry Battalion
> Logistic Unit – 84 men.

The Army would be represented by a mere 39-man platoon of the 25th Regiment. This platoon was the advance party of its parent regiment which was the one chosen to fly to Stanley immediately after its capture, replace the landing force and assume the responsibility for providing a permanent garrison. The platoon was the only unit in the landing force not located at or close to Puerto Belgrano from where the expedition would sail; it flew from its barracks at Colonia Sarmiento in Argentina's Chubut Province, a thousand miles to the south. The last element in the landing force was a 41-man team of 'Civil Affairs' officers and men who would help to set up an Argentine administration in the Falklands. The total strength of the landing force at Stanley would be 904 men. A further two platoons of the 25th Regiment would be embarked and taken to Goose Green after the capture of Stanley. The units were loaded into various ships, with the *Cabo San Antonio* taking the greatest number of men. Every spare corner was filled. The naval transport ship *Isla de los Estados* would not carry troops, only supplies, mainly a large reserve of food for both the garrison and the island population in the uncertain period which would follow any landing.

The last ship to be made ready would face the longest voyage. The frigate *Guerrico* was in dry dock at Puerto Belgrano. Work was finished in a rush, and, taking aboard a reinforced platoon from the 1st Marine Infantry Battalion, she set out on the 1,400-mile voyage to South Georgia, hoping to start the operation against the British there at the same time as the Falklands operation.

There were no major setbacks, and the troops started loading in the ships at Puerto Belgrano at 8.00 a.m. on Sunday 28 March. Secrecy had been well maintained. There had been no general mobilization and no major disruption of air services, but some movement of troops was noted and reported to Britain. The Argentine newspapers announced that a joint anti-submarine exercise was to be carried out with the Uruguayan Navy. The Argentine marine units were told that they would be on exercises in Patagonia with officer cadets. But these explanations were not believed by all the men involved; the presence of so much ammunition and of an army platoon brought up by air *from* Patagonia, together with so many media reports about trouble with the British in the South Atlantic, led to much excitement and speculation as to the destination. Rear-Admiral Büsser sums it all up:

> Those of us who knew where we were going were very proud. We felt very lucky that we had been chosen and extraordinarily fortunate to have the opportunity to regain the Malvinas. Those NCOs who had guessed our destination obtained a lot of Argentine flags ready to fly on their arrival; they felt they were taking part in an historic action and every one of them had a flag wrapped up under their kit. That is why there were so many Argentine flags to be seen in the Malvinas after we landed.
>
> It was a Sunday. Our chaplain jokingly gave the men dispensation from going to Mass that morning. It didn't matter, we had a Mass in the *Cabo San Antonio* that evening. The loading went smoothly and was finished by midday. It was a sunny day, with a very bright sun, a nice autumn day without wind. April was a lovely month that year.

The fleet of ships sailed. The officers of the units on board the various ships were informed of their destination at lunch that day and given their first briefing. The other men on the ships were not yet told that they were bound for the Falklands. The intention was to sail down the coast of Argentina until well past the Falklands and then approach the islands from the south, but a fierce storm which blew up on the next day – Monday the 29th – lasted for forty-eight hours and spoiled that plan. The broad-bottomed *Cabo San Antonio*, designed to carry 450 men but now loaded with 880, suffered the most, rolls as much as 44 degrees being recorded; there was much seasickness.

On the morning of Wednesday 31 March, with the planned landing less than twenty-four hours away, it became obvious that the proposed timetable could not be met, even by sailing directly to the Falklands from the north. It was decided to postpone the landings by one day, until Friday 2 April. The decision was taken by General García and Rear-Admiral Allara, who were together in the *Santísima Trinidad*. President Galtieri had appointed General García the overall commander of the 'Malvinas Theatre of Operations'. The storm subsided the next day, but it now became necessary to change some of the details of the landing plan. A signal was received which stated that there was a double garrison of Royal Marines at Stanley, and that the Governor was aware that an attack was imminent and was preparing a defence, particularly at the airport and near the beach chosen for the main landing. This information was all accurate. The annual change-over of the small British garrison in the Falklands had been interrupted by the South Georgia crisis, and there were seventy Royal Marines and eleven armed sailors ashore at Stanley. British Intelligence had picked up orders for an Argentine submarine to carry out a reconnaissance of the landing beach and had informed Governor Hunt. The Royal Marines had immediately come to the alert and established armed posts at various places, including the airport and the proposed landing beach. Governor Hunt had broadcast a warning to the civilian population and ordered the airport runway to be blocked. This recent information undoubtedly came from inside Stanley, almost certainly from the Argentine airline office based there. The Falklands were served by L A D E (Líneas Aéreas del Estado), a section of the Argentine Air Force which operated non-profitable routes as a government service; this was the Falklanders' only air link with the outside world. A L A D E officer,

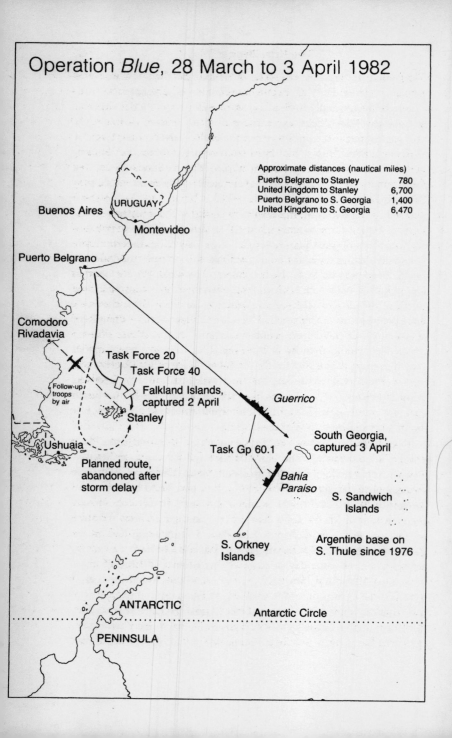

# Operation *Blue*, 28 March to 3 April 1982

Approximate distances (nautical miles)
Puerto Belgrano to Stanley          780
United Kingdom to Stanley          6,700
Puerto Belgrano to S. Georgia      1,400
United Kingdom to S. Georgia       6,470

Buenos Aires

URUGUAY

Montevideo

Puerto Belgrano

Comodoro Rivadavia

Follow-up troops by air

Task Force 20

Task Force 40

Falkland Islands, captured 2 April

*Guerrico*

Stanley

Task Gp 60.1

South Georgia, captured 3 April

Ushuaia

Planned route, abandoned after storm delay

*Bahía Paraíso*

S. Sandwich Islands

S. Orkney Islands

Argentine base on S. Thule since 1976

ANTARCTIC

Antarctic Circle

PENINSULA

Vicecomodoro Hector Gilobert, had left Stanley a few weeks earlier at the end of his twelve-month tour of duty but had just returned unexpectedly to Stanley, ostensibly to check some financial documents. This officer, experienced in local conditions, was probably the source of the intelligence now reaching the landing force.

Rear-Admiral Büsser had been studying the problems of landing in the Falklands since January: 'My overall plan was to capture Government House and the Royal Marines' barracks at Moody Brook by surprise and, if possible, without bloodshed. To do this I decided to come in from many directions and with a crushing superiority. I hoped for a psychological effect that would be overwhelming.' Büsser's original plan was to land the Amphibious Commando Company during the night on a beach two miles south of Stanley, to march overland and seize the barracks at Moody Brook and various key points in the town, with the main landing force coming ashore north of the airfield at dawn and sending the army platoon quickly ahead to capture Government House while the marines completed the occupation of Stanley. As soon as it was judged safe to do so, a small plane would then fly in from the mainland, and its occupants would prepare the airport for the arrival of the large army contingent which would replace the landing force and form the first garrison. Alongside these operations in the Stanley area, two further army platoons were to land by helicopter from the *Almirante Irizar* to occupy the Goose Green–Darwin area.

But several new factors endangered parts of Büsser's plan. There would be no surprise. The beach chosen for the main landing was likely to be defended and the airport runway blocked. Finally, the Puma helicopter on the *Almirante Irizar* had broken loose in its hangar during the storm and was now out of action. Büsser crossed by helicopter from the *Cabo San Antonio* to the *Santísima Trinidad* to discuss with Rear-Admiral Allara the changes required in the plan. The two were old friends; they had entered the Navy Academy as cadets on the same day in 1947. Büsser arrived on the flagship at 9.40 a.m. Allara told him that any new decisions would have to be taken by 10.15 a.m. in order to avoid a further postponement. The two officers, joined by General García, quickly made a new plan. The main landing beach was switched to a more westerly one known as Yorke Bay. The direct flight from the mainland to the airport was cancelled. The army platoon earmarked for the capture of Government House was switched to the seizure of the airport and the clearance of the runway. A small Amphibious Commando party allocated to the securing of the key places in Stanley was relieved of that task, because surprise was gone, and given instead the mission of capturing Government House. The Goose Green–Darwin operation also had to be cancelled because of the damaged helicopter. The two army platoons released from that operation were added to the reserve of the Stanley force, making a total of about 940 Argentine troops who would be attacking eighty-one British marines and sailors.

These hasty decisions left at least one weakness in the new plan. The capture of Government House had earlier been the task of a 39-strong army platoon which had studied the task and prepared a careful plan. That task was now given to just sixteen Amphibious Commandos under Lieutenant-Commander Pedro Giachino. The original plan had been based on the assumption that surprise would be achieved and that Government House would be undefended. Despite the fact that it was now known that the British were on the alert, no reinforcement was given to Giachino; in fact, very little information about his task was available because the army unit originally designated for it was in another ship. It was an apprehensive Giachino who would have to lead his small party to the British seat of government in the Falklands.

The whole operation could be cancelled at any time up to 6.30 p.m. on the evening before the landing.[1] The submarine *Santa Fé*, carrying the beach reconnaissance party, would submerge at that time and be out of touch. That vital time came, and there was no message of postponement from the junta. The invasion of the Falklands was to go ahead, happen what may during the night. (The Argentines refuse to use the word 'invasion'; they viewed the operation as the 'repossession' of their own territory.) Rear-Admiral Büsser remembers that 6.30 p.m. deadline:

It was a very impressive moment when no cancellation order came. It was the hour of meaning in the whole of my life; the time for me to show exactly whether I was a good soldier or a

---

[1]  The time being used by the Argentines was three hours behind the time in Britain.

bad soldier, a good commander or a bad commander. The fact
that it was the recovery of the Malvinas was not quite so strong
in my mind; I had been living with that for some time by then.

The weather had become much calmer; one officer said 'it was like
sailing on a swimming pool'. Every man in the landing ship *Cabo
San Antonio* was given a hot bath or shower and the first good meal
since before the storm. At 7.00 p.m. Büsser spoke on the ship's
loudspeaker; other ships had copies of the statement:

> We have been chosen by destiny to carry out one of the dearest
> ambitions of the Argentine people, to recover the Malvinas
> Islands. For years you have been preparing your muscles and
> minds for the fight. Tomorrow you will prove the quality of the
> Argentine soldier. I expect from you bravery in battle, respect
> for your enemy and generosity in victory. I warn you that if
> there are any excesses against the enemy troops, women or
> private property I will impose the maximum penalty. Tomor-
> row you will be victorious but disciplined, and carry out your
> duty with the blessing of Our Lord. God save Argentina.

There was 'an explosion' among the men in the *Cabo San Antonio;* it
was 'just like a goal being scored at a football match!' Everyone was
ordered to their quarters at 9.00 p.m.; reveille would be at 4.30 a.m.

The British Government was almost certain that a landing was
imminent. It was relying upon President Reagan to intervene. Reagan
tried to talk on the telephone with President Galtieri, but Galtieri
would not accept the call at first. Reagan persisted, and the two
leaders eventually spoke, but to no effect. Galtieri could not stop the
operation even if he wanted to at this stage, and there is no evidence
that he did want to. What the Argentines called Operación *Azul* –
Operation *Blue* – had already started. (It had been known as Operación *Rosario* – Operation *Rosary* – during the planning stage but
this was changed to *Blue,* after the robe of the Virgin Mary; the
planners were anxious that the operation should be seen by the
Argentine soldiers and public as a semi-religious crusade.)

# 4 · Operation *Blue*

At 9.30 p.m. on 1 April, half an hour before President Reagan finally managed to speak to President Galtieri on the telephone, the Type 42 destroyer *Santísima Trinidad* anchored one mile south of the Falklands coast. Twenty-one inflatable rubber boats were lowered into the sea, and the marines of the Amphibious Commando Company transferred to the small craft.[1] It took an hour and a half to load the boats. A small advance party under Lieutenant Bernard Schweitzer went ahead, but the main group waited near *Santísima Trinidad* until the last boat was ready.

When the main group did proceed, it had to be careful to find the entrance into Port Harriet leading to the planned landing place at Mullet Creek. Unfortunately, the boats went in a little too far north and found themselves among beds of tough seaweed – the local 'kelp' which gave its name to the 'kelper' islanders. The propellers of the boats became entangled with the kelp, and there was some confusion. The noise of engines being revved to get clear was heard by a Royal Marines look-out and reported; this was the basis of the later British belief that these first troops ashore were landed by helicopter. Some boats suffered engine breakdowns and had to be towed by other boats. An attempt to use oars and row out of the kelp was abandoned as being too slow. All the boats struggled through

[1] An error in the Argentine press prevented the Amphibious Commando Company from receiving the credit for its part in this operation. The magazine *Somos* was anxious to publish the first account of the capture of Stanley and was given some information by a naval officer who had once served with the Buzos Tácticos, a smaller unit specializing in underwater demolition and coastal reconnaissance. This officer is believed to have hinted that the Buzos Tácticos played a prominent part in the action, and *Somos* rushed the story out, giving the main credit to that unit, even naming as being members of Buzos Tácticos all the casualties which were officially announced. The Amphibious Commando Company, which did most of the fighting and suffered all the casualties, was not mentioned. That mistake by *Somos* spread all round the world and has been repeated many times since.

eventually, but it was decided to land at the nearest beach instead of pressing on to Mullet Creek. The first Argentines to land in the Falklands thus came ashore at a small unnamed beach near Lake Point. The time was 11.00 p.m.

The ninety-two marines were all present. They removed their neoprene outer suits, took their weapons and other equipment out of waterproof packs and prepared to move. The small party under Lieutenant-Commander Giachino who were to capture Government House had the shortest distance to go — two and a half miles due north — but Moody Brook Barracks, the destination of the main party, was six miles away over a high ridge. It will be convenient for us to follow the main party; Lieutenant-Commander Sánchez Sabarots, the company commander, describes its progress:

> It was a nice night, with a moon, but the cloud covered the moon for most of the time. We were only a few minutes late but we had further to go now. We didn't take a direct route; there would have been no landmarks that way. We went along the coast to Mullet Creek and set out from there, following a fence line which was shown as running due north on the map.
>
> We were very surprised at the difficulty of the ground. What the reconnaissance photographs showed as 'grass' we found to be great hummocks. It was very hard going with our heavy loads; it was hot work. We eventually became split up into three groups. We only had one night-sight; the lead man, Lieutenant Arias, had it. One of the groups became separated when a vehicle came along the track which we had to cross. We thought it was a military patrol. Another group just lost contact, and the third separation was caused by someone going too fast. This caused my second-in-command, Lieutenant Bardi, to fall. He suffered a hairline fracture of the ankle and had to be left behind with a man to help him. But, except for Lieutenant Bardi and his helper, we all got there by various means; I think we had a certain amount of luck. We were at Moody Brook by 5.30 a.m., just on the limits of the time planned, but with no time for the one hour's reconnaissance for which we had hoped.

It had taken this party six hours to travel six miles over the rough Falklands terrain in the dark, an early example of the manner in

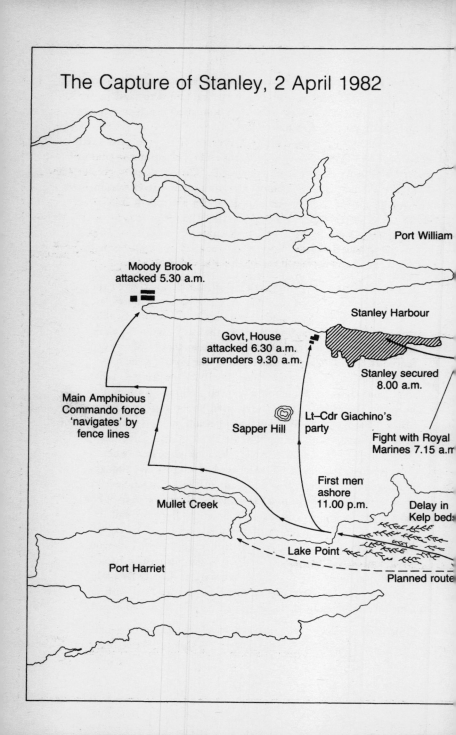

# The Capture of Stanley, 2 April 1982

Port William

Moody Brook
attacked 5.30 a.m.

Stanley Harbour

Govt, House
attacked 6.30 a.m.
surrenders 9.30 a.m.

Stanley secured
8.00 a.m.

Main Amphibious
Commando force
'navigates' by
fence lines

Sapper Hill

Lt–Cdr Giachino's
party

Fight with Royal
Marines 7.15 a.m.

First men
ashore
11.00 p.m.

Mullet Creek

Delay in
Kelp beds

Lake Point

Port Harriet

Planned route

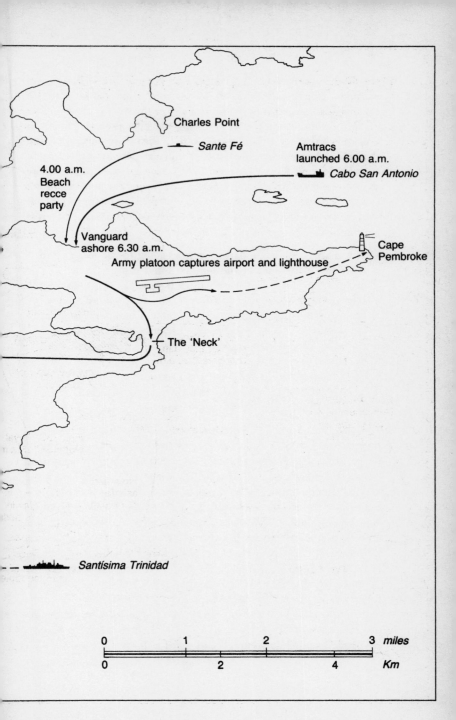

Charles Point

*Sante Fé*

Amtracs
launched 6.00 a.m.

*Cabo San Antonio*

4.00 a.m.
Beach
recce
party

Vanguard
ashore 6.30 a.m.

Army platoon captures airport and lighthouse

Cape
Pembroke

The 'Neck'

*Santísima Trinidad*

| 0 | | 1 | | 2 | | 3 | *miles* |

| 0 | | | 2 | | | 4 | | *Km* |

which all the troops who came to the islands would find that distances on maps would be deceptive. Lieutenant Jorge Bardi, with his cracked ankle bone, was the first casualty of the war.

The Argentines were still following the plan prepared before it was known that the British were aware of the coming operation and they still assumed that the barrack huts at Moody Brook might contain sleeping Royal Marines. It was soon established that there were no sentries. An electric light was seen switched on in one room, later found to be the office of the Royal Marine commander, but there was no other sign of life. Lieutenant-Commander Sabarots continues his description:

> It was still completely dark. We were going to use tear-gas, to force the British out of the buildings and capture them. Our orders were not to cause casualties if possible. That was the most difficult mission of my career. All our training as commandos was to fight aggressively and inflict maximum casualties on an enemy. We surrounded the barracks with machine-gun teams, leaving only one escape route along the peninsula north of Stanley Harbour, so that anyone who did get away would not be able to reach the town and reinforce the British there. Then we threw the tear-gas grenades into each building. There was no reaction; the barracks were empty.

Sabarots had been ordered to make as much of a display of noise and firepower as possible, as part of Rear-Admiral Büsser's overall plan. Giachino's force should have been attacking the rear of Government House two miles away, and the main landing force should have been coming ashore well away to the east, all at the same time. Büsser hoped that this simultaneous display of Argentine presence on three sides would induce the British commander at Government House to surrender quickly. Sabarots could hear nothing of any action at Government House, nor from the more distant landing area, but he ordered his men to fire machine-guns over the barracks, not to damage the buildings – the Argentine army units which were to follow the landing force would need the accommodation – but only to make a display of tracer fire. The lights of Stanley were seen to go out soon after the first burst was fired. The Argentines at Moody Brook then settled down to rest and wait for dawn.

Pedro Giachino and his smaller party had reached Government House but were not able to deploy and carry out their part in the operation at the planned time of 5.30 a.m. The Royal Marine log kept at Government House shows Giachino's first action as taking place at 6.15 a.m. Giachino faced the difficulty of capturing this important objective with a force of only sixteen men. Earlier in 1982, Governor Hunt had been visited by an Argentine tourist who stated that he was an architect and asked for a photocopy of the plans of Government House. 'Like a fool', said Hunt later, 'I gave him them.' Giachino did not have these plans; they were probably with the commander of the army unit originally designated for the Government House operation and were in another ship of the landing force. Giachino approached his objective from the high and rocky hillock immediately inland from it. He split his small force into groups, placing one on either side of the house and one at the rear. In the slowly growing light, he could see men moving in and around the house and some vehicles arriving. Despite this, and the fact that the Argentine landings were clearly disclosed by the bursts of fire at Moody Brook, Giachino went ahead with the original plan given to him, a plan based on the dual policy of assuming surprise and hoping not to cause casualties. Fantastic as it may seem, he simply moved with four other men to the rear of the house, with the intention of entering the back door and demanding the Governor's surrender.

The lack of detailed plans caused an early failure. Giachino and his party did find a door, broke it open and entered, but they were in a separate, smaller building which contained the servants' quarters. It was empty. The five Argentines came out again and made for the back of the main building. Unknown to them, Government House was the main concentration point of the British defence. The building contained thirty-one Royal Marines, eleven armed Royal Navy men, one local man – an ex-Royal Marine – with a rifle, Governor Hunt with a pistol and his driver with a shotgun. A hail of fire from the defenders in the rear of the house fell on Giachino and his men. Giachino fell, bleeding profusely from a cut artery caused by a bullet wound in his upper thigh. One of his companions, Lieutenant Quiroga, was hit by two bullets, one in the arm and one in the chest; he was saved from severe injury by a Swiss army penknife in his breast pocket which took the main impact of one bullet. The three other

Argentines took shelter in the servants' block, where they were later captured by the Royal Marines. Giachino called to his own men for help, and a first-aid man, Seaman Urbina, came over from one of the other parties. He was injured by a British grenade. The Argentines who recount these events make no complaint about Urbina being hit; the red cross on his satchel would not have been visible in the gloom.

Giachino's 'snatch party' was thus completely neutralized. Giachino was left in the open, bleeding badly and holding a grenade in his hand from which he had withdrawn the pin. The Argentines in the other parties had returned the British fire, and Government House had been hit many times, but there were no British casualties. When the firing died down, the British called to Giachino to throw away the grenade, so that they could help him. There are two versions to what happened next. The Argentines say that Giachino agreed to allow the British to come out and tie down the handle of the grenade, if they would bring him medical aid. But, say the Argentines, the British never did this and left Giachino lying there. Major Norman, the Royal Marine commander who was actually on the spot, denies this, saying Giachino was shouting out 'aggressively' and brandishing the grenade, so he was left. It is probable that there was some language misunderstanding at what was a tense moment for all involved. Little more would happen at Government House for the next two and a half hours.

The main Argentine landing was coming ashore when Giachino's party became pinned down outside Government House, but the landing was four miles away to the east, and it would be at least two hours before help could reach Giachino. The landing force was preceded by a small beach reconnaissance party of men from the Buzos Tácticos landed by the submarine *Santa Fé*. These men were in position by 4.30 a.m., ready to guide in the main landing. Their move had taken place at the same time as the march of the two parties of Amphibious Commandos to Government House and Moody Brook. Rear-Admiral Büsser had kept in touch with all three parties by radio, using short messages in an English voice code, 'although our men's English was not perfect, and I was not sure the ruse would work. But it all went well. I am a lucky man to have had such well-trained units available; those three groups, all on the move at the same time, were all true professionals.'

The landing ship *Cabo San Antonio* approached the land escorted by the frigate *Drummond*. Büsser realized that these ships would be detected by the English radar but he used that as part of his plan, hoping that the radar report of ships to the east, coinciding with the display of fire at Moody Brook in the west and the attack at Government House, would combine to have a demoralizing effect upon the British defenders. The Argentine ships were detected, firstly by the radar of the small local ship *Forrest*, and then visually by the light-houseman at Cape Pembroke. The *Cabo San Antonio* stopped two miles offshore. The time was just before 6.00 a.m. The amphibious vehicles in the vehicle deck of the ship were loaded and ready. There were twenty of the American-built armoured FMC troop-carrying Amtracs and some unarmed stores-carrying LARC5 vehicles. The engines had all been run up, creating an enormous din in the enclosed deck, and communication between vehicles was only possible by radio. All the vehicles proved to be serviceable. Then, right on time at 6.00 a.m., the bow doors opened, and the dim shape of land could just be seen. Lieutenant Mario Forbice, the Amtrac commander who had worked so hard to get his unit ready, remembers the moment: 'Everyone was very emotional. We were going into a real action for the first time, an action to recover the Malvinas. It was a particularly proud moment for the Marines, because every man had trained for action and this was our first opportunity. We were recovering something that belonged to us and had been taken from us.'

The amphibious vehicles were in three groups. The first, of four Amtracs, was the 'vanguard'. This was followed by the main group of fourteen Amtracs, including those of Rear-Admiral Büsser and Commander Alfredo Weinstabl, the commander of the 2nd Marine Infantry Battalion, which provided most of the men in the landing force. The third group of vehicles contained the battalion second-in-command, a recovery Amtrac and one of the load-carrying LARCs. As soon as each Amtrac entered the water, it sheered off to the left or right to make way for the one following. When the controller in the ship saw that the way was clear, a red lamp gave way to green, and the next Amtrac drove forward. The average time between departures was thirty seconds.

The Amtracs churned their way towards the beach. The *Cabo San Antonio*'s radar guided them safely past a rocky outcrop – Yorke Point – and then a red lantern placed by the beach reconnaissance party marked the final run-in to land. It was a well-executed operation carried out by well-trained troops.

Zero Hour for the first vehicle ashore was 6.30 a.m., half an hour before dawn. The timetable had been brought forward that half-hour when it had become known that the British were aware of the approach of the Argentine ships. That change of time and the change of beach meant that the approach of the Amtracs was not observed by the two Royal Marines on the next beach, three-quarters of a mile away. Lieutenant-Commander Hugo Santillón was in command of the vanguard and was in the leading Amtrac. This is his account:

It all went just as though we were on an exercise in Patagonia. My call sign was 'Alborada' – 'Dawn', very poetical. My group of four Amtracs approached the beach in a diamond formation. If I got ashore safely, the others would form a column and follow me in, but if I bogged down in mud or something, the others could swing right and lead the battalion on to Purple Beach and be prepared to fight their way in there.

When I felt the Amtrac touch bottom, I radioed 'Touch-down'; it was 6.30 a.m. exactly – a credit to the people on the *Cabo* who guided us in by radio. Then, ten or fifteen seconds later, the driver engaged the tracks, and I radioed that the ground was firm, that the tracks were running well and that there was no enemy in sight. I gave the order, 'Everyone up!' The three forward hatches were opened – one for me, one for the driver and one for the gunner – and the two long hatches at the sides were opened for the marines to man their weapons.

All went well. The beach was incredibly white, to my sur-prise, with a steep slope ten metres from the waterline, a few rocks; there was no cover for my huge Amtrac, and I thought I was a sitting duck as I came up that slope – but the place was deserted. When I was up on the slope, Commander Weinstabl came on the radio and said that he could see me on his night-sight and was following me in. I ran on to the south, over open ground, through a narrow valley only 200 metres wide, with my other three Amtracs following in column. It was rocky, and we could not go fast. I thought the Royal Marines were being very clever, that they were allowing me to come off the beach and had prepared a killing zone in that valley; I thought I was a sitting duck again.

I reached the track and could see details of the ground now, because it was getting light. It was going to be a beautiful day, no wind, very mild. I hit the track and turned east towards my first objective, the airport. I could see that the main group were following us.

All twenty Amtracs were ashore, the only setback, ironically, was to Rear-Admiral Büsser's command vehicle – 'Charlie One'. On entering the water, the deflector plates which controlled the flow of water behind one of the propellers became jammed, and the Amtrac would only go round in circles while in forward gear. The driver had to change to reverse, and the Argentine commander thus invaded the Falklands backwards until his vehicle beached and the land tracks could be engaged.

One of the vanguard Amtracs contained the army platoon detailed to secure the airport runway. This party was under the command of Lieutenant-Colonel Mohamed Ali Seineldin, the main part of whose 25th Regiment would fly into the airport later in the day. The three other Amtracs took up supporting positions, and Seineldin's vehicle then went at the fastest speed possible over the rough ground, machine-guns in the vehicle at the ready, riflemen running along on either side. The airport was also deserted but many items, from old vehicles to blocks of concrete, were blocking the runway. A company of marines was detached to clear the blockages.

The Amtrac force continued on the road to Stanley, but first having to negotiate a narrow stretch of land which the Argentines called 'The Neck', where it was anticipated the British would put up a defence. But, again, there was no opposition. Carlos Büsser showed me the notes he made at the time:

05.25 Ojo, localizar enemigo. [Watch out! Locate the enemy.]
06.45 Dónde está el enemigo? [Where is the enemy?]

The British were finally encountered two and a half miles further on, just outside Stanley, where a small group of Royal Marines were defending the approaches to the town with anti-tank rocket launchers and machine-guns. It was 7.15 a.m. when the Amtracs bumped into this position. Lieutenant-Commander Santillón, now with only three Amtracs in the vanguard, describes the action:

> We were on the last straight stretch of road into Stanley. I saw a yellow road repair machine which appeared to be broken down on a bend in the road, partially blocking the road. We were running fast by then, and I told my men to be careful. Perhaps the road was mined or the repair machine was booby-trapped. I never finished the message. A machine-gun fired from one of the three white houses about 500 metres away and hit the right-hand Amtrac. The fire was very accurate. Then there were some explosions from a rocket launcher, but they were inaccurate, falling a long way from us.
>
> We followed our standard operating procedure and took evasive action. The Amtrac on the right answered the fire and took cover in a little depression. Once he was out of danger, I told all three vehicles to disembark their men. I needed to evaluate the situation. I ordered my subordinate leaders to report what they could see. I radioed to the battalion commander, and he told me to stop and wait for him to come forward. He soon arrived. He told me to organize a fire base from my position, so that the other two companies could deploy to the north and swing round into the town.
>
> The same group of Royal Marines opened fire on my position again, fortunately ineffectively, and no one was hit. Commander Weinstabl and I decided it was time to force the British to withdraw. I ordered the crew with the recoilless rifle to fire one round of hollow charge at the ridge of the roof of the house where the machine-gun was, to cause a bang but not an explosion. We were still following our orders not to inflict casualties. The first round was about a hundred metres short, but the second hit the roof. The British troops then threw a purple smoke grenade; I thought it was their signal to withdraw. They had stopped firing, so Commander Weinstabl started the movement of the two companies around the position. Some riflemen

in one of those other houses started firing then; that was quite uncomfortable. I couldn't pinpoint their location, but one of my other Amtracs could and asked permission to open up with a mortar which he had. I authorized this, but only with three rounds and only at the roofs of the houses. Two rounds were short, but the third hit right in the centre of the roof; that was incredible. The British ceased fire then.

Thus ended the only action of the day for the 2nd Marines. The fact that no one was observed to emerge from the first Amtrac to be engaged encouraged the Royal Marines to think that one of their rocket rounds had punched a hole in it and that some of the machine-gun fire had penetrated the hole and caused severe casualties among the men inside. Local civilians who observed the action optimistically supported this view later. There was no rocket hit, however, just the scars of ninety-seven machine-gun bullets. Only one Argentine marine was slightly wounded by a sliver of metal cutting his hand.

Rear-Admiral Büsser was becoming very anxious about the position at Government House, having received no reports from Giachino's party for several hours. He ordered the Amtracs to push on into Stanley and the six guns of his artillery force and the infantry reserve all to come ashore. The Amtracs moved through Stanley, their tracks clattering, their engines being deliberately revved so that the roar would contribute to the psychological pressure of Büsser's plan. The town was occupied soon after 8.00 a.m. The artillery was soon ashore and in position near Yorke Bay, and aircraft were starting to bring in the follow-up force at the airport. The Amtracs of the advance guard roared along the coast road outside Government House to see what was happening at Moody Brook, but met the tired Amphibious Commandos halfway; they were hurrying into Stanley to help their colleagues at Government House.

Governor Hunt had already decided that further resistance was hopeless. He sent for Vicecomodoro Gilobert, the L A D E airline officer who had been held in custody all night with the other locally based Argentines, and asked him to negotiate. Radio contact was made with the *Santísima Trinidad*, and the ceasefire proposal was

passed back to Rear-Admiral Büsser in Stanley. Büsser proposed a
meeting in front of St Mary's Catholic church, which was on the
waterfront near the Government House end of town. Büsser describes what happened:

We were ready for this, and I had ordered a white flag to be
packed. But when I told the officer concerned to get it out the
flag wasn't there. He had thought the order was a joke and had
not packed it! We had to take a white waste-disposal bag from
one of the Amtracs. I walked several streets to reach the meeting
place. We were a party of three officers, unarmed to show that
we were quite sure of success. There was no one there. We
waited for a few minutes, then I saw a small party walking along
the road at the water's edge. I had seen photographs of Governor Hunt, but he was not there. I thought of refusing to talk,
but then I recognized one of them as Héctor Gilobert. Gilobert
told me about our wounded men outside Government House.
We all went back there. Some shooting was still going on, but I
ordered our men to cease fire.

I went into the house. The first person I met was a British
soldier, his rifle pointed at my stomach. I was not armed, and I
thought that in the next few moments I would be either a
prisoner or the victor. I thought it was advisable to act coolly,
so I introduced myself and offered to shake his hand. He was
surprised at this but shook hands, as did a whole line of other
soldiers behind him. Then I met the others. I recognized the
Governor and Major Noott from photographs. I shook hands
with Major Noott and with Major Norman, the new Royal
Marines commander, but the Governor refused. He said I was
an intruder.

I asked him to surrender, but he was reluctant. I told him
that I had a crushing superiority. I told him that he had his job
to do and I had mine. His job was to prevent my men killing all
his men, and my job was to prevent British soldiers killing
some of mine. I invited him to carry out his duty. I insisted
that they had no chance and told him we had the airport and
were receiving reinforcements, that we had captured Moody
Brook and the town, and that Government House was all that

was left. The Governor asked the two Royal Marine officers what they thought; I think they answered more with their eyes than anything else. The Governor agreed to surrender. I wanted to get it over with, to tend to my men I knew were wounded.

Attention could now be turned to Lieutenant-Commander Giachino and the other wounded Argentines who had been lying on the ground outside the house for more than two hours. Blankets and bandages were taken out. Giachino was in a poor way. Rear-Admiral Büsser describes a moment of Anglo–Argentine compassion:

We were lifting the body of Giachino into a blanket, to take him to the hospital. I was lifting one side of the blanket, but Giachino was a very big man, very heavy, and suddenly two hands appeared at my side, helping me to lift. It was Major Norman. I have a very good feeling towards him; his attitude is something I shall never forget.

But poor Giachino died from loss of blood. He had been given a near-impossible task. His country gave him the posthumous award of the Cruz-La Nación Argentina al Heroico Valor en Combate, its highest decoration, and a posthumous promotion to Commander (*capitán de fragata*). His body was flown back to the mainland, and he was buried at Mar del Plata where his unit was based. The other two wounded men survived.

The fighting was over. Excited and proud Argentine marines were everywhere; the flags which they had brought with them were soon flying. General García and Rear-Admiral Allara came in by helicopter and landed at the football field near Government House. Rear-Admiral Büsser met them, and the three set out to walk along the town's waterfront road. Büsser says: 'That was when I felt the deepest emotion. We had achieved all our objectives. We had suffered one man killed and two wounded, and caused no casualties to the Royal Marines or to the civilians.' Out on the airport peninsula the army platoon which had secured the airport swept the open ground to the east and occupied the lighthouse where a local man, Basil Biggs, had been on duty all night and had been reporting the Argentine ships' movements to Government House. Mr Biggs described how an officer placed an Argentine flag over the rail at the top of the lighthouse and ordered that it was not to be touched.

Mr Biggs said: 'OK. It's only temporary; the British will soon sort this lot out.'

'No. No,' replied the Argentine officer. 'This is for ever.' The officer concerned was probably the platoon commander, Second Lieutenant Roberto Reyes.

The remainder of the Army's 25th Regiment was already flying in from the mainland airfield of Comodoro Rivadavia to replace the marine landing force. It would be followed by the 9th Engineer Company; and these two units would constitute the first Argentine garrison in the Falklands. Four Pucarás of the 3rd Attack Group carried out a fly-past and then landed to represent the Air Force. The choice of the 25th Regiment to be the main element in the garrison deserves some explanation. Some publications state that this was a 'symbolically national' unit, with men selected from every part of Argentina to provide the first garrison in what was regarded as a recovered part of the homeland. The green berets worn by its men were believed to mark them as superior troops to the men of other regiments. This is another misconception. The 25th Regiment was chosen for this duty solely because of its geographical location in Argentina. It was part of IX Brigade, based in Chubut Province which is close to the Falklands. It was a normal Argentine infantry unit, with professional officers and NCOs but with all of its 'private soldiers' being young conscripts. A possible origin of the 'national unit' story may be the fact that Chubut is a sparsely populated province, and, with not enough local conscripts to complete the regiment, others were often brought down from the more populated north. This was a long-standing arrangement, but it is possible that it was the basis of the impression given that a 'national unit' was now stationed in the Falklands. The green berets had no significance; many units were allowed to choose their own distinctive headgear. What is clear is that all but a few officers who had been in the know were amazed to be ordered from their barracks at Colonia Sarmiento, loaded into transport planes at Comodoro Rivadavia and flown 600 miles to these islands in the South Atlantic which had again become part of Argentina.

The responsibility for the Falklands passed from the Argentine

Navy to the Army before the day was over. There was a slight anxiety that a British submarine might be at sea in the area, and most of the marines returned to the mainland in the transport aircraft bringing in the army units. The Buzos Tácticos and the amphibious commandos went first, and many of these men would be back in their own quarters at Mar del Plata, more than a thousand miles to the north, by nightfall. General García also returned to the mainland, leaving in command Brigadier-General Américo Daher, from whose IX Brigade the arriving troops had come. Daher had just 630 men available that night to garrison this multitude of islands whose combined size equalled that of Wales, but these plans had been prepared on the assumption that there would be no active British response.

The agents of British authority were quickly removed. Most of the Royal Marines were quickly rounded up. Major Norman commented that his men were reasonably treated by their original captors, the Amphibious Commandos, but that the men of the 2nd Marine Infantry Battalion acted as 'arrogant victors' who had done no fighting and who set out to humiliate the Royal Marine prisoners. The British marines were allowed to go in small groups to Moody Brook and pack their personal belongings; they complained that many of their possessions – money, cameras and radio cassettes – had been stolen. They were loaded into a C-130 Hercules at the airport that evening and flown to Comodoro Rivadavia. Governor Hunt, his family and other officials left at the same time in a Fokker F-28. Both groups were flown on to Buenos Aires, then to Montevideo and from there to England. Six Royal Marines were not immediately captured. They had been in a position near the entrance to Stanley Harbour and they withdrew to open country, hoping to avoid capture and maintain a British military presence, however small, for as long as possible. It was a brave effort, but they were members of the newly arrived Royal Marines detachment, did not know the area and eventually had to give themselves up. The claim made on their behalf that they holed and sank an Argentine landing ship with a rocket projectile at the harbour entrance is unfounded.

The intention to seize South Georgia on the same day as the Falklands could not be achieved because of the rushed nature of the preparations and the recent storm at sea. The frigate *Guerrico* arrived at Leith to reinforce Lieutenant Astiz and his men who had been keeping a lonely vigil there. There was a platoon from the 1st Marine Infantry Battalion on the *Guerrico,* and these men, with Astiz's party, set out on 3 April in *Guerrico* to capture the British base at Grytviken where there were twenty-two Royal Marines. (Captain Carlos Alfonso of the *Guerrico* was in overall command of the landing force, but Captain César Trombetta, the commander of Argentina's Antarctic Naval Squadron, was also present.)

It is a story which can be quickly told. The Argentine force had firepower in the shape of *Guerrico*'s 3.9 -inch gun and mobility in the form of two helicopters – a Puma and an Alouette. The British put up a good fight, firing a rocket round into *Guerrico*'s side as well as hitting it with other weapons, and forcing down the Puma with small-arms fire. A seaman on the *Guerrico* and two marine conscripts in the helicopter were killed, and several men were injured. But the Royal Marines were eventually forced to surrender and were later returned to England.

Seven hundred miles away in the Falklands, the Argentines were that same day consolidating their position. Advance parties were flown out by helicopter to Goose Green and to Fox Bay. The main garrisons for these places followed by ship. The 9th Engineer Company went to Fox Bay, the only men to be placed on the huge island of West Falkland, and two platoons of the 25th Regiment went to Goose Green. The men at Fox Bay would see little of the war, but those sent to Goose Green were destined to see more of it than any other Argentine troops. They were commanded by First Lieutenant Carlos Esteban,[2] who could not have realized that his journey to Goose Green was only the beginning of what would prove to be a dramatic sequence of events. Twenty-seven-year-old Esteban – son of an air force NCO – had graduated second from a class of 250 at the Army Academy and would prove well suited to the independent command for which he was now chosen. He soon made contact with the local civilians. When he called at the home of Brooke Hardcastle,

---

[2] Eric Goss, the settlement manager at Goose Green, described Lieutenant Esteban as a 'real soldier', but Mr Goss's use of the English translation of Esteban – 'Stephen' – led me to make the mistake of describing this officer as 'Lieutenant Stephen' in my earlier Falklands book and to assume, wrongly, that he was killed in the war because the name of Lieutenant Stephen did not appear in the list of prisoners of war.

the manager of the Falkland Islands Company for the whole of the Falklands, who lived at nearby Darwin, Esteban found a photograph of his own wife, Viviana, and Mr Hardcastle's daughter when they had been fellow students at boarding-school in Córdoba.

Alongside the movements of troops came the establishment of Argentine government. On the day of the landings, General García, in his capacity of Military Governor of the Malvinas, South Georgia and the South Sandwich Islands, had come ashore and issued a series of proclamations which were broadcast from the local radio station. But García soon returned to the mainland, and Brigadier-General Mario Menéndez arrived on 3 April to become what the Argentines called their eighth Governor of the Malvinas, the first seven having served in the islands between 1821 and 1833. A 41-strong civil affairs team, all military officers or NCOs, had sailed with the landing force and come ashore earlier, but the senior members of Menéndez's administration team were late arriving. Their assembly had been a hurried affair, another example of the hasty nature of the landing decision.

The first member of the team to be switched from his previous post of duty was Comodoro Carlos Bloomer-Reeve, who had been serving as Air Attaché in Bonn and was recalled to Argentina 'for urgent duty' on 26 March. He knew the Falklands, having been in charge of the LADE airline office at Stanley seven years earlier; he now became Chief Secretary to Menéndez. Another air force officer, Comodoro Guillermo Mendiberri (serving at Comodoro Rivadavia), was given 'Intelligence'; and, from the army, Colonel Oscar Chinni (an accountant on the General Staff at Buenos Aires), became Treasurer, and Colonel Manuel Dorrego (an engineer at the Army Arsenal) took over Public Works. The last appointment to be made was the only naval officer in the team, Captain Barry Melbourne Hussey, who took charge of Education and Public Health. Hussey had no connection with the Falklands or apparent qualification for his selection but was told that it was because of his excellent understanding of the English language and people. As far back as his cadet days, Hussey had been nicknamed 'the Englishman', and his friends had even forecast, jokingly, that he would be the next Argentine Governor of the Malvinas. When I asked how much English blood he had, he replied, 'Not a lot, about as much as Eisenhower had German blood.' After several briefings in Buenos Aires, the team arrived in Stanley on 4 April. They moved into the residence of the former Chief Secretary of the Falkland Island Government, who had been sent back to Britain, and they worked from the Secretariat Building. They believed that theirs was a transitional role and that a fully civilian Argentine administration would follow. Comodoro Bloomer-Reeve was told that he would only be in Stanley for forty days and would then return to his post in Germany.

The first, uneasy meetings took place with those local officials who had not responded to Argentine invitations to leave. Some of these people were native Falklanders, others were British expatriates working under contract. When Colonel Chinni took over the treasury, he checked all the notes and silver in the safe and handed them back to Harold Rowlands, the Falklands-born official who had agreed to carry on in the interests of the civilian population, but only for a limited time. The Argentines nicknamed Rowlands 'Beethoven' because of his shock of hair. The Falklands civilians protested when an order was issued that all local vehicles should change from driving on the left to the right-hand side of the road. Captain Hussey pointed out that one reason for the change was concern for the safety of the civilians. 'Which would you prefer, that our eighteen-year-old conscripts, with their big lorries, should try to drive on the left, or that you, with your little vehicles, change to the right?' Goods were purchased by the Argentines from the Falkland Islands Company, whose officials asked the Argentines for a document stating that they had been forced to provide goods and services. This request was later used to criticize the company, but the civil team (who reassembled in full to talk to me in Buenos Aires) agreed that if the company had not sold these items then 'the normal procedure of war would have followed'. Did this mean confiscation? 'Yes.'

Within four days of the landing of the first Argentine commandos, the whole of the Falklands, together with South Georgia, was occupied and administered by the Argentines. In 1976 the Argentines had quietly set up a small base manned by naval personnel on Cook Island, one of the South Sandwich Islands which were claimed by Britain. When the presence of the base was detected by the British, the Argentines claimed that it was purely a scientific station and pointed out that they also claimed these islands. The British Government of the day decided not to use force to remove the station. That event and the moves of the past few days now left Argentina in control of every island in the South Atlantic previously held by Britain. Behind those islands was that part of the huge, unexploited Antarctic continent also claimed by both countries.

# 5 · The British Are Coming

The Argentine euphoria could hardly have been shorter lived. On 2 April, the very day of the landing in the Falklands, the British representative at the United Nations placed the issue before the Security Council in New York. A British resolution was debated the following day; it was interrupted by the news that an Argentine force was attacking the British in South Georgia. In the vote at the end of a tense debate, Security Council Resolution No. 502 was passed in these words:

Deeply disturbed at reports of an invasion on 2 April by armed forces of Argentina,
  Determining that there exists a breach of the peace in the region of the Falkland Islands (Islas Malvinas):
  1 Demands an immediate cessation of hostilities;
  2 Demands an immediate withdrawal of all Argentine forces from the Falkland Islands (Islas Malvinas);
  3 Calls on the Governments of Argentina and the United Kingdom to seek a diplomatic solution to their differences and to respect fully the purposes and principles of the Charter of the United Nations.

Ten members of the Security Council voted in favour of Britain, only one – Panama – voted against, and there were four abstentions. It could hardly have been a worse setback for Argentina. Far from securing the blessing of world opinion for her action, the vital vote of the United States had been cast against her, and even the blood ties with Spain only produced an abstention by that country.

The remainder of the month was to see move and counter-move, but no more fighting. Two aspects of that period made the tragedies of May and June inevitable. The junta, backed enthusiastically by what appeared to be the entire Argentine nation, refused to accept the United Nations call to withdraw their forces from the Falklands but instead poured more and more troops into the islands. The British, led by Mrs Thatcher, were equally determined to send a military force 8,000 miles down the Atlantic to liberate an 1,800-strong population of Falklanders who regarded themselves as British. There was some opposition to this rescue operation in Britain but it was never more than by a minority. The month would also see intense diplomatic activity in attempts to solve the problem, but these were all unsuccessful; they are not the subject of this book.

The first troops of the new Argentine build-up were the men of the 8th Regiment which left its barracks at Comodoro Rivadavia and started to move to the Falklands by air on 6 April, just three days after the United Nations debate. Orders were also issued that the 5th Marine Infantry Battalion and detachments of marine field and anti-aircraft artillery should follow; these units started to fly across on 8 April. The 8th Regiment was sent to Fox Bay Settlement on West Falkland, and the 5th Marines and the artillery units were deployed around Stanley. This instant response by the junta was to demonstrate Argentina's determination to remain in the Falklands and hopefully to deter Britain from making any military move.

This policy did not succeed. Eight British warships, a supply ship and a tanker were already on the move south. These ships had been exercising in the Atlantic off North Africa but were still many days steaming from the Falklands. Their orders to sail south on 3 April were not announced by the British, but two days later the aircraft-carriers *Hermes* and *Invincible*, their decks packed with Sea Harriers and helicopters, sailed from Portsmouth amid a deliberate display of publicity. The requisitioned liner *Canberra* sailed four days later, again with much public display; she was carrying four élite commando and parachute units. This was the British way of telling Argentina that Britain was prepared to fight for the islands.

The junta and the other Argentine military commanders were stunned. Their plan to repossess the Falklands with the support of world opinion and on the assumption that Britain would remain passive was now in ruins. I asked Vice-Admiral Lombardo about the reaction of his superiors:

They couldn't believe it. It seemed impossible that the British would go to so much trouble, to mobilize so many ships and modify so many merchant ships and liners over such a place as the Malvinas. For example, when Menéndez was put in charge of the Malvinas with a large party of senior officers and politicos, no one told him that it would be his task to defend the Malvinas. I sent him a message on 8 April, telling him I was coming to see what he was doing in the military sense. Menéndez said: 'What the hell are you talking about?' His only problems until then had been to look after the kelpers.

Lombardo went on to say that there was a sense of unreality in Buenos Aires at this period, with a strong feeling that the British moves might be all bluff. But four battalion-sized British units, all manned by long-term professional soldiers trained to NATO standards and supported by a powerful force of warships and aircraft, were now on the move. The Argentines only had three units of battalion size in the Falklands; most of their men were young conscripts with less than a year's service. Lombardo compared the junta's response to the betting in the next round of a game of poker; it was either 'upping the ante' or 'calling the bluff'; neither of us knew enough about poker to know which was the more appropriate term. The junta decided to double the strength of its forces in the Falklands and ordered the dispatch of a complete new brigade of infantry. Those two events – the sailing of the *Canberra* loaded with troops and the junta's decision to commit a further brigade – changed the whole nature of this potential conflict. The Argentine Navy had been the most enthusiastic element in the Falklands venture and had made all the early moves, but now the large-scale troop movement by both sides would result in the Army being forced to bear the main burden in the war.

The Argentine Army possessed nine brigades of front-line troops. There was no divisional system; the country was divided into corps areas in which the brigades were stationed. The main army units which had so far been sent to the Falklands were the 25th and 8th Regiments, which were from IX Brigade in Chubut Province. The new brigade now selected to reinforce the Falklands garrison was X

Brigade, [1] whose units were based in Buenos Aires Province. This was a well-equipped formation, with armoured personnel carriers and an armoured car squadron, but with no experience of cold weather conditions. Its commander was the bluff and physically imposing Brigadier-General Oscar Luis Jofre, known by the nickname of 'the Horse' because of his powerful stature and the shape of his face; but it was an affectionate term, and he seems to have been well respected by his men – even by the conscripts, which was not always the case with Argentine officers. The three regiments in the brigade were the 3rd, 6th and 7th based at La Tablada, Mercedes and La Plata respectively. These places were all around Buenos Aires city, and many of the conscripts came from there, contrary to hostile reports that the junta only sent men to the Falklands from distant parts of the country for fear of dissatisfaction in the capital.

The time has come to explain the Argentine conscript system, because the experiences of the young conscripts – the *chicos* ('boys') – became such an emotive part of the war. Every Argentine youth becomes liable for a twelve-month period of military service in the year in which he attains his nineteenth birthday, with a further liability for later recall from the reserve in a national emergency. The military year for an Argentine unit starts in January when the career officers and NCOs prepare to receive the year's conscripts; there is no such thing as a 'regular' private soldier. It is usually February before the 600 conscripts in an infantry regiment have all been received. The recruits are trained during the ensuing months, but then the first releases start as the year draws to a close. The effective term of service for the average conscript is only about ten months. The service is not harsh; the young men are usually posted to local units and can go home on most weekends and sometimes at night during the week as well. But they only have a lowly status, and there is no promotion. Young men could have their service deferred by up to seven years, but the opening of the Falklands War found most army units manned by *Soldados Clase '63* – 'Privates of the Class of 1963'. The weakness of the system was that units were no more than perpetual training cadres, albeit with cores of professional

---

[1] This was actually X Mechanized Brigade but the brigade left most of its transport on the mainland, and it will be more convenient to drop the 'Mechanized' subtitle from the brigade and its regiments in this description of the Falklands campaign.

# Argentine Build-Up, 6 to 29 April 1982

..... Provincial boundaries
Nearly all personnel crossed to the Falklands by air;
heavy equipment and stores were carried by ship.

Corrientes Province

III Bde

BRAZIL

4th Artillery

Córdoba

URUGUAY

B.A. City

Buenos Aires Province

X Bde

CHILE

601st AA

Marine units

Mar del Plata

Puerto Belgrano

Chubut Province

8th Regt

Comodoro Rivadavia

Puerto Deseado

25th Regt

Original garrison –
in Falklands from 2 April

Río Gallegos

5th Marines

Río Grande

British Exclusion Zone

statute miles

0          250          500

0          400          800 km

officers and NCOs, and that the Army had a particularly low operational ability in the early months of the year. That was one of the
reasons why the long-term Falklands plan had not envisaged any
action before September.

Brigadier-General Jofre was woken at one o'clock in the morning
of 9 April by a telephone call saying that his brigade was to prepare
to go to the Falklands: 'In the past week I had been warned for the
possible defence of the whole of the I Corps area. This new order
came as a complete surprise, but I had been hoping like mad that we
would have the chance to go.' There followed hectic days of decisions
and preparations. The armoured personnel carriers would not be
taken to the Falklands, but the Panhard armoured car squadron and
some of the lorries would. A furious recall of reservists took place in
a frantic effort to replace the current year's conscripts with the more
fully trained men from the previous year. Major Guillermo Berazay,
the Operations Officer of the 3rd Regiment, describes how he heard
the news:

I was out with some of the new recruits on their first exercise in
the countryside near Ezeiza International Airport. My commanding officer came on the radio at four o'clock in the morning
and told me to wake up all the men. We had to be in the
Malvinas in thirty-six hours! So we returned to La Tablada to
start recalling the reservists. Part of this was done by wireless,
part by telegram and part by vehicles calling at the men's
addresses. There was no holding back; they were very enthusiastic, an immediate reaction to the recent television and newspaper coverage of the occupation of the Malvinas. We managed
to change two-thirds of our new men for reservists and off we
went. We were even processing reservists right up to the last
minute. I remember a convoy of lorries loading up with men to
go to El Palomar Airport, with reservists still coming in, hurriedly changing their civilian clothes for uniforms and jumping
on the lorries. There were many civilians stood at the side of
the roads from the barracks to El Palomar, cheering and ap-
plauding. You could see that the soldiers felt very proud.

Another job that had to be done was to get all the heavy weapons – machine-guns, heavy and light mortars, anti-tank guns –

out of store. The new men had not started training with these weapons; they only had rifles at that stage. We took the heavy weapons out of store and they were all given to the reservists.

Alan Craig was one of the recalled reservists:

I was called back only one month after finishing my service. I wasn't going to go at first. I knew enough about the British forces to know what we would be up against; my father was a Mosquito pilot in the RAF in the Second World War, and my grandfather won the DSO with the Scots Guards in the First World War. My mother was Swiss, so I was the first Argentine in our family. But my father insisted that I went, and I reported for duty.

X Brigade managed to replace almost all of its new recruits with reservists, and the small number of new men who were taken to the Falklands were kept out of the front line; not one of them died in the war. The first regiments to go to the Falklands did not have the opportunity to make this exchange, but the marine units, which operated a two-monthly intake of conscripts rather than an 'all-in, all-out' system, were also able to take only 1962 men into action. It is also probable that X Brigade's proximity to Buenos Aires enabled it to make up its deficiencies of equipment and officers from the various military establishments in the city; there was an abundance of officers anxious to go to the Falklands. At the Military Academy at El Palomar, the entire senior class of 260 officer cadets were granted emergency commissions, becoming *sub tenientes en comisión*, and were posted to various units. A selected few, no more than twenty, went to the Falklands, where six of them would be decorated for bravery and one would die.

The first unit of X Brigade – an advance party of the 3rd Regiment – left El Palomar Airport in the early hours of 11 April in a Boeing 707 of the national airline, Aerolíneas Argentinas; the airliner had all its seats removed to enable a maximum load to be carried. After a refuelling stop in the south of the country, Stanley was reached in the first light of dawn, the aircraft captain not liking the appearance of the short runway but managing to land safely. Major Berazay was on that plane: 'My first impressions on seeing the Malvinas were:

one, that our clothing would be inadequate and, two, that we had never carried out exercises in country like that; it was going to be very difficult to defend with no cover and no trees and with such unsuitable soil in which to dig positions.' The rest of the brigade followed during the next five days. The heavy material, including the cooking equipment, would not reach Stanley by sea until 22 April. It was the start of hard times for the Argentine troops. The entire brigade was deployed to open ground in various sectors around Stanley, and the men became acquainted with the unforgiving nature of the Falklands climate and of the soggy, peaty, rocky ground where they dug the holes or pitched the tents which would be their homes for the next two months.

The arrival of X Brigade created a command difficulty at Stanley. There were now three brigadier-generals – Menéndez, Daher and Jofre – and the staffs of one part and one complete brigade headquarters – Daher's and Jofre's. There was actually sufficient infantry to form two brigades, but if this move was considered, it was soon discarded. Menéndez was secure in his position as Governor and Commander-in-Chief, but Daher, the Land Forces Commander, now found that the units from his brigade were outnumbered by Jofre's newly arrived units. Daher proposed that there should only be one Land Forces Commander and asked Menéndez to decide between himself and Jofre. Menéndez chose Jofre because he had most troops and a complete headquarters. Daher returned to the mainland, with no hard feelings against Jofre but disappointed to lose this interesting position and to hand over two of his regiments to another commander. He was soon back again, however, his corps commander allowing him to return to Stanley and become Chief of Staff to Menéndez. Menéndez and Jofre now settled down to decide their policy. An appreciation from Buenos Aires arrived showing that the British task force could arrive as early as 18 April. Jofre ordered all of his units to complete their defence works by that date and to be prepared to repel a British landing. Five of his six infantry units were deployed around Stanley, defending what was thought to be the natural objective of any British landing. But the Argentine units would have a long and uncomfortable wait before they saw their first British soldier.

*

The escalation of forces involved in the conflict was not over. A series of one-day visits by senior officers to Stanley took place. Admiral Anaya came on 19 April, Brigadier Lami Dozo on the 20th, General Nicolaides on the 21st – probably on a fact-finding mission for General Galtieri, who followed one day later. The events of that day, Thursday 22 April, were important.

We can go back to noon on 18 April when firm information reached Buenos Aires that a force of British ships had sailed south from Ascension Island. All Argentine merchant ships and commercial airliners had been asked to help in observing British warships' movements. The merchant ship *Río de la Plata*, on a routine voyage, was specifically ordered by the Argentine Navy to linger off Ascension. Her master, Captain Carlos Benchetrit, was one of those merchant marine officers who had attended a naval liaison course. It was Benchetrit who observed and reported the sailing of the British ships from Ascension; he was later decorated for this service. The Argentine Air Force now took over, sending unarmed Boeing 707 transport planes to detect the progress of the British task force. Argentina did not receive any help from Russia, whose merchant ships and Tupulov 'Bear' reconnaissance aircraft were also following the progress of the British force. The very first Boeing flight, captained by Vicecomodoro Jorge Ricardini, was fortunate enough to pick up the British force, coming into visual contact soon after noon on 21 April at 19.39 South, 21.35 West, which showed that the British ships were already about one-third of the way from Ascension to the Falklands. 'Two light aircraft-carriers and eight destroyers or frigates' were counted and reported by radio before a Sea Harrier appeared. The Argentine aircraft was quite clearly marked as an Air Force plane and was obviously on a reconnaissance mission, but British forces did not yet have permission to open fire in such circumstances, and, after each aircraft had photographed the other, the Boeing flew home to land at Buenos Aires.

So, when Galtieri came to Stanley on the day after that first Boeing 707 flight, it was clear that British intentions were serious and that the garrison in the Falklands must be prepared to defend itself, possibly within days rather than weeks. The Argentines also knew by now the composition of the British units which might be carried in the ships. Any landing in the Stanley area would find four

professional British battalion-sized units attacking six Argentine conscript units. A fifth British unit, a parachute battalion, was being
prepared and would sail from England on 26 April, but this may not
have been known to the Argentines.

Galtieri, together with Brigadier-Generals Menéndez and Jofre,
made long helicopter flights across the Falklands to study the extent
of the area to be defended. An important conference at Moody
Brook followed. Jofre describes what was discussed:

> The appreciation reached was that the British possession of so
> many helicopters would give them all the options. Their main
> landing would probably take place on the beaches south and
> south-east of Stanley, but there could be diversionary landings,
> even a main landing, at Uranie Beach on Berkeley Sound twelve
> miles north-west of Stanley. Stanley could thus be attacked
> from the south, the south-east, the south-west or the north. We
> decided that we could not oppose a landing on those lines with
> our present forces. San Carlos was mentioned but was dismissed
> as being too far away.
>
> So it was decided that our main force would remain around
> Stanley, with only our special forces to harass any landings
> further away while the main force waited for the British to
> arrive near Stanley and fight there. Galtieri said we did not
> have enough reserves, and we agreed; we only had two infantry
> companies in reserve, with a few helicopters and the twelve
> armoured cars. Galtieri suggested sending a further regiment
> of infantry. Menéndez and I agreed, providing he could solve
> the logistic problems we had with our existing forces, plus that
> of the new regiment. We had come in by air, and our cooking
> equipment took twelve days to follow by ship. At that time I
> only had fifteen days' rations and fifteen days' ammunition
> reserve in the *Formosa* in Stanley Harbour.
>
> Galtieri went home, and that night, at 11.30 p.m., a tele-
> printer message came from V Corps Headquarters on the
> mainland that a whole new brigade was being sent. I queried
> this, saying that they must mean a regiment. But, no, it was to
> be a complete brigade, plus the helicopters we had asked for. I
> cannot say I was unhappy with these extra troops, but I knew

that it was the start of a lot of new problems, fundamentally logistic problems. One regiment would have been a useful reserve. It would have given us a good helicopter-borne force to control the outer sectors.

The Argentine Army now had to decide which brigade to send. There were still seven complete infantry brigades left in Argentina but these were all stationed close to the frontiers, and there was reluctance to move them. The one that could be best spared was Brigadier-General Omar Parada's III Brigade, near the small and friendly country of Uruguay, and it was this brigade which was ordered to the Falklands. It contained ordinary conscript units recruited from Corrientes Province. The policy of leaving the other frontier units untouched left the excellently equipped VI and VIII Mountain Infantry Brigades along the Andes facing Chile and XI Brigade, equipped for cold-weather operations in the extreme south, also facing Chile. The long-standing hostility with Chile, particularly the dispute over two small islands in the Beagle Channel in Tierra del Fuego, thus robbed the Falklands garrison of the most suitable troops for fighting in the islands. III Brigade, coming from the subtropical north of Argentina, was a completely unsuitable force to be sent to the Falklands, where it would be located in places away from the town of Stanley with only a minimum of accommodation nearby.

The hapless III Brigade, destined to suffer the heaviest casualties in the war, had already been moved 1,300 miles south from its peacetime location. That move had started on 16 April when the three regiments left their barracks and were moved by rail and air down to Chubut Province, which was now regarded as the most vulnerable area of Argentina because its local brigade had already lost two regiments sent to the Falklands. III Brigade was in the process of deploying its units, to the west to strengthen the defences against any Chilean move and along the coast in case there was any British action against the mainland, when the unexpected order came to move to the Falklands. One company of the 12th Regiment was actually moving out west towards the frontier with Chile on the night of 22 April, when a police car overtook the truck convoy with the new orders. Most of the brigade had to cross to the Falklands by air, with little more than the equipment each man could carry. The units were well up to strength with conscripts and recalled reservists but would arrive in the Falklands severely deficient in many items of equipment. Most of the support weapons, radios, vehicles and other equipment – even such things as spades, rifle-cleaning equipment and reserve ammunition – were loaded on to a merchant ship, the *Ciudad de Córdoba*, but this ship never reached the Falklands. The units departing by air even had to go to local shops to buy spades to take with them on the aircraft. The air move of the personnel started on 24 April, the units arriving in the Falklands on that day being greeted with hail and rain at Stanley Airport and winds so fierce that tents could not be pitched that night. The move was completed on 29 April. The last unit to cross was the 4th Regiment. It was fortunate; there were sufficient aircraft available on that day for this regiment to bring its heavy weapons.

When this large body of troops reached the Falklands, the units could not all be located near Stanley, and the brigade was broken up and distributed to various locations. Most units suffered the detachment of companies or platoons for various duties. The 4th Regiment was added to the Stanley defences, being allocated a new westerly sector in order to extend the defended coastal area. The 12th Regiment was sent to Goose Green, to increase the strength of the garrison protecting the air base being established there, but it had to leave behind its B Company in the hills outside Stanley as a helicopter reserve. The 5th Regiment, which contained Menéndez's son, Second Lieutenant Mario Menéndez, went to Port Howard, a settlement on the island of West Falkland.

The arrival of III Brigade also created command difficulties. There were now two brigade headquarters staffs, one of which, Jofre's, was acting as that of the Land Forces Commander. It was decided that Brigadier-General Menéndez should become Land Forces Commander and that Jofre should command all the units in the Stanley area, which now became Agrupación Puerto Argentino. The newly arrived Brigadier-General Parada would command the huge outer area containing the western part of East Falkland island, including Goose Green, and the whole of West Falkland; this area became Agrupación Litoral. Parada was supposed to move his headquarters out to Goose Green but never did so. Brigade organizations

# Argentine Units in the Falklands, 30 April 1982

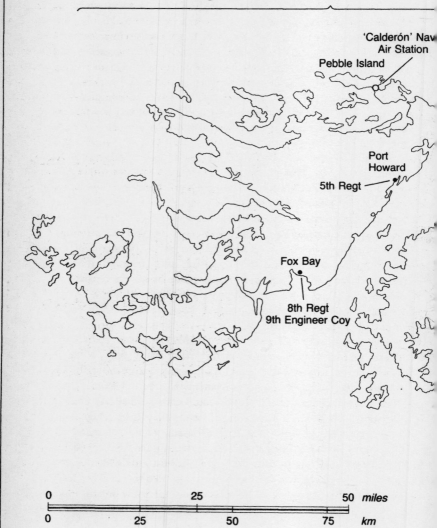

Coastal Sector (Agrupación Litoral)
Brig.-Gen. O. E. Parada

'Calderón' Nav
Air Station

Pebble Island

Port
Howard

5th Regt

Fox Bay

8th Regt
9th Engineer Coy

```
0                    25                    50  miles
├─────────────────────┼─────────────────────┤
0          25         50         75  km
├──────────┼──────────┼──────────┤
```

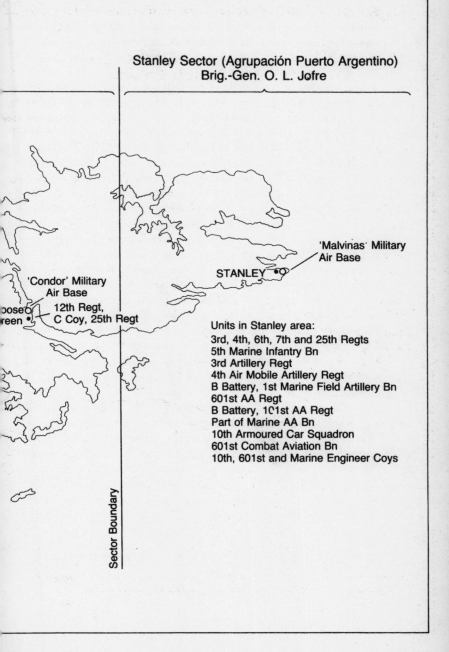

Stanley Sector (Agrupación Puerto Argentino)
Brig.-Gen. O. L. Jofre

'Malvinas' Military
Air Base

STANLEY

'Condor' Military
Air Base

oose
reen    12th Regt,
        C Coy, 25th Regt

Units in Stanley area:
3rd, 4th, 6th, 7th and 25th Regts
5th Marine Infantry Bn
3rd Artillery Regt
4th Air Mobile Artillery Regt
B Battery, 1st Marine Field Artillery Bn
601st AA Regt
B Battery, 101st AA Regt
Part of Marine AA Bn
10th Armoured Car Squadron
601st Combat Aviation Bn
10th, 601st and Marine Engineer Coys

Sector Boundary

now had little meaning. Parada lost one of his regiments to Jofre's command but gained the 8th Regiment at Fox Bay, a unit which now found itself under its third brigade commander in less than a month.

There were many other units in the Falklands besides the infantry regiments so prominently mentioned. There were three artillery units. The first to arrive was B Battery of the 1st Marine Field Artillery Battalion, which was equipped with six Italian-made 105-mm Otto Melara field guns. This battery always worked with the 5th Marine Infantry Battalion and came over with that unit early in April. When Jofre's X Brigade arrived, as the first full brigade on the islands, it did not bring its own artillery unit, the 1st Artillery Regiment,[2] because that unit's old-pattern American 105-mm guns were considered too old and too unwieldy for deployment on the Falklands terrain. Instead, the 3rd Artillery Regiment was transferred from III Brigade and crossed to the Falklands by air with its eighteen modern Otto Melara 105-mm guns. These were easily moved along the tracks around Stanley and were immediately deployed, mostly to the south of the town to face the expected British landings there. When III Brigade followed, it in turn had to borrow an artillery unit and was given the 4th Air Mobile Regiment from IV Brigade; and this unit, with eighteen similar 105-mm guns, arrived to give the Argentine commanders in the Falklands a force of artillery which would outnumber the guns eventually landed by the British.

The first anti-aircraft unit to arrive was also from the marines, with a detachment of twelve 30-mm Hispano Suiza guns and three British-made Tiger Cat missile launchers. The Army's 601st Anti-Aircraft Regiment followed, with twelve twin-barrelled radar-controlled 35-mm Oerlikons, three 20-mm Rheinmetall guns, three Tiger Cat launchers and one Roland twin missile launcher, the last being a very effective modern weapon which would much influence British air tactics in the Stanley area. 'We were very sad,' said the

---

[2] Argentine Army artillery units are organized in 'Grupos', normally of three batteries and thus the equivalent of the artillery regiments of most other armies; for this reason, the term 'Regiment' will be used in this English-language work.

regimental commander Lieutenant-Colonel Arias, 'that we only had one Roland.' Arias's unit had considerable difficulty in getting its equipment across to the Falklands. The guns were loaded into the transport ship *Ciudad de Córdoba*, but this ship never sailed, and the equipment had to be unloaded and sent over piecemeal by air. The unit was only just able to complete its full deployment by the end of April, on the eve of the first British air attacks. Two of the twin-barrelled Oerlikon units were sent to Goose Green, and two more to Moody Brook, but the remaining anti-aircraft weapons – both marine and army – were deployed in an integrated screen covering Stanley town, harbour and airfield; eight 20-mm guns of the Air Force were also stationed at the airfield. A further unit, B Battery of the 101st Anti-Aircraft Regiment, was also dispatched, but its guns came by sea, and the battery would not be operational when the first British attacks came.

In listing the smaller units in the Falklands, the versatility of the Argentine Marine Corps was shown in the action taken by Rear-Admiral Büsser after a visit to his 5th Marine Infantry Battalion in its hill locations west of Stanley. Büsser decided that the unit would be vulnerable to attack by troops landed by helicopter just outside the range of its regular weapons. He returned to Argentina and hurriedly formed a company of no less than twenty-seven 12.7-mm heavy machine-guns, some of which were fitted with infra-red night-sights. The British never used the helicopter attack about which Büsser felt anxious; the machine-guns were later distributed among many of the other positions defending Stanley and were much feared by the British infantry who eventually had to attack those positions. It was also a marine engineer company, sent early in April, that was the only fully equipped engineer unit to reach the Falklands. Two army engineer companies followed – the 10th and the 601st – but these were without most of their equipment because of the sea blockade; most of the army engineers had to be used as infantry because of this deficiency. The marine engineers were ordered to fortify the beaches around Stanley but did so without much enthusiasm because their amphibious experience led them to believe that the beaches were too small to sustain a major British landing and that the main threat would be from elsewhere. Most of their effort was put into laying mixed anti-tank and anti-personnel minefields in the western approaches to Stanley, a degree of forethought that proved to be a valuable investment.[3]

The policy of the Argentine commanders in the Falklands was that any landings away from Stanley should be harassed by the helicopter infantry reserve at Stanley and by special forces units, but the special forces were non-existent when the war started. Commando companies had been formed in the early 1970s, but had then been disbanded because, it is thought, the military junta feared the existence of such highly trained groups which might be used in a coup. The companies were reformed in 1975 for the internal war but disbanded again, then formed temporarily for security during the World Cup soccer tournament held in Argentina in 1978, but then disbanded after the games. The Falklands War thus found a number of trained commandos, 'still with the old spirit' as one said, but dispersed throughout the army and without recent commando training. These men were hurriedly collected, and the 601st and 602nd Commando Companies were formed with about forty men each and sent to the Falklands.[4] The commandos were supplemented by a detachment of the Gendarmería Nacional, Argentina's tough frontier police.

A number of air units also arrived. The Air Force had sent four Pucará propeller-driven ground-attack aircraft of the 3rd Attack Group on the day Stanley was captured by the marines and then eight more of these aircraft a week later. The Navy then sent six Aeromacchi 339A light jet aircraft and four propeller-driven Turbo-Mentors of the 1st and 4th Attack Squadrons on 24 April. Most of these aircraft were based at Stanley Airport, which became the Base Aérea Militar Malvinas; but a few of the Pucarás went to the grass airstrip at Goose Green, which became the Base Aérea Militar Cóndor; and the Mentors went to yet another grass strip at Pebble Island, which became the Base Aérea Naval Calderón. Twenty-six helicopters of various kinds from all of the armed services were transferred to the Falklands, as were two Skyvan transports of the

---

[3] Lieutenant-Commander Luis Menghini, the commander of the Marine Amphibious Engineer Company, had some strong comments to make about minefields. He was very incensed that a British officer had declared at a conference in the United States that 'no details' of minefields were handed over. He handed over full details of the minefields laid by his unit to a Major Roderick MacDonald of the Royal Engineers the day after the Argentine surrender in the Falklands, thus fulfilling the rules of the Geneva Convention. If the British had 'no details', he says, 'then they must have lost them!' But he agreed that army engineer units laying minefields may not have been so careful with records.

[4] The commander of the 602nd Commando Company was Major (later Lieutenant-Colonel) Aldo Rico, who later in the 1980s led small mutinies against the civilian government in Argentina.

Coast Guard. This made a total Argentine air strength in the Falklands of fifty aircraft by the end of April. The Navy provided no warships to help defend the island it had captured earlier in the month; the only ships to be sent from the mainland were the small Coast Guard vessels *Río Iguazú* and *Islas Malvinas* which were only armed with machine-guns. Two local ships, the *Forrest* and *Monsunen*, were taken over for the transport of military supplies between the various Argentine garrisons, and a third small ship, the *Yehuin*, a smaller oil-rig tender, was requisitioned in Argentina and sent to the Falklands to perform the same duty. The local air and naval commanders were Brigadier Luis Castellano and Captain Antonio Mozarelli, but Mozarelli was replaced by Rear-Admiral Edgardo Otero at the end of April.

With only a few small exceptions, the Argentine forces which would defend the Falklands were complete by the end of April. There was almost the strength of a complete division (although the Argentine Army did not possess divisional organizations). There were about 13,000 troops, three-quarters of whom were located in the Stanley area. The force which had numbered one Argentine soldier for every three Falklands civilians immediately after the occupation now outnumbered the local people by seven to one; it was almost twice as large as the landing units with the original British task force, which numbered about 7,300 men, although plans were already maturing in Britain to increase that strength by a further brigade of 3,200 soldiers.

Brigadier-General Menéndez and his commanders could do little now except wait for the British to come and show their hand. The Argentines had a powerful force of troops, with locally based air support and capable of being further supported from the mainland by the Air Force and Navy. But their defence policy was still based on the twin misconceptions that the approaching task force carried the main British landing force and that any landing would be near Stanley. There were many other shortcomings in the Argentine ability to repel a British attack. All of the Argentine units were based upon the conscript system. Nearly all had suffered sub-units detached and dispersed. An example of this was the army garrison at Goose Green, which would be the first to be in major action. At

Goose Green were the 12th Regiment – less its B Company, which was a mobile reserve near Stanley – C Company of the 25th Regiment, the original garrison at Goose Green, and a platoon which had somehow been detached from the 8th Regiment. There were many other examples of men who would have to fight in strange company. One of the reasons for this was a chronic lack of mobility. There were no roads connecting the various garrisons. Movement by sea would quickly prove hazardous when the British arrived, and the 26-strong helicopter force had to be carefully husbanded; the British task force would eventually operate more than 200 helicopters, and even these would not be judged sufficient during some parts of the campaign! Then there were the shortages of weapons and equipment caused by the British sea blockade. Some units had left behind all of their mortars, machine-guns, radios and cooking equipment. Argentine soldiers constantly mention the lack of such basic items as batteries for radios and weapon-cleaning lubricants. Men whose personal weapons were pistols often had no more than the six rounds of ammunition actually in the weapon; some conscripts had rifles which were unserviceable, while a few were completely without a personal weapon.

But morale was still high in those last few days of April. One conscript says that 'the spirit of the Malvinas' was felt by all of his comrades, and another felt that the war had already been won for Argentina on 2 April and that there would be no more fighting. Lieutenant Ignacio Gorriti of the 12th Regiment says that, on his departure from Argentina with the last reinforcements, 'there was no need for speeches. From the beginning we knew how important the Malvinas were. It was a kind of love; we were going to defend something that was ours.'

Captain Giaigischia was the pilot of a Chinook helicopter:

> I feel very excited at the sight of the islands on the radar screen of my helicopter. Then – there they are; I am right over them. I am deeply moved to be overflying the heart of millions of Argentines. I wish I could share this with my first grade teacher! These damp, low lands, alternating between sea and yellowish-green land, criss-crossed by thousands of streams and sprinkled with sheep!

We reached Puerto Argentino, well aware that we were now the actors of this war. Our blue and white flag flying proudly at the top of the pole, for a while, made me think that it was all a dream.[5]

Augusto La Madrid, one of the cadets given an emergency commission, was sent to the Falklands with the 6th Regiment:

I did not know we were actually going to the Malvinas until we'd left Río Gallegos by air; then we guessed where we were going. No one had told a junior officer like me. There was an excess of joy; we were quite thoughtless of any danger. The feeling of patriotism was high. No one wanted to be left in Argentina.

I was thrilled to arrive. First, as an Argentine, coming to defend the Malvinas; second, because I heard people speaking English which was a language I had heard in my home. I wanted to speak to the people, but the only ones who would speak to me were little children. I gave some sweets to them, but when the mothers saw this they took the sweets away and fetched the children inside. I remember my mother saying that the English were a proud people and would not accept us in the Malvinas and would never forgive us. She also told me to be aware and to keep on my guard. My mother was a Spencer-Talbois – one of the oldest English families in the Argentine. My great-grandfather fought in the Crimean War – he was a relative of Kitchener and Buller – and he came to Argentina soon afterwards. My grandfather was in the First World War and was gassed in the trenches in France.

But there was no conflict in my mind about the Malvinas. I was proud to be an Argentine and I believed completely that the islands were Argentinian.

Major Guillermo Berazay of the 3rd Regiment viewed the future more realistically:

[5] This and similar accounts by air force personnel are from a typewritten English translation of *Dios y los Halcones* (*God and the Hawks*) by Captain Pablo Marcos Carballo, an air force Skyhawk pilot in the war who collected accounts from fellow airmen for his book. Captain (now Major) Carballo kindly gave me a photocopy of the translation. With his permission, I have carried out some editing of the accounts.

I always thought it would come to fighting and that we would lose. You cannot fight against the third or fourth military country in the world and win. So, if the British really did come, then I knew many of us would die out there. We listened to the radio news about the ups and downs of the negotiations, but the British task force was still coming. When we heard that it had reached Ascension Island I realized they would definitely come down to the Malvinas. Until then, we thought it was too far for them.

We really wanted to fight as soon as possible. To have to wait for so long, that was the worst part of it for us.

## 6 · Distant Action

The Argentine fleet returned to its base after the initial landing on 2 April, its welcome as the force which had regained the islands somewhat muted by the United Nations resolution calling for a withdrawal and the news that the British were dispatching a task force. There would be nothing much that the Argentine Navy could do for at least two weeks until the British task force arrived, so all ships were replenished, and their mechanical defects were repaired. The British Government declared that a 'Maritime Exclusion Zone' would exist within the area 200 nautical miles from the centre of the Falklands; any Argentine ships attempting to enter that zone after 12 April were likely to be attacked. This move, which was to have such a weakening effect on the Argentine build-up, was made possible by the British possession of nuclear-powered submarines with their almost unlimited underwater endurance. Two of these vessels, *Spartan* and *Splendid*, had actually sailed for the South Atlantic on 1 April, as soon as the British realized that an Argentine force was about to land in the Falklands. The British press even suggested that a third submarine was already in the South Atlantic at the beginning of April, but this was an error, albeit a source of Argentine anxiety. *Spartan* and *Splendid* were both on station by 12 April, when the Maritime Exclusion Zone came into effect. What the Argentines did not know was that the British submarine commanders had not yet received permission to attack ships, because of the hope that negotiations to persuade the Argentines to withdraw from the islands might still succeed. The Maritime Exclusion Zone was, therefore, largely a bluff at this stage, but the Argentine leaders could not rely upon this.

The Falklands could not be supplied by air alone, and what might be called the Argentine 'blockade-running' operation can be split into three phases. Four ships were sailed before the Maritime Exclusion Zone came into effect. The *Río Cincel* and the *Lago Argentino*, both loaded with air force stores, were able to deliver their cargoes and return to the mainland before 12 April. The *Cabo San Antonio* and the *Bahía Buen Suceso*, carrying mainly naval stores, vehicles and equipment for the marine units ashore, reached Stanley just before 12 April. *Cabo San Antonio* was actually in the periscope sights of the submarine *Spartan* on four consecutive days when she was anchored in the approaches to Stanley Harbour. But *Spartan* did not attack, and this ship later returned safely to the mainland. The *Bahía Buen Suceso* was kept at Stanley, firstly to make use of her accommodation and later to distribute stores around the island garrisons.

But the introduction of the Maritime Exclusion Zone caught four other ships still in mainland ports. These were the *Formosa*, loaded with army rations and with X Brigade's heavy equipment, the *Río Carcaraña* with army weapons and stores, the *Ciudad de Córdoba* with III Brigade's equipment, and the *Isla de los Estados* also with army stores. The junta decided to suspend the sailings of these ships. It reasoned that if any of them were sunk then there would be criticism in Argentina over the loss, and that if the ships arrived and the news became known in Britain that the garrison had been so heavily resupplied then it would become harder to get a favourable response from Britain in the current negotiations.

The army commanders in the Falklands were, however, desperate to have their supplies, particularly of food; the level of reserves was down to forty-eight hours at one stage, and the scale of ration issues had to be reduced. So the junta reluctantly authorized the sailing of the four ships. They were sailed independently and unescorted, it being correctly assumed that the British would not attack unarmed, solitary merchant ships while negotiations continued. The *Formosa* sailed first and reached Stanley safely, bringing the food reserves up to fifteen days, but this was reduced by half when the units of III Brigade were sent over by air soon afterwards. III Brigade's equipment, in the *Ciudad de Córdoba*, never arrived; this ship struck a rock soon after sailing and had to return to the mainland. The *Río*

*Carcaraña* and the *Isla de los Estados* sailed later and both managed to reach Stanley before hostilities commenced, but they were not able to unload quickly and would be trapped in the islands.

A good contribution is available to illustrate these events. It comes from merchant navy Captain Edgardo Dell'Elicine, master of the *Río Carcaraña*, who was between voyages when the Falklands situation developed. His employers were E L M A (Empresa Líneas Marítimas Argentinas), a large, state-owned company with more than fifty cargo ships. The *Río Cincel, Lago Argentino* and *Formosa*, mentioned earlier, were all E L M A ships chartered by the Argentine Navy for their voyages to the Falklands. This is Captain Dell'Elicine's account:

I had volunteered my services on 2 April, asking if I could do anything to help in the Malvinas. I was called to the head office by the Operations Manager on 13 April. I didn't think that the army could keep up its logistic effort without ships, and E L M A's help would be needed. I knew the private shipowners would not be very keen. I was asked if I was still willing to go. Looking back on it, I think I made a big mistake, but there was no turning back.

I was ordered to take over the *Río Carcaraña*, which had been laid up for nearly a year; they had thought that its useful life was over. I had to prepare the ship for operations; we had her seaworthy in forty-eight hours. There was a lot of indecision over what we were going to do. I went to Navy Headquarters several times but kept coming back without orders. Then on the 19th, there was a big commotion, and I was ordered to be ready to sail that night. I had no crew at that time, and the ship was not loaded. We got a crew, moved berth and loaded on the 20th. There were lorries, much fuel in drums – jet fuel, diesel, etc. – and containers, at least one of which was full of television sets for the kelpers; as an Argentine, I could not understand that one. There was also 200 tons of fresh food as frozen cargo; the army in the Malvinas thought that food was the most welcome part of the cargo.

We sailed on the 22nd. I was ordered to keep my mouth shut

about the destination, not even being able to tell the crew, but the whole port of Buenos Aires knew we were loading for the Malvinas. We made a good voyage, and I cheated the British Navy in their Exclusion Zone by sailing down to the deep south and approaching the islands from due west. I made landfall on the little Isla Pájaro – what you call Bird Island; I think the naval liaison officer was impressed with our navigation. We came into Puerto Argentino – Stanley – on the 26th. I don't think they were expecting us because a reception committee of four navy jets met us on the way in. They circled round us for several minutes; I could see they were armed to the teeth. The flight leader eventually identified the colours on my funnel as belonging to E L M A and knew we were friendly. I am pleased they were navy pilots; the air force might have been more trigger-happy. Then we were met by a Coast Guard ship which handed over on a long pole a very rough chart of the local minefields. We came in very close to the coast, between the land and the minefields, and anchored in the outer harbour. I was surprised to see the *Formosa*, another E L M A ship, there.

I reported to the navy: 'Well, here we are. It's all yours.' The very first thing they wanted off was that container of television sets for the kelpers. I thought that was disgusting; the army needed ammunition and food far more urgently than the kelpers needed those television sets, but it was a political decision.

Those television sets were part of the 'hearts and minds' policy by which the Argentine administration hoped to win over the Falklands civilians. Two hours of transmission were relayed each evening from the mainland. There was an interesting sequel. The sets were sold on generous hire-purchase terms, but the war ended, and the Argentines departed, leaving the civilian buyers with the sets after paying only two monthly instalments – but only able to play video recordings.

An 'air bridge' had been put into operation when the Maritime Exclusion Zone came into being. A major effort was made using C-130 Hercules and Fokker F28s of the Argentine Air Force, Lockheed Electras and F-28s of the Navy, Boeing 737s of Aerolíneas Argentinas and BAC 111s of the internal airline Austral.[1] When that first air bridge closed in the evening of 29 April, just before the British task force arrived, more than five hundred successful flights had been made to Stanley, bringing in approximately 10,700 men and 5,500 tons of cargo, mainly ammunition and weapons. But this means of supply could not satisfy the garrison's entire needs, and the units in the Falklands would be left with grave shortages of food and many items of equipment.

The Argentine high command overestimated the ability of the British to reach the Falklands with a force capable of making a landing on the islands. The British ships and military units had been dispatched in haphazard fashion, with big public displays being given to some departures while others were in secret. The British policy over this was twofold, firstly hoping to persuade the Argentines to withdraw from the islands by a public display of strength and determination, secondly to confuse the Argentines over the exact composition of the task force. The first aim was not achieved, but the second one was.

The next British moves were determined by two factors. An early success was desirable, to sustain support at home and to put further pressure on Argentina to conform to the United Nations resolution to withdraw, but no major landing would be possible in the Falklands until the equipment of the landing units had been sorted and re-stowed at Ascension Island after being loaded so haphazardly in the rush to sail from Britain. South Georgia, with its small Argentine garrison, was chosen for the early success needed. The British task force thus split into three parts. Most of the British warships were pushed on to the Falklands to carry out preliminary operations there. The main landing ships and military units remained at Ascension to sort out their equipment and to await a further reinforcement – a parachute battalion whose ship would not reach Ascension until 7 May. A small force of ships containing troops made for South Georgia.

The Argentine Navy was responsible for South Georgia, with

[1] When I visited Argentina in 1987, the Argentine Navy booked my return flight from Puerto Belgrano to Buenos Aires on an Austral plane, probably one of those that had taken part in the air bridge; emblazoned on the side were the words LAS MALVINAS SON AR-GENTINAS. The same words are on a large roadside sign which greets every passenger travelling from Ezeiza International Airport to Buenos Aires city.

Admiral Anaya taking personal control. His intentions for the area went through several phases. Initially, he wanted to set up a scientific station as a practical example of Argentine sovereignty, but this idea was overtaken by military events. When news arrived that British ships were approaching South Georgia, Anaya's first reaction was to write off the place as untenable and order his men there to give up without a fight. But Anaya changed his mind again and dispatched a reinforcement of a composite marine platoon of about forty men under Lieutenant-Commander Luis Lagos aboard the submarine *Santa Fé*, with orders to make a stand if attacked but then to surrender if the British proved to be in overwhelming strength. In this way Anaya hoped that an easy recapture of South Georgia would satisfy British honour and that the British would not proceed with operations against the Falklands. The British attacked, being successful because of exactly the same factors as had been available to the Argentine attackers earlier in the month, the gunfire support of warships and the availability of helicopters, although the British lost two helicopters early in the operation when they crashed in a snowstorm. No one was killed in the fighting on South Georgia, but a crewman from the *Santa Fé* was badly wounded when the submarine was attacked by British helicopters, and another man in its crew was tragically killed by his Royal Marine guard after the submarine was captured when the guard thought that the Argentine sailor was trying to scuttle the submarine. Petty Officer Quartermaster Félix Artuso thus became the first fatal casualty in Argentina's attempts to hold the places taken from the British earlier in April.

The brief action in South Georgia ended on 26 April. Argentina's presence here lasted just twenty-three days. The British took 180 prisoners in South Georgia, a figure which includes Sr Davidoff's hapless scrap-metal workers, the various marine parties and the crew of the *Santa Fé*, which was damaged and beached, the first ship lost to Argentina in the war. The prisoners were soon returned to Argentina, via the Uruguayan city of Montevideo, which would act as a neutral exchange point for many more men later in the war. Only one prisoner was not immediately returned. Lieutenant Astiz was taken to Britain to be questioned about several foreign people who had disappeared in Argentina in the 1970s, but the British respected his status as a prisoner of war, refused to hand him over to other governments and returned him to Argentina later in the year.

The fall of South Georgia marked the start of a massive distortion of events by the junta. Official communiqués described a prolonged and heroic defence against overwhelming British forces, with commando parties dispersing into the wilderness and holding out long after the main fighting ended – the last part of which was completely untrue. The senior Argentine officer ashore, Lieutenant-Commander Lagos, was court-martialled in 1983 'for contravening Argentina's military code by surrendering without having exhausted his ammunition and without three-quarters of his men becoming casualties'. Vice-Admiral Lombardo attended the court martial and testified as to the exact nature of the orders issued, and this enabled the officer to be acquitted.

Sr Davidoff's scrap metal remained uncollected, and after the war he was not able to obtain a refund of his payment to the owners.

As the last days of April passed, the Argentines made their final preparations to meet the British. Their fleet had sailed and was exercising hard, but only in shallow coastal waters which British submarines could not enter. Air force and naval aircraft had been extensively practising attacks on ships. Most of the air units were now deployed to makeshift bases in the south of Argentina from where they would be within range of the Falklands. A few ships had to go into port again after the hard exercises but these soon returned to sea, and the entire surface navy stood ready for action. It was still believed that the support ships seen with the British task force were carrying landing units. A detailed plan was prepared; most of this will be more usefully described in a later chapter. I asked Vice-Admiral Lombardo if the Argentine plans would have been any different had it been known that the main British landing units were still on Ascension Island. After a few seconds of thought, he answered that it was an interesting question but too difficult to answer.

The only warship sent into the exclusion zone around the Falklands was the submarine *San Luis*, which sailed from Mar del Plata on 11 April. After two days spent exercising and testing its equipment, the submarine reached the edge of the zone on 17 April and was ordered to remain just outside it while negotiations were still taking place; the Argentine ships were ordered not to fire the first shots. Then, after the loss of South Georgia, the *San Luis* was ordered into the zone and it reached its patrol area north of Stanley on 29 April. The British commanders were apprehensive about the dangers posed by Argentina's submarine force, but the *San Luis* would be the only one to operate. Her sister ship *Salta* was not allowed to sail because a defective propeller shaft caused too much noise which would have attracted attack. The older *Santa Fé* was put out of action in South Georgia, and her sister ship the *Santiago del Estero* was not even able to submerge; she sailed from her base at Mar del Plata, in the hope that the British would believe her to be at sea, but was hidden in Bahía Blanca harbour for the remainder of the war. Two modern submarines of German design, the *Santa Cruz* and the *San Juan*, were still under construction and could not be made ready, although the British did not know that.

The Argentines received the final confirmation that the British task force was about to reach the Falklands area when it was spotted and reported on 29 April. The report came from the *Narwal*, which was one of several deep-sea fighting trawlers with naval officers aboard which, under orders from Naval Intelligence, were looking out for the British task force. *Narwal* gave particularly good service, spotting and reporting the task force on this day and making contact again later.

Friday 30 April was an important day. It was apparent that negotiations were failing and that serious action was about to commence. The United States ended its period of even-handed neutrality and firmly declared itself in favour of the British cause, a severe diplomatic setback for Argentina. It was on this day also that Britain had announced that the Maritime Exclusion Zone was to become a Total Exclusion Zone, with aircraft, as well as ships, now being liable to attack in the zone. A note spelling out the full implications of British policy had been delivered by the Swiss Embassy in Buenos Aires to the Argentines on 23 April. It read:

In announcing the establishment of a Maritime Exclusion Zone around the Falkland Islands, Her Majesty's Government made it clear that this measure was without prejudice to the right of the United Kingdom to take whatever additional measures may be needed in the exercise of its right of self-defence under Article 51 of the United Nations Charter. In this connection Her Majesty's Government now wishes to make clear that any approach on the part of Argentine warships, including submarines, naval auxiliaries or military aircraft, which could amount to a threat to interfere with the mission of British Forces in the South Atlantic will encounter the appropriate response. All Argentine aircraft, including civil aircraft engaging in surveillance of these British forces, will be regarded as hostile and are liable to be dealt with accordingly.

The main implication of this warning for the action about to commence was that any ship or aircraft *approaching* the exclusion zone might now be attacked if it was considered a threat to British units. I asked Vice-Admiral Lombardo if, in the light of the later sinking of the *General Belgrano* just outside the exclusion zone, he fully understood the intent of the message. He answered, without any hesitation or qualification, that he and his colleagues realized the implications of the note. He went on to say that his first thought was that the British would use the new conditions to attack the mainland air base at Río Grande to neutralize the Exocet-equipped Super Étendard aircraft there, and he sent four battalions of marine infantry to that area and asked the army to provide an anti-aircraft unit.

The fear that the British might land special forces to attack the mainland air bases led to a tragedy on 30 April. A Huey helicopter of the army's 601st Combat Aviation Battalion was searching the coastline near the Comodoro Rivadavia air base, following a report that men had landed from the sea, when it crashed in mist and early-morning darkness. All eleven men on board were killed – the three-man helicopter crew, together with two officers and six soldiers from the staff of a military college. One of the officers was Colonel Clodoveo Arévalo, who would be the most senior-ranking Argentine serviceman to die in the war.

# 7 · First of May

The British task force entered the 200-nautical-mile exclusion zone during the night of 30 April. That 200-mile limit had no particular significance for the British, but they needed to approach the Falklands in order to commence operations. The British Government had decided that negotiations were unlikely to persuade the Argentines to withdraw and that offensive action should now be pressed ahead as quickly as possible. There were twelve warships in the task force – the aircraft-carriers *Hermes* and *Invincible*, each with a squadron of Sea Harriers and many helicopters, and ten destroyers and frigates, together with three supply ships. The only troops present with the task force were detachments of the Special Air Service (SAS) and Special Boat Service (SBS).

The mission given to the task force was to conduct operations in such a way that the Argentines would believe that a major landing was about to take place and so to draw into action the main Argentine naval and air strengths from the mainland. Major engagements were hoped for so that these elements of the Argentine forces could be neutralized before the vulnerable landing ships arrived. The only British to set foot on the islands would be the special forces parties, who would gather as much information as possible about the Argentine defences, but who would avoid direct contact if possible. The British commanders were prepared to allocate at least two weeks to this preliminary phase. The first shots would be fired on 1 May. For the British, this undeclared war had started on 2 April, but many Argentines view 1 May as the first day of war; the operation of 2 April, they say, was one of repossession, not one of war.

The first attack came in a manner which caught the Argentines by surprise. A single Vulcan bomber came in from the north, flying

nearly 4,000 miles from Ascension Island and having been refuelled
many times on the way by a fleet of Victor tankers. Its task was to
bomb the runway at Stanley airfield. At 4.40 a.m. the Vulcan dropped
its long stick of twenty-one bombs in just the manner planned, and
one bomb burst nearly halfway along the runway, making a large
crater. To obtain this accuracy, the Vulcan had made its bombing
run at only 10,000 feet, within the range of the 35-mm anti-aircraft
guns and of the Roland missile launcher defending the Stanley area.
The Skyguard radar of the guns had been detected by the Vulcan's
electronic counter-measures devices and jammed. Lieutenant-
Colonel Arias, the commander of the 601st Anti-Aircraft Regiment,
says that the sophisticated A N T P S-44 'Alert' radar on Sapper Hill
detected 'various aircraft' to the north but that there was a delay while
a check was made to establish whether any Argentine aircraft were in
the area. Whatever happened, the Argentine defences were slow
coming into action, and the Vulcan turned back and eventually
landed safely at Ascension Island.

Major Alberto Iannariello was an air force officer who experienced
the bombing:

> I was sitting in an armchair in the Control Tower, deep in
> thought, when the explosion of the first bombs suddenly shook
> me back to reality, and I found myself facing a red cloud which
> swept towards the tower, smashing all the window panes and
> shaking the building. When I came round, I found myself under
> an armchair and heard Captain Dovichi moaning. He had fallen
> down the stairs and badly hurt his spine. I went down and outside
> as quickly as possible with my rifle and my helmet and found a
> chaotic situation – people running here and there, wounded
> moaning, the red flashes of our anti-aircraft guns exploding in
> the sky, white-orange missiles. . . . It was our baptism of fire.[1]

It is probable that three men were killed: Raul Romero, a member of
the Marine Anti-Aircraft Battalion who was with an air force communications post at the airfield, and two air force men – Héctor
Bordon and Guillermo García. All three men were conscripts from
the Class of 1962 and all were buried in the civilian cemetery at
Stanley later that day. Several other men were injured.

[1] From the unpublished English translation of *Dios y los Halcones*.

The damage to the runway was serious. It could not be perfectly repaired with the available local resources, and the hit put paid to any plans the Argentines might have been considering to use the airfield as a forward operating base or an emergency landing ground for their high-performance jets, a factor which enabled the British task force to remain closer to the islands for the conduct of its operations for the rest of the war. The crater was roughly repaired but would even then cause problems for the rugged Argentine transport aircraft which continued to fly into Stanley; one Hercules nearly crashed after a rough take-off over that section of the runway. The remaining bombs burst in a long line across the airfield area and caused minor damage to some parked aircraft and to equipment.

The next attack came soon after dawn when eighteen Sea Harriers took off from their aircraft-carriers. The first two of these flew over Stanley airfield to photograph the results of the Vulcan bombing and then joined four other Sea Harriers flying air patrols, in case any Argentine fighters turned up to engage the bombing raids which were about to commence. Nine more Sea Harriers then attacked Stanley airfield. They flew in two groups, from the north-east and from the north-west, and roared in at low level, dropping twenty-seven bombs of various kinds in the airfield area. A fuel store was set alight, producing an impressive fire and a tall column of black smoke, but this was the only serious damage, although there may have been some light surface damage to the runway. Argentine guns fired furiously, and at least two missiles were fired. The crew of the *Río Carcaraña* believed that their ship was strafed by cannon fire from a Sea Harrier which flew right over the ship and the crew cheered 'as in a football match' when they saw a missile from the airfield area follow that aircraft into the cloud. They were convinced that the missile scored a hit. A log kept at the Argentine headquarters at Stanley recorded various reports and claims. The 3rd Battery of the 601st Anti-Aircraft Regiment reported two Sea Harriers destroyed and another departing trailing smoke and unlikely to reach its aircraft carrier. Then the Coast Guard ship *Islas Malvinas* 'confirmed' that a Tiger Cat missile had scored a success. The local Air Force Headquarters now made the tally two Sea Harriers definitely destroyed and two probables. An hour and a half later, having studied all the reports, this was amended to three definites. In fact, only one Sea

Harrier had been hit in the tail by a single 20-mm cannon shell. This aircraft returned to its carrier safely and was quickly repaired.

The remaining three Sea Harriers attacked the air base at Goose Green. A Pucará air patrol was just taking off when the three Sea Harriers came in from the north and dropped their bombs. One Pucará was actually starting its take-off; it slowed down and broke its nose wheel in a hole. The 'bomblets' of a cluster bomb fell right across another Pucará, and there were numerous explosions, both of the bomblets and of the plane's own ammunition. The Pucará broke in half and burned. The pilot was killed, together with five mechanics – all career air force men – who were nearby. It was a horrible scene of carnage and destruction. The grass airstrip was cratered, and two other Pucarás were damaged so much that they were never repaired to fly again. The army units at Goose Green escaped most of the bombing; their commanders had been warned of the possibility of air attack and had moved their men away from the airstrip. Captain Giaigischia, an air force Chinook helicopter pilot, describes the evacuation of the wounded to Stanley and the deaths of two more men:[2]

All those who were still alive were carried to the helicopter, and First Lieutenant Bower and I started our flight towards Puerto Argentino. We had to land twice on the way because Harrier air patrols were about.

When we put down at our base at Puerto Argentino, a chaplain made the Sign of the Cross towards the interior of the plane while speaking the words of absolution. I shouted, 'For heaven's sake, get an ambulance! These men are dying!' In fact, two of them had died during the flight. To one side of the helicopter I saw an NCO from the crew crying, so I asked him what was wrong with him. 'Sir, he died in my arms. We studied and graduated together; we were always close friends. And he died in my arms, begging me not to let him die!'

He was deeply moved and kept shouting the same thing, completely out of control. Affectionately, yet firmly, I struck his chest and ordered him to laugh. But he kept on crying. So I persisted, until at last he started to smile, then giggled, and finally roared with laughter. I must have needed some relief

---

[2] From the unpublished English translation of *Dios y los Halcones*.

myself, for suddenly I found myself laughing with him. So we saved ourselves. We had to overcome the weakness of our human nature, for many lives depended on us, and this was just the beginning of the war. Maybe there would be time to cry at night.

There was a lull of several hours after the Sea Harrier attacks. The next actions involved five British warships which left the task force to carry out two separate operations. In the first of these, the frigates *Brilliant* and *Yarmouth* steamed to a position twenty miles off the north-east corner of East Falkland island on an anti-submarine sweep. They were hunting the Argentine submarine *San Luis*. British intelligence was good; it had picked up the signal which two days earlier had ordered the *San Luis* to come into this area. The two frigates, together with three anti-submarine Sea King helicopters from *Hermes*, carried out a long search. Several contacts were gained and many depth-charge attacks made. A suspected oil slick was seen, and there were hopes that the *San Luis* may have been sunk, but the wrecks of many old iron whaling ships were in this area, and it was probably these that were depth-charged, because the *San Luis* was not attacked. The submarine's captain was Commander Fernando Azcueta. His was the only boat of the Argentine submarine service to take part in the war and it had an unhappy voyage, gaining no successes, but it did tie down British resources — particularly anti-submarine helicopters — as long as it was known to be in the area. Commander Azcueta was most anxious to talk about his experiences and to dispel the impression that the *San Luis* was not handled vigorously enough:

> We were sent to sea unready for operations, under conditions very far from suitable. I think we could have had a successful operation in better circumstances. Also, the crew was not fully trained because it was so early in the year; we had taken a complete new crew aboard in January. I was very proud of what they did in difficult circumstances; they did the best they could.
>
> That morning, we detected a British ship on our 186 Sonar. I believed there were three ships but it was difficult to be sure because there was so much noise in the water. They were

steaming at high revolutions, about 20 knots, with medium propeller noise. I could not see them visually by periscope; all the work was done by the passive sonar equipment. We attacked at a range of between 10,000 and 14,000 metres. I fired one torpedo at 10.05, a German wire-guided A E G S S T-4. The attack was not successful because the main control computer, the heart of the firing system, was unserviceable; it had failed on 19 April. In the absence of the computer, a team of people working manually had to control the firing. I had a good team; they had been practising ever since the computer failed. Also, I think the wire guide broke a few minutes after the launch of the torpedo.

We heard some depth charges in the distance, and I also believe that we heard an anti-submarine torpedo, but the British attacks were nowhere near us.

The second group of British ships to leave the task force came in much closer to land. The destroyer *Glamorgan* and the frigates *Arrow* and *Alacrity* approached to within seven miles of the coast south of Stanley with the intention of shelling six targets: the airfield parking area, the road between the airfield and Stanley, two suspected gun positions and two suspected radar stations on Sapper Hill and Mount William. The ships opened fire at about 1.30 p.m. The British did not know for sure where the Argentine gun positions and radar posts were, but they were shelling likely locations with two objects, to continue the process of wearing down the Argentine defences started that morning by the Vulcan and the Sea Harriers, but, more importantly perhaps on this day, to act as though they were firing a preparatory bombardment for a major landing. Two young conscripts, Horacio Benítez and Juan Diez, in the positions of the 3rd Regiment south of Stanley, saw the twinkling of the ship's guns firing out at sea:

We were on sentry duty. We had lit a fire and were listening to Bob Dylan on Stanley Radio. We saw this light; we didn't know what it was. We kept on chatting. Then there was a second light, then a third. We thought perhaps they were Argentine ships, but they were not. The guns of the 3rd Artillery Regiment started to fire at those lights. We thought that the British were trying to land but our artillery drove them off.

The ships settled down to their task. Their 4.5-inch guns easily out-
ranged the Argentine field artillery, and the Argentine gunners soon
realized that they could not hit back. Shells fell steadily around the
airfield targets; there are no reports of casualties there, but the batter-
ing of the equipment and facilities started that morning continued.

Some helicopters were working with the bombardment ships, cor-
recting the fall of the shells. Two of these had brushes with the
Argentine defences. The Coast Guard ship *Islas Malvinas* opened
fire on a Lynx helicopter from *Alacrity*, and the helicopter crew
fired back. Both the ship and the helicopter were hit by machine-
gun bullets, and one Argentine was wounded. Another helicopter, a
Wessex, was outside Stanley Harbour hoping to catch and attack any
ships forced out of the harbour by the shelling, but it was driven off
by two Tiger Cat missiles fired from the airfield. These helicopter
incidents were the basis of the report sent to the mainland that
landings were taking place by helicopter and landing barge in the
Berkeley Sound area, eight miles north of Stanley.


The presence of the British ships brazenly shelling the Stanley area
drew the Argentine mainland air units into action, but only a small
force of aircraft was committed in the first operation, and only
twelve aircraft were dispatched, with the main emphasis being on
fighter action. The 5th Fighter Group[3] sent four of the old second-
hand American Douglas Skyhawk A-4Bs with which the unit was
equipped, each carrying two 500-lb bombs. The 8th Fighter Group
provided a top-cover escort of four of its much newer, French-built
Mirage IIIE As; each of these aircraft was fitted with two air-to-air
Matra Magic missiles and two 30-mm cannons. Both units were
flying from Río Gallegos. The final element in these morning missions were four Dagger I A Is (Israeli-built copies of the Mirage) of
the 6th Fighter Group based at Río Grande; these aircraft were also
flying in the purely fighter role; each was armed with two Shafrir
missiles and two 30-mm cannons. One of the twelve pilots involved
would not survive the day, and four more would die later in the
month.

The twelve aircraft all reached the Falklands area, where they

[3] This was Grupo 5 de Caza; its *caza* – 'fighter' – designation indicated its main role, but most of
the fighter units would be required to operate in the fighter-bomber role during the war.

came under the direction of the local air force controllers. Everyone was experiencing their first active service conditions. The controller at Stanley directed the Skyhawks to a target north-east of the islands, and the Argentine pilots made for that area, searching for ships to bomb. But the controllers were confused and had made a mistake; the Skyhawks were being directed towards the echoes of two Sea Harriers! Two of the Mirage pilots realized what was happening and intervened. Although they were short of fuel and about to return to the mainland, they dived and launched one (possibly two) missiles at the Sea Harriers, but without scoring hits. There was a little more manoeuvring between the rival fighters but no further direct contact. The Skyhawks found no targets for their bombs, and neither did the Daggers make any firm contact with Sea Harriers; they all returned to their bases after an unproductive first mission.

A flight of three locally based aircraft were also in action. These were Turbo-Mentors of the 4th Naval Attack Squadron flying from Pebble Island. They were ordered to attack suspected helicopters landing troops north of Stanley. The Turbo-Mentor was only a tiny aircraft; its primary role was that of training naval pilots to fly. The more suitable Aeromacchis based at Stanley airfield were not used, probably because of the damage caused to the runway by the bombing of the Vulcan and the Sea Harriers that morning. The Turbo-Mentor pilots flew to the north-east tip of East Falkland and spotted just one helicopter to the south. The situation developed into a real game of who caught whom first. The Turbo-Mentors turned and made for the helicopter, which would have had little chance of escaping their combined attack if two Sea Harriers had not arrived on the scene. Sub-Lieutenant Daniel Manzella was flying Number Two in the Turbo-Mentor flight:

We did not know where the Sea Harrier patrols were. We were searching for the helicopters for half an hour when I spotted one, near Cow Bay. We were about two miles out. We all went in and prepared to attack. But, at that moment, while very close to Cow Bay, Number Three cried out on the radio: 'Lobos a las seis' – 'Wolves at six o'clock.'

I instinctively broke to the right; at the same time I heard the sound of the 30-mm cannons of the Sea Harriers. I jettisoned my pods of rockets and of machine-gun ammunition, and the Sea Harrier passed over me at that moment. I would have run right into its fire if I had turned to the left. The Sea Harrier came round and attacked again, but I evaded it and escaped into a cloud. I think he missed me because we were too slow and so got away.

The Sea Harriers might easily have shot down these low-performance aircraft if the British pilots had been prepared to use their Sidewinder missiles. But, as one of the British pilots explained: 'It was not considered the done thing at that time to waste an expensive Sidewinder against a cheap, propeller-driven aircraft.' The pilots of both sides would soon shed such inhibitions. Only one of the Turbo-Mentors was slightly damaged, by a cannon shell which went through the cover of the empty rear cockpit. This would be the only time the Turbo-Mentors were used in action.

The Argentine morning air missions had been tentative and the results inconclusive, but more determined moves were planned for the afternoon now that the situation around the Falklands had become clearer. A total of at least fifty sorties was planned, with the main emphasis now being on ship attack. Every front-line Argentine air force unit of the mainland would be involved. Many of the sorties were planned to be as near simultaneous as possible in their arrival over the combat area so that the British defences would be overwhelmed. It will be more convenient to describe the experiences of the attack units first, then of the escorting fighters.

It is not known exactly how many anti-ship sorties were planned; the possible number may be thirty-seven. The first to appear were three Daggers of the 6th Fighter Group flying from San Julián. The formation, led by Captain Dimeglio, flew round the north of the Falklands, seeking to attack the group of British ships which were on the anti-submarine sweep north of Stanley. An account is available from one of the pilots, First Lieutenant César Román. A small point to emerge from the account is how the British helicopters operating near the islands led a charmed life that day; 'Puerto Argentino' is Stanley:[4]

---

[4] From the unpublished English translation of *Dios y los Halcones*.

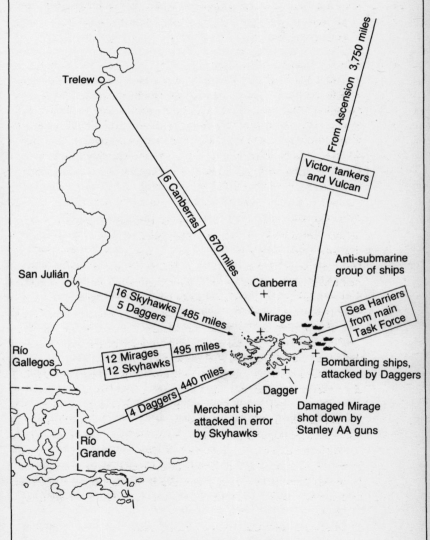

# Air Operations, 1 May 1982

○ Air bases
+ Aircraft losses

Trelew ○

From Ascension 3,750 miles

Victor tankers and Vulcan

6 Canberras
670 miles

San Julián ○

Canberra
+

Anti-submarine group of ships

16 Skyhawks
5 Daggers  485 miles

Mirage
+

Sea Harriers from main Task Force

Río Gallegos ○

12 Mirages
12 Skyhawks  495 miles

Bombarding ships, attacked by Daggers

4 Daggers  440 miles

Dagger
+

Merchant ship attacked in error by Skyhawks

Damaged Mirage shot down by Stanley AA guns

Río Grande ○

*(All distances are in statute miles)*

We had been seated in our planes all morning, ready to take off
at five minutes' notice. At midday, we were told to take off and
that we would be informed of the mission during the flight. We
took off but then were ordered to land again. Our commander
gathered the three of us to plan a high-level outward flight with
a low-level final leg. The name of our mission was *Torno* –
'Drum' – and the target was to the north of Puerto Argentino,
about fifteen miles from the coast.

Our high outward formation was a loose one, then we went
down low and flew one close each side of the leader. I caught
sight of a helicopter to our left, but we were only four minutes
away from our target, so, when I informed the leader, he said
we must carry on to the target. Suddenly, we saw something on
the horizon and started the attack – but it was only a rock.

We changed course, always following the coast, and reached
the target area, but there was nothing there, so we headed
towards Puerto Argentino. We could see that the shore was
being fired at, and right in front of us the explosions looked like
fireworks. All of a sudden, we caught sight of them. There
were three frigates, all firing rapidly, very near Puerto Argentino. I heard on the radio the flight leader say: 'Number One,
take the centre frigate, Number Two the left, Number Three
the right.' We skimmed over a calm, grey sea at a height of about
300 metres. It was 15.00 hours.

We opened full throttle preparatory to attacking. I saw flashes
in the water in front of me and thought I was being fired at, but
they were only the spitting flames of my leader's guns. It was
our first attack upon the British fleet, and we took them totally
by surprise. I didn't fire my guns, as I couldn't believe those
were their ships and not ours. Number One dropped his bomb.
Number Two told us later that, after climbing to get into
position for a cannon attack, he had been heavily fired upon by
the ships. An officer on the island, Major Catala, later reported
that he saw the frigate launching two missiles at Number Two,
but they went past below him. He fired all the rounds from his
guns, and dropped his bombs. I only dropped my bombs.
Then – 'Number One, leaving!' '*Torno* Two, leaving!' '*Torno*
Three, leaving!' Good! I saw a large explosion on the surface

of the water, with a lot of fire in it. We went up through the cloud, trying to gain altitude, and disappeared in the distance.

It was my first return from a combat mission. Once on land, we embraced each other, had our post-flight briefing and then off we went to rest. As time went by, a reaction set in, and my fear gradually increased as I recollected our experiences, but at the same time I felt comforted and at peace, having fulfilled my duty.

The ships attacked were not the originally intended target – the anti-submarine group – but were the three ships of the bombardment group off Stanley: *Glamorgan*, *Alacrity* and *Arrow*. The sudden attack had taken the ships by surprise. *Glamorgan* managed to launch a Sea Cat missile, and *Arrow* fired a few cannon shots, but the Argentine aircraft were not hit. *Glamorgan* had bombs explode either side of her, and *Alacrity* also had near misses, but both escaped with no more than a severe shaking and, in *Glamorgan*'s case, some side plating dented by blast. Both ships were also hit by cannon fire, and one seaman on *Arrow* was slightly injured by a splinter of metal. None of the ships was put out of action, but the attack did make the captains realize how vulnerable they were so close to the coast, and they broke off the bombardment and withdrew.

The attack and the resulting retreat of the ships were observed by the Argentines on land, where the event was a major boost to morale on what, so far, had been a bad day. It was believed that one of the ships had been severely damaged and set on fire, a belief based on the emission of much smoke from one of the ships – probably the older *Glamorgan* steaming away at speed. It was an exciting incident and was a good attempt by the Argentine pilots in their first action. It is interesting to speculate on what success might have been achieved if the attacking aircraft had been flown by naval pilots, who had practised ship attack frequently, rather than by air force pilots more used to land targets.

The next effort – mounted by the 4th and 5th Fighter Groups based at San Julián and Río Gallegos respectively – involved no less than twenty-four Skyhawk sorties, all in flights of four aircraft, all equipped with bombs. But only one flight found a target. This was the 5th Fighter Group's *Trueno* – 'Thunder' – flight, led by Captain Pablo Carballo, who has provided the following account.[5] One of his flight returned early with mechanical trouble:

> While I was checking the controls before take-off, I realized that my hands and knees were shaking. This really distressed me, for it was not the image I had in mind for the warrior who faces two terrible truths; first, the fact that he may die; second, whether he is a man of courage or a coward. In spite of this, while giving the routine signals to the groundcrew, I was a picture of steadiness and determination which I was far from feeling. Three little holy medals and my rosary clinked on my chest. These would protect me throughout the whole war. The ground staff, with tears in their eyes, shook hands with me; that wasn't very reassuring! We got to the runway head, turned on full throttle, and as soon as the wheels left the ground I was invaded by that feeling of peace and tranquillity I had always prayed to God for in the previous days. I got to know later that this same thing happened to everybody.
>
> When I caught sight of land, I felt a mixture of fear and courage; it was the moment of truth. I was acutely aware of the historical importance of the coming events. At the suggestion of one of my flight, we came down even lower, very close to a calm, greyish sea, while to my left I could see the coastline. We flew on for some time, sometimes over land and sometimes over the sea again. Then, in the darkening sunset, I saw the imposing shape of a ship silhouetted to the east on the horizon. It was the first time in my life I had seen a ship sailing in the open sea. We were to face our first trial. I shouted: 'Viva la Patria', and pushed the throttle to its maximum forward position, flying the plane as close to the sea as possible. The ship began to grow larger in my sight as we waited for their firing, but nothing happened. On getting nearer, I could see a rectangular metal superstructure, similar to the ones we had seen in pictures of tankers that, according to what we had been told at previous briefings, accompany the fast frigates which sail with half fuel loads to be able to move more freely in action. When I

[5] From the unpublished English translation of his own book, *Dios y los Halcones*.

came within range, I climbed, dropped my bombs, and so did the others.

Later, on my return flight, there in the red sunset I saw again the silhouette of the ship I had bombed. I felt disappointed that I hadn't fulfilled my mission, for it was intact. After making an intimidatory dummy run over the ship, so that its crew might take shelter, I came in again and opened fire with my cannons; I was not interested in killing men, but only in destroying their equipment. I watched my tracer ammunition go into the upper works, rebounding everywhere. As we made off westwards I listened on the radio to the joyful expressions of the others who commented on how wonderful it was to return alive.

But the ship Carballo and his flight attacked was the E L M A merchant ship *Formosa*, which had delivered a large cargo of military stores to Stanley in the build-up period and had been hurriedly sailed from Stanley that morning, ironically to get her out of the danger zone. The attack took place off the south coast of East Falkland. The ship was hit by two bombs but was most fortunate because one bounced off and fell into the sea and the other did not explode. There were no casualties. The ship's master, Captain J. G. Gregorio, not surprisingly reported that he had been attacked by Sea Harriers. This was the only attack carried out by the twenty Skyhawks dispatched; none of the others made contact either with ships or with the Sea Harrier patrols.

The remaining anti-shipping strike was provided by six Canberra bombers which had once served with the R A F and were now operating with the 2nd Bomber Group, flying from Trelew. Two flights of three Canberras were dispatched. It was perhaps fortunate that neither flight came upon British warships. These old aircraft would have bombed from medium level and, at that height and with only their obsolete counter-measure equipment, would have been most vulnerable to the modern missile systems on the British ships. But one flight of Canberras was interrupted by a pair of Sea Harriers, and a Sidewinder missile shot down one Canberra into the sea.[6] Its crew ejected but they were never found.

---

[6] This was Canberra B110 (Argentine serial number), which, as the RAF's W610, had served with no less than five squadrons and survived an accident while in RAF service before being sold to Argentina ten years earlier.

The result of the large Argentine air effort dispatched against the British ships was thus one successful attack, causing damage to two ships, and one attack on an Argentine ship, with the loss of one Canberra and its crew.

The aircraft operating purely in the fighter role were also in action. These were Daggers and Mirages of the 6th and 8th Fighter Groups flying from Río Grande and Río Gallegos. They flew in pairs and were intended to provide high escort cover for the anti-shipping flights. They were partially successful in this because their presence attracted the Sea Harrier patrols away from all of the bombing missions except the unfortunate Canberras. But this was at a high cost to the fighter aircraft. A pair of Mirages met two Sea Harriers over the north of the Falklands, and a brisk missile combat ensued. The tactics and the missiles used by the British pilots proved to be superior to those of the Argentines, and both Mirages were hit. One crashed into the sea off Pebble Island; the pilot ejected and was fortunate enough to come down so close to land that he could wade ashore. The fate of the other Mirage created one of the most dramatic moments of the day. Captain Gustavo Cuerva's plane was badly damaged by a Sidewinder, and Cuerva realized that his aircraft would not survive a flight of more than 400 miles to the mainland. He decided to attempt an emergency landing on the airfield at Stanley and approached it from the west. The liaison necessary between air force and anti-aircraft gunners in circumstances like this was not achieved. The gunners believed the approaching aircraft was a Sea Harrier, and many of them opened fire. Major Jorge Monge, himself commander of an anti-aircraft battery, was walking near Government House, a helpless spectator:

> Some men later said they saw the Mirage jettison its fuel tanks; these fell and burst, looking like bombs. It continued on, very low, on a direct approach to the airfield. It flew right over my head, and I realized it was one of ours. I saw a machine-gun nearby shooting, but everything along the way was firing as well. I felt a terrible anguish because I knew it was one of ours. It was very frustrating. I wanted to shout to everyone that it was ours, but it was too late. As an anti-aircraft officer I knew

they would not miss at that range. I think it crashed in the airfield area. He could have ejected and saved himself but he was definitely trying to save his plane. It took me some time to get over that incident.

Captain Cuerva was killed. Meanwhile, a Dagger flight had encountered further Sea Harriers, and after another missile combat one Dagger was hit and exploded over the south coast of East Falkland somewhere near Lively Island. The body of the pilot, First Lieutenant José Ardiles, cousin of a famous footballer, was never found. The Argentines thus lost three aircraft, either during or as a result of combats with Sea Harriers which had themselves survived unscathed. This was a major setback for the Argentines, demonstrating that their aircraft, training and equipment, together with the distance from the mainland, would always leave Argentine aircraft operating in the fighter role at a disadvantage. This type of escort mission and fighter sweep would have to be abandoned in future, thus conceding air superiority over the islands to the Sea Harriers.

Darkness came, but the action and bloodshed were not yet finished. The three British warships which had retired after the Dagger air attack returned to resume their bombardment programme, the evening targets being mainly to the west of Stanley. There were further casualties. A man of the 3rd Regiment was killed on Sapper Hill, and at least five men were injured there; the dead soldier – Private Jorge Oscar Soria – was the first man of the Argentine Army to die for the Malvinas. Another conscript was killed by gunfire in the positions of M Company of the 5th Marine Infantry Battalion, but it is not known whether he died in the afternoon bombardment or this evening continuation. He would prove to be the only fatal casualty in his company during the whole campaign.

Another British activity started as soon as it became dark. Sea King helicopters came in and landed reconnaissance parties of special forces at several points along the north coast of East Falkland island. The last shells from the British ships fell at about 10.00 p.m., and the other ships on various outlying duties rejoined the task force, which withdrew from the scene of action, leaving everyone to consider the results of a momentous day's events.

The civilians at Goose Green settlement were ordered to leave
their homes and concentrate in the settlement's community hall that
evening. First Lieutenant Esteban says that the decision was his:

> I had already decided that, if air attacks came, I would move
> my defences from around the school, which was separate from
> the settlement, to new positions around the houses, with the
> idea that the British would never bomb the settlement area. We
> believed that a landing was imminent, and I did not want the
> children around; also, some of the civilians had seemed hostile
> and uncooperative. They had left lights on at night, let animals
> out on to our minefields and sometimes cut off the water and
> petrol. I thought it was better to concentrate them all in one
> place in that hall in the centre of the settlement, with a red
> cross painted on the roof.

More than a hundred people would have to remain in that hall for
nearly a month. The Argentines moved into their homes.

The British task force had tried to make radio contact with the
Argentine command during the day. The Argentines had not replied,
but some civilians at Salvador Settlement heard the message. The
British wanted the Argentines to discuss the possibility of a ceasefire
to avoid further bloodshed. The settlement manager and his family
acknowledged the message on their radio and tried to relay it to the
Argentines at Stanley but, for their pains, were visited by two helicopters full of troops who took the manager back to Stanley, where he
was rigorously questioned by the military police and forced to
remain for the remainder of the war. The Argentines were in no
mood yet to consider surrendering, but this incident did start an
anxiety about the development of a local resistance movement spring-
ing up among the civilians and working with the British special
forces which had such a high reputation and whose men were now
obviously present on the islands.

It had been a very bad day for the Argentines. The runway at
Stanley airfield had been badly damaged, and a Pucará had been
destroyed and two more damaged at Goose Green airfield. Positions
had been bombarded. Two Argentine ships had been damaged, one
by the fire of its own side's aircraft. Three Argentine aircraft had

been shot down by Sea Harriers and a fourth destroyed by the fire of its own side after being damaged in air combat. Seventeen Argentines were dead – four aircrew in the air, one pilot and seven technicians at Goose Green and five men killed around Stanley by the Vulcan bombs or by naval shelling. One officer and twenty-seven men were injured. Several observation parties of British troops had been successfully landed. The British casualties consisted only in superficial damage to two ships, a cannon shell hole through the tail fin of a Sea Harrier and one seaman slightly injured.

It is interesting to examine how the Argentine public relations system dealt with these setbacks. Overclaiming in the heat of action of casualties inflicted upon one's enemy is a common and understandable occurrence; the armed forces of all countries do it. The Argentines at Stanley really were convinced that they had shot down three Sea Harriers on the morning of 1 May; although none of the wrecks had fallen on land, radar indications led to the belief that three aircraft had crashed into the sea. British forces would make similar mistakes later in the month during the Argentine air attacks on the British landing area. Similarly, the sight of three of their own aircraft bombing and strafing the bombardment ships in the afternoon, followed by the high-speed withdrawal of those three ships, one of them seemingly belching black smoke, was a reasonable basis for the claim that all of the ships were damaged, one seriously so. The Argentines did not know that the ships which returned after dark and resumed the shelling were the same ships, still capable of effective action.

But this understandable overclaiming was to be followed by deliberate lying. Immediately after this day's action, Brigadier-General Menéndez ordered the publication of a local newspaper for the troops in the Falklands. The first issue of the *Gaceta Argentina* (*Argentine Gazette*) appeared one week later, its editor being named as an army chaplain, Friar Salvador Santore, assisted by a press officer of the military government, Captain Fernando Mayo. The presence of that last name showed that the newspaper would reflect the line ordered by the junta. In describing the actions of 1 May, the *Gaceta* admitted the death of one man of the 3rd Regiment but made no mention of four other men killed at Stanley and eight at Goose Green. The losses in air combat were given as a 'Skyhawk' and a Canberra –

both old types of aircraft, when the actual losses were a Dagger, a Mirage and a Canberra, the losses of the more modern Dagger and Mirage thus being concealed. The crew of the Canberra were described as being safely recovered; in fact they were never seen again. To account for the loss of the second Mirage, seen by so many men to be shot down by their own fire when it was trying to land at Stanley, the *Gaceta* stated that this aircraft had been in collision with a Sea Harrier, with both aircraft crashing but with the Argentine pilot surviving. I do not know exactly what was publicly announced on the mainland, but it is probable that the media releases there followed the same line. The junta press office in Buenos Aires added a further lie. Lieutenant Antonio Jukic, the young Pucará pilot killed in his aircraft when Goose Green airfield was bombed, was described as dying in a gallant, lone attack on the British aircraft-carrier *Hermes* which Jukic's bombs set on fire. Dramatic sketches of this imaginary action were also issued.

These were all blatant lies, designed to cover up the Argentine setbacks of the day. They set the scene for future treatment of bad news. It would create a cruel disillusionment for those Argentines who either knew at the time or would soon discover the truth. The men at Goose Green knew that Lieutenant Jukic had died there, and the whole of the Argentine Air Force would soon know the truth and resent the lie. The men at Stanley had seen the Mirage shot down by their own guns, and someone must have removed the dead pilot from the crashed plane. But there were many Argentine soldiers, as well as most of the civilian population on the mainland, who did not realize that this was all propaganda and who believed that their forces were doing so well. It would be a very long process to correct these misconceptions. The process was still not complete when I visited Argentina five years after the war. I was recommended to buy a book, described to me as 'the most reliable book about the Argentine side of the war'. Most of the untruths were repeated in that book.

The Argentines still remain desperate to claim some success for that day's actions. Even while I was writing this book in 1988, Brigadier-General Jofre sent me a copy of a new book written by him and the officer who was his Chief of Staff in the Falklands. The book even quotes the serial numbers of two Sea Harriers – XZ 458 and XZ 491 – claimed shot down near Stanley that morning, the first by a 35-mm gun, the second by a Roland missile.[7] In fact both aircraft were that day flying from England to Ascension Island and were then taken to the Falklands on the *Atlantic Conveyor*. They returned safely to England after the war but both aircraft were then lost in accidents, XZ 458 crashing in Scotland after a bird strike in 1984 and XZ 491 running out of fuel and crashing into the sea while flying from the new aircraft-carrier HMS *Ark Royal* in 1986. The Argentines might say that these are cover stories, concealing the losses of the two Sea Harriers at Stanley, but my son-in-law was serving in HMS *Ark Royal* as a technician in 1986 and had often worked on XZ 491.

[7] O. L. Jofre and F. R. Aguiar, *Malvinas – La Defensa de Puerto Argentino* (Sudamericana, 1987), p. 100.

# 8 · Task Force 79

The Argentine Navy was trying to play its part in combating the anticipated British landings, but there was no direct contact between the two task forces on that first day of action. Every serviceable Argentine warship had been at sea since mid-April, rehearsing their parts in what was expected to be a major clash when the British arrived. The Argentine ships were operating under the overall designation of Task Force 79. Rear-Admiral Allara was the seagoing commander, flying his flag in the aircraft-carrier *Veinticinco de Mayo*. Vice-Admiral Lombardo, who had gone to sea in command of a task force when the Falklands were occupied at the beginning of the month, now stayed ashore at Puerto Belgrano and directed operations from there. Task Force 79 was originally divided into three 'task groups' which were thought to be the best tactical groupings to operate against the British. The three groups were:

> Task Group 79.1: *Veinticinco de Mayo* (aircraft-carrier), *Hércules* and *Santísima Trinidad* (Type 42 destroyers), *Drummond*, *Gránville* and *Guerrico* (frigates).
>
> Task Group 79.2: *Comodoro Py*, *Hipólito Bouchard*, *Piedra Buena* and *Segui* (destroyers).
>
> Task Group 79.3: *General Belgrano* (cruiser).

Task Groups 79.1 and 79.2 were to operate against the main British task force. Task Group 79.1 would use the eight Skyhawk attack aircraft on the aircraft-carrier as its strike element, and the four destroyers of Task Group 79.2 would operate as a 'surface-attack group', their main weapon being their Exocet missile launchers. The old cruiser *General Belgrano* was to do no more than take station in the deep south with two duties – to guard against the possibility of

British ships coming round Cape Horn from the Pacific and to counter any hostile move which Chile might make.

But these plans were changed on 26 April. There were two reasons. The recent loss of South Georgia showed that the British now had ships in the deep south, and at the same time a report was received that HMS *Exeter*, the British Type 42 destroyer on duty at Belize, had been seen with a tanker going through the Panama Canal into the Pacific, which – if true – would have given *Exeter* the opportunity to come round Cape Horn and strike up from the south. (It is probable that the '*Exeter*' sighting was of the older ship *Norfolk*, which had been sold to Chile and had passed through the Panama Canal in March.) The composition of the task groups now changed. Task Group 79.2 was broken up; two of its destroyers – *Comodoro Py* and *Segui* – were transferred to the aircraft-carrier group, and the *Hipólito Bouchard* and the *Piedra Buena* were sent south to reinforce the *General Belgrano*. At the same time, the new Task Group 79.4 was formed by taking the frigates *Drummond*, *Gránville* and *Guerrico* from the carrier group to form a new surface attack group, this time of more modern ships. All groups now had a strike capability, of either aircraft or Exocets. It should also be remembered that ashore at Río Grande there was a fourth strike element, the Super Étendard naval squadron with its Exocets, its aircraft capable of being air-refuelled and of operating well out to sea.

It was with these dispositions that the Argentine Navy awaited the arrival of the British task force. The three groups were all in position by 30 April, all ships topped up with fuel, tankers in reserve positions ready to refuel later if the operation was a long one. The Argentine ships were ordered not to fire the first shots. Each group was positioned between 50 and 90 nautical miles outside the British declared exclusion zone. I asked Rear-Admiral Allara whether he believed that the positioning of his ships just outside the exclusion zone would bring him immunity from British attack. He replied that he was aware of all the implications of the recent British warning that attacks were now likely outside the zone but said that it was hoped that Britain would not allow attacks on Argentine ships at that stage because such attacks would prejudice the last negotiations which were still taking place. The Argentine commanders were quite correct in this assumption. The British submarine *Splendid* had seen all five escort ships in the old-style Task Group 79.1 on 26 April and it spotted the three frigates of the new Task Group 79.4 on 29 April, but British submarines still had orders not to engage targets. The Argentines were quite prepared to cross the border of the exclusion zone once fighting broke out, and they did not consider that the 200-mile limit held much relevance after the events of 1 May.

Everything changed on that morning of 1 May, with the reports that the British had opened the action with their air attacks at Stanley and Goose Green. The three Argentine task groups were all ordered to move towards the estimated position of the British task force, although they did so cautiously, steaming round the outside edge of the exclusion zone rather than striking into it at this stage. This caution was probably a mixture of tactical reasoning and a reflection of the hope that, by not yet entering the zone, British submarine attack could still be avoided. This last was again correct; the British submarines still did not have permission to attack, even though HMS *Conqueror* was now in contact with Task Group 79.3 in the south and could have made a torpedo attack on the *General Belgrano* at any time on that day.

But it was in the north where the greater chances of a clash existed. The British task force had come in so close to the Falklands, in order to carry out its various operations, that it was less than 300 nautical miles away from the approaching Argentine aircraft-carrier and the surface attack group. The Argentine admirals would never have a more favourable opportunity to strike than on that day, when the opposing forces were so close and so much of the British effort was devoted to the opening attacks on the islands; but initially at least, neither side knew the exact location of the other. The Argentine ships were keeping radio silence, and British intelligence had not on this occasion been able to locate the Argentine groups. The only Argentine move they knew of with certainty was that of the *Belgrano* group in the south, but that did not yet pose a serious threat. The Argentines had three reconnaissance aircraft operating from the *Veinticinco de Mayo*. These old, slow, twin-engined Grumman Tracker aircraft were not ideal for reconnaissance work in these days of sophisticated weapons. They ran a considerable risk flying out to find the British ships but they were helped by some hastily added electronic surveillance equipment recently fitted into the aircraft by the workshops at their mainland base. This enabled the Trackers to detect British radar emissions at a greater range than the aircraft's ordinary radar sets. 'That equipment saved our lives several times,' says one Tracker pilot.

On the first Tracker mission of 1 May the new equipment immediately detected British radars working, but only the approximate range, not the bearing. At midday, however, another Tracker, flown by Lieutenant-Commander Alberto Dabini and his crew, obtained both range and bearing but went in so close that the Tracker found that it was being positively 'illuminated' by British ship radars. The Tracker was now in great danger, because any Sea Harrier in the area could easily have caught this 120-knot aircraft. But it was also important that the location of the British ships be firmly established. Dabini continued his climb just long enough to use his own radar briefly, but this was sufficient to confirm the bearing and show the echoes of six ships, 55 miles distant. He turned back at once, went down low, radioed his information back to the aircraft-carrier and flew back, taking a zigzag course so as not to disclose the exact route back to his own task group. Dabini and his crew were fortunate that they had been beyond the range of the British Sea Dart missiles and that all the Sea Harriers were tied up with other operations.

The Tracker report provided Rear-Admiral Allara with vital information which could form the basis of a successful air strike. The escape of Dabini's Tracker showed that the Sea Harrier cover was not complete, but ships' missiles were considered to be a greater danger at that stage of the war; experience would quickly show that this was an incorrect assumption. Allara hesitated. He was undoubtedly concerned about British submarines. Also, there was only a light wind, which would have necessitated the aircraft-carrier closing the range with the British task force. The day passed without any air strike being ordered.

A further Tracker sortie took place after nightfall in an attempt to plot the further movement of the British ships. Lieutenant-Commander Emilio Goitía and his crew detected the British ships, coming within 60 miles of them, but were followed by a Sea Harrier on their return. The British aircraft was then detected by the radars of the Argentine ship *Hércules*, but, in turn, the Sea Harrier pilot realized that he had been detected and turned away, although coming back again later to obtain a quick glimpse on his radar of five

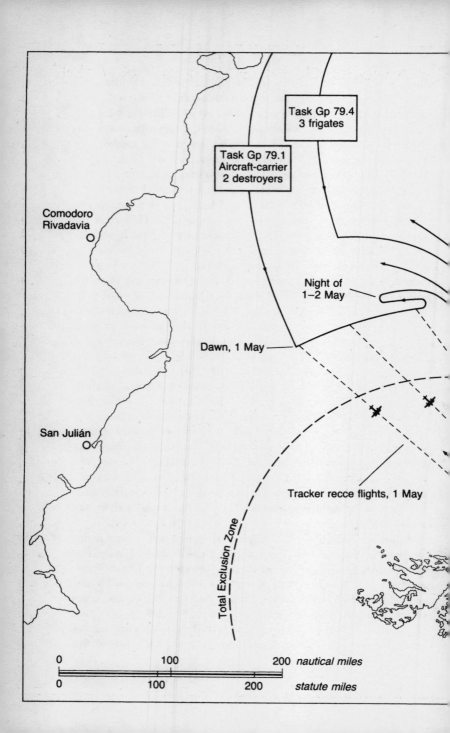

Task Gp 79.4
3 frigates

Task Gp 79.1
Aircraft-carrier
2 destroyers

Comodoro
Rivadavia

Night of
1–2 May

Dawn, 1 May

San Julián

Tracker recce flights, 1 May

Total Exclusion Zone

| 0 | 100 | 200 nautical miles |
| 0 | 100 | 200 statute miles |

# Naval Moves (North), 30 April to 2 May 1982

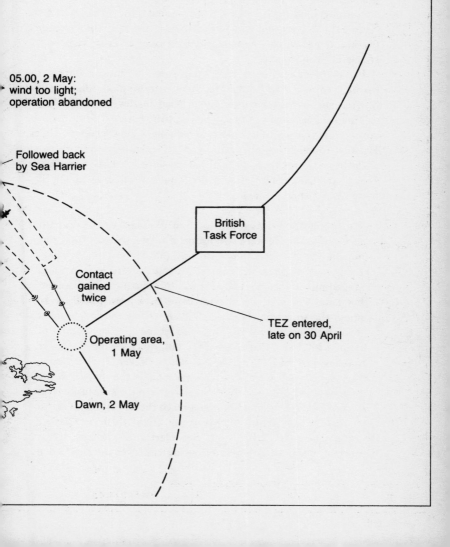

05.00, 2 May:
wind too light;
operation abandoned

Followed back
by Sea Harrier

British
Task Force

Contact
gained
twice

TEZ entered,
late on 30 April

Operating area,
1 May

Dawn, 2 May

Argentine ships. Both sides now knew exactly where the other's ships were and could prepare for the morrow. Having recovered the Tracker, Rear-Admiral Allara ordered his carrier group to turn back towards the Argentine coast for several hours, intending to return at dawn and attempt an air strike the next morning. The three frigates of the surface attack group to the north complied with these moves; any action by them would be in conjunction with an air strike or against isolated British units. Rear-Admiral Woodward, the British commander, having successfully completed the opening actions against the Argentine forces on the islands, turned to the south-east, putting all his ships on the alert to defend themselves against possible attack in the morning.

Fresh information was received by the Argentines during the night. A report from Stanley reached Rear-Admiral Allara, telling him that the suspected British landings had not developed. To Allara, this meant two things – first that the British ships would now be concentrated, second that there was no longer the urgency to attack. He still proceeded with his plan to return and attempt a morning air strike but not to come in so close that his ships would be endangered. Lieutenant-Commander Alberto Philippi was the leader of the Skyhawk sortie being planned:

We started the briefing at 11.00 p.m. We only had six aircraft serviceable. There were two teams of pilots, and my team was on the roster that time. In the middle of the briefing, Lieutenant-Commander Castro Fox came up from behind and tapped me on the shoulder. He was the squadron commander, but I was senior to him, having come back from a staff job to rejoin the squadron. He said: 'Please, this is the first combat mission of my unit. Will you please let me have the honour of leading it?' I said that I was sorry but, no, I was on the roster and I would take the mission. Later, however, I talked alone with the intelligence officer who was making the analysis of the English ships and their missiles; he came to the conclusion that only four of the six aircraft would reach the target and only two of them would return. I was really afraid then. It was the surface missiles – Sea Wolf, Sea Dart and Sea Cat – that worried me most. It was only during and after the war, when

things had been tested in action, that we realized the fighters
were a greater danger.

But dawn did not bring favourable conditions. The wind was still
very light, and the meteorological officer's forecast was that there
would be no change for twenty-four hours, an unusually long period
of calm in this area. A minimum wind speed of 15 knots was needed
to allow the Skyhawks to take off with two 500-lb bombs and sufficient fuel to attack a target 200 miles away; the current conditions
only permitted an 80-mile sortie and one bomb to be carried because
of the reduction in the aircrafts' loads necessary for take-offs in the
light wind. (Ironically, the British manufacturers of the Sea Harrier
had tried to sell some of these aircraft to the Argentine Navy when
the *Veinticinco de Mayo* was purchased from the Netherlands Navy
in 1969 but had been unsuccessful; Sea Harriers could have taken off
in the light wind prevailing that morning with almost full loads.)
The six Skyhawks were still fuelled and armed for the flight but they
never took off. Vice-Admiral Lombardo, at Puerto Belgrano, had followed every move and he now ordered that the operation be abandoned. I asked Rear-Admiral Allara whether the order was a political
one originating from the junta; 'No. Definitely not. None of our plans
envisaged an all-out engagement between the two task forces; the difference in strength made that impossible. My orders were to carry out
limited operations, taking favourable opportunities. The important
factor that morning was that the British were not making a landing
on the Falklands, and their ships were now concentrated.' Lombardo's new order was to return not to port but only to the mainland
coast to await further developments. The British ships remained on
the alert all day. Rear-Admiral Woodward did not know that the
Argentine ships were leaving the scene of potential action. The
Super Étendards at Río Grande attempted an attack that day, dispatching two Exocet-armed aircraft, but the necessary in-flight refuelling was not successful, and that operation was also abandoned.

So the opportunity for a major clash passed. Some Argentine
officers were bitter that the chance to launch the air strike the
previous day had not been taken. One says, perhaps overstating the
situation a little: 'It would have been the great battle of the war, the
Midway of the South Atlantic.'

# 9 · The *Belgrano*

Vice-Admiral Lombardo's order to the aircraft-carrier group to turn west and steam towards the Argentine coast was also transmitted to the most southerly element of Task Force 79 – the cruiser *General Belgrano* and the destroyers *Hipólito Bouchard* and *Piedra Buena*. The destroyers had been to sea before during the Falkland operations, as part of the naval force which covered the original landings in the Falklands one month earlier, but this was the first war sortie for the *Belgrano* since she had been part of the United States Navy and as the USS *Phoenix* had fought against the Japanese in the Second World War. Because the sinking of the cruiser caused the greatest single loss of life during the war and also the greatest controversy, it is important that her exact mission should be described.

The *Belgrano*'s *original* role, in the first days of this voyage, was to guard the south-western approaches to the potential war zone in case British supply ships or warships came round Cape Horn from the Pacific or in case the Chileans intervened. But, when the British task force approached the Falklands and commenced operations, the *Belgrano* group was ordered east to conform to the movements of the main elements of Task Force 79 in the north. I asked Rear-Admiral Allara what his intentions were for the *Belgrano* at that time. This was his answer:

In addition to blocking the way in for any British ships coming in from the Pacific and showing a presence in the south because of our problems with Chile, she could now move east, basically as a diversion but capable of taking advantage of any favourable opportunities. One of these might have been the separation of a small group of ships from the main British task force. The

*Belgrano* would have created a useful source of menace in the south. There was no need to keep her presence secret; we assumed that the British were getting satellite information, and the *Belgrano* might have attracted a small group of British ships. Don't forget that there was air support in that area – the Super Étendards with their Exocets – and there were Neptune reconnaissance aircraft.

The *Belgrano* and the two destroyers carried out their orders, steaming eastwards all day on 1 May. The ships remained just outside the old exclusion zone, but all concerned knew that there could be as much danger in or out of the zone, and everyone I spoke to willingly agreed that the zone would have been entered if conditions for successful action arose. One Argentine naval officer who was at sea at that time, though not with the *Belgrano* group, was anxious to tell me that he had decoded a signal to the *Belgrano* group on the evening of 1 May, telling the group to be prepared the next day 'to flit in and out of the exclusion zone to test the reaction of the British'. That was not admitted or confirmed by other officers. Just what the *Belgrano* group would have done that next day will never be known, because the group was ordered to reverse course at 5.30 a.m. on 2 May. This was to comply with the movement of the units in the north when the planned air strike was abandoned that morning for lack of wind. The furthest point reached was 55.15 South, 57.50 West, which was 240 nautical miles from the British task force. The group was ordered back towards the coast, but not to port. Captain Hector Bonzo, captain of the *Belgrano* and commander of the group, stresses: 'We were heading towards the mainland but not going *to* the mainland; we were going to a position to await further orders.'

What the Argentines did not know was that the British nuclear-powered submarine HMS *Conqueror* was following every move the *Belgrano* made. The submarine had made long-range sonar contact with the Argentine ships on the evening of 30 April, even before they started their voyage to the east. Visual contact by periscope was gained the following day, and the group was followed without difficulty to its furthest point east and then back again when course was reversed, a total of almost 500 nautical miles. The *Conqueror* could have made a torpedo attack at any time, but the British Government

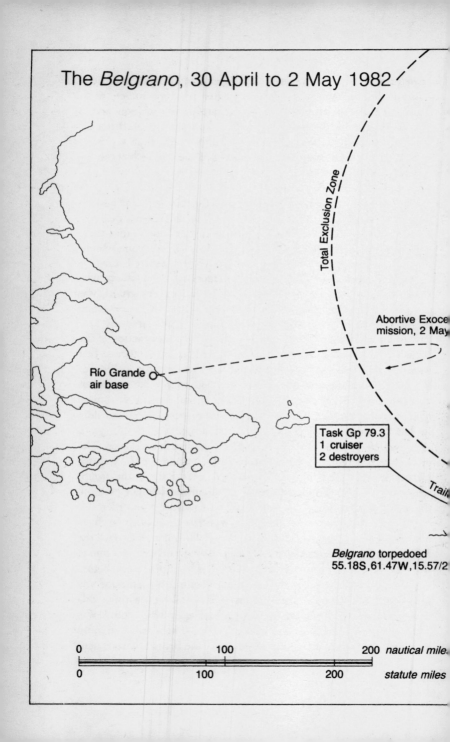

The *Belgrano*, 30 April to 2 May 1982

Total Exclusion Zone

Abortive Exoce[t]
mission, 2 May

Río Grande
air base

Task Gp 79.3
1 cruiser
2 destroyers

Trail

*Belgrano* torpedoed
55.18S,61.47W,15.57/2

| 0 | 100 | 200 *nautical mile[s]* |
|---|-----|-----|
| 0 | 100 | 200 *statute miles* |

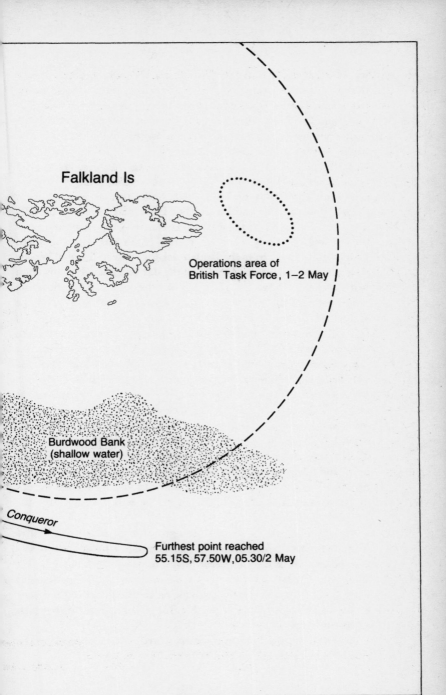

Falkland Is

Operations area of
British Task Force, 1–2 May

Burdwood Bank
(shallow water)

Conqueror

Furthest point reached
55.15S, 57.50W, 05.30/2 May

was still not willing to attack ships outside the exclusion zone despite the ten-day-old warning, and the *Conqueror*'s captain was only permitted to attack ships if they entered the zone.

It is important now to study just what the British knew about the various groups of Argentine ships during the day of 2 May and, based on that knowledge, what the British could expect the future Argentine moves to be. The movements of the *Belgrano* group were being reported by *Conqueror*; these ships were steaming westwards at medium speed. But the British had no idea that the major units in the north were also withdrawing. The last contact with the aircraft-carrier group had been through a Sea Harrier's electronic device in the evening of 1 May when the carrier group was only about 150 nautical miles away from the British task force. Rear-Admiral Woodward expected an attack all through the day of 2 May, but no action had developed. Now he had to look to the future. The Argentine units, both the aircraft-carrier group and the three frigates in the surface attack group, which he believed still to be to the north, could approach during the night and be in a position to launch attacks the following day. If the *Belgrano* group came in from the south, over the shallow water of the 200-mile-long Burdwood Bank, then the *Conqueror* might be unable to follow and would certainly lose touch with two of the three ships if the group split up. The *Belgrano* might be an old ship but she had fifteen 6-inch guns, and the two destroyers were equipped with Exocets with a range of over twenty miles. To Rear-Admiral Woodward, therefore, the coming day appeared to be filled with great danger, with attacks possibly coming in from both north and south. He decided to ask London for the Rules of Engagement for submarines to be changed, allowing attacks outside the old exclusion zone and thus implementing the policy declared to the Argentines on 23 April.

There was a delay while the request was considered by a hastily convened meeting of the British War Cabinet – it was a Sunday – but the captain of the *Conqueror* finally received the new rules that afternoon. These did not specify the *Belgrano*; any Argentine warship outside the exclusion zone could now be attacked, but the *Belgrano* group was the only one with which a British submarine was in touch at that time.

At 3.57 p.m. on 2 May, *Conqueror* fired three torpedoes at the

*Belgrano*. They were the older Mark 8 torpedoes, relatively unsophis-
ticated weapons but with huge warheads. *Conqueror*'s captain chose
those weapons because he knew that the *Belgrano* had a 6-inch-thick
band of armour plating along most of the ship's side; even the Mark 8
torpedo might not penetrate that armour. The torpedoes were
fired in a 'spread' in the near certainty that one and possibly two
would hit. The range was very close, only 1,400 yards, the recommended optimum for such an attack. Two of the torpedoes scored
hits.

The *Belgrano* had presented an easy target – course steady, no
zigzags, speed about 10 knots. The two destroyers were both to the
north, on the far side from the submarine. They were zigzagging
within what was called 'sector formation', varying their distance
from the *Belgrano* between 7,000 and 10,000 yards. The weather is
described as being 'indifferent, sea state 3 or 4, steadily worsening'.
The short period of daylight in that deep southern latitude was
coming to an end. The number of men aboard was 1,093, the pre-
war complement of 792 having been increased to this number. Although only 30 per cent of those on board were conscript sailors, the
main part of the crew had only been together since February, and
the extra wartime element had been aboard for less than a month.
But the ship was not overcrowded – she could have taken a further
200 men – and the relative newness of the crew was not a major
factor in the heavy loss of life.

There is some confusion over the sequence of the hits. It is gener-
ally believed that the hit near the bow was the first one, but two of
the eight members of the crew I met, including Captain Bonzo,
believe this was the second hit. But there were only three or four
seconds between the hits, and it will be convenient to describe the
effects of the one near the bow first. The torpedo struck between ten
and fifteen yards back from the bow, outside the forward limit of the
side armour and of the internal anti-torpedo bulge. The effect was
dramatic. The front of the ship simply disappeared, being blown
away to leave segments of the deck plating hanging over the separation. But the bulkheads behind held, and there was no inrush of
water. The powder magazine just behind those bulkheads did not
explode, although the 40-mm ammunition store was blown away
with the rest of the bow; the shattered timber of the ammunition

boxes was later seen spread across the surface of the sea. There was probably no one in that forward part of the ship. (This was the third time the cruiser had lost its bows. The first time was in action in the Second World War; the second was when, as an Argentine ship, she collided with a sister ship, the *Noveno de Julio*.)

The second torpedo hit was the one which caused so much loss of life. It struck about three-quarters of the way back along the ship, unfortunately a few feet outside the rear limit of the armour plating. The ship gave a huge shudder; Captain Bonzo said it was 'just as though it had reared up on a sandbank, coming to a dead stop'. The nearby magazines were just aft of the hit but did not explode; that was the only good fortune going. The torpedo easily pierced the side of the ship before exploding in the after machine room, wiping out the watch on duty there. But the effects of the huge explosion spread much further. Just above the machinery room were two messes – one for petty officers and one for senior seamen – and, then, on the next deck up, were two dining halls and a general relaxation area called 'the Soda Fountain'. These places were crowded, particularly the Soda Fountain and the dining halls, because the watches were being changed at 4.00 p.m. The blast of the internal explosion had to find an outlet and most of it went upwards, blowing away these compartments and leaving a 20-yard-long hole in the main deck. There were no survivors from these places; it was later estimated that 275 men – 85 per cent of the total dead – were in this area. Most of them were career sailors; there were a smaller number of conscripts but no officers. The officers' cabins and posts of duty were all in other parts of the ship. Badly burned and injured men who survived on the fringes of the explosion area reported a huge fireball rushing down the companion-ways. There was no fire after this expended itself, but the interior of the ship filled rapidly with dense smoke.

The cruiser was crippled. The forward bulkheads held, but the inrush of water through the after torpedo hole could not be checked, and the water inside could not be pumped out. Lieutenant-Commander Jorge Schottenheim, the ship's chief electrical officer, describes why:

> I went down to the forward machinery room; I could already hear the water rushing in and sloshing about down there. There

was no one there – complete silence. The watch had all gone up
on deck; the smoke had driven them out. I had to go down
through the smoke; it was thick and choking, and I could only
find my way back by shining my torch on the wall. I reported
to Captain Bonzo that nothing could be done; there was no
electrical solution because, of the two emergency diesels, the
one aft was destroyed and the forward one needed to be linked
to the distribution panel which was underwater in the forward
machine room. Actually, I believe that the shock of the two
torpedo explosions had shaken up the distribution panels in all
of the machine rooms.

(This officer and I then had an interesting discussion, comparing the
complete electrical breakdown in the *Belgrano* with a similar situation
which occurred in the British battleship *Prince of Wales* when it was
hit by Japanese torpedo bombers in 1941. I pointed out that the
*Prince of Wales* was sunk forty years earlier. 'Yes,' he replied, 'but
don't forget that the *Belgrano* was built at the same time as the
*Prince of Wales*.')

The *Belgrano* was clearly sinking, a list to port steadily increasing
at the same time as she started going down by the bows. Hundreds
of men tumbled out on to the deck from below, some from the area
of the rear torpedo explosion being completely naked and badly
burned. Twenty minutes after the attack, Captain Bonzo ordered:
'Abandonar el buque' – 'Abandon ship.' The majority of the crew
got away in the purpose-made rubber life-rafts which were stored in
plastic containers along both sides of the ship. On the order to
abandon ship, the containers were thrown into the sea attached to
the ship by a line; when this was jerked, a carbon dioxide capsule
was activated and inflated the raft. There were more than enough of
these for that part of the crew who survived the torpedo explosions.
It was still just light, and there was no panic. There were a few
incidents which led to the further loss of some lives, but there were
no large groups of men trapped below decks. Lieutenant Juan Meunier, who had been asleep, describes his escape:

I put my clothes and life-jacket on and went up to the upper
deck. After reporting to my own departmental senior officer, I
heard the order given to abandon ship. I went to my own life-

raft; the petty officers threw the raft container into the sea and
it inflated and the men got in. I didn't go myself; I remained to
help my chief who was responsible for seeing that the bow
sector on the port side was abandoned properly. We got into
the last raft to go in that section; it may have been the last one
to go on the whole ship, because we had to climb *up* to the raft
from the ship's side.

We couldn't seem to get away from the ship, even though we
tried to row away. We kept moving nearer to the bow – or what
was left of it. We eventually had to jump overboard from the
life-raft because it was being torn apart by the jagged metal
there. I started to swim and climb into another life-raft, and
someone helped me into it. There were twenty-seven of us, and
I was the senior officer.

Hundreds of men in the life-rafts watched the ship sink.
Lieutenant-Commander Schottenheim again:

The ship settled further on its port side, very slowly, but eventually reaching 90 degrees, quite vertical, with the three guns of
Number Two turret sticking starkly into the air. Then she
started going down by the stern. It slid down backwards, just as
though it was a sledge. The last we saw was the remains of the
bow disappearing. The men in my life-raft immediately started
to sing 'The March of the Armada'; it was a song of the Petty
Officer Mechanical School; most of those in the life-raft were
machinery and electrical men. The words were:

> Valiant boys of the Navy,
> Who far from loved ones and home,
> Watch over the far reaches of our nation's sea.

Night fell with no sign of immediate rescue. The wind increased.
Lieutenant Meunier describes the conditions:

I stood near the door of the life-raft hoping to attach a rope to
another life-raft nearby, but had to give up because the storm
was banging us together. Then I sat down and slept a little
until a big wave threw me back into the interior of the raft and
over the men there. They were all behaving very well. We kept
very warm – human heat. The only problem was the movement

of the sea. We kept the life-raft fairly dry by bailing, but things became a bit messy with all the movement. Many men were sick; I was the first. That was it until the morning.

The two destroyers – *Hipólito Bouchard* and *Piedra Buena* – were unaware that the *Belgrano* had even been attacked, let alone sunk. They were out of visual touch in the gloom when the torpedoes struck, although in radar contact. The *Belgrano*'s radio had failed when the torpedoes struck, and her distress rockets and battery-operated lamp signals were not seen. One reason for this failure to detect that the cruiser was in serious trouble was that *Hipólito Bouchard* believed that she had been struck by a torpedo. Her crew felt a firm impact, although there was no explosion. The two destroyers, already steaming westwards, continued on that course and started dropping depth charges. This took them well away from the scene of the *Belgrano*'s distress. When the *Hipólito Bouchard* was examined after this voyage, the mark of a possible impact was found, and it is just possible that *Conqueror*'s third torpedo struck the destroyer at the end of its run, but with insufficient momentum to trigger an explosion. The effect of the destroyers' torpedo scare was to leave the *Belgrano*'s crew in their life-rafts without any immediate prospect of rescue. It eventually became obvious to the destroyers that something had happened to the cruiser when she could not be contacted by radio and was no longer to be seen on their radar screens. The two ships turned back and commenced a search; but it was now dark, they had no clear idea of where the cruiser had met trouble, and a storm blew up. Captain Bonzo estimates the wind at 120 kph (75 mph) and the waves to have been six to seven metres high. The life-rafts were thus swept rapidly downwind and became well scattered.

Conditions in the life-rafts were unpleasant but not desperate. They were of excellent construction, each with a canopy and a good stock of rations, although the standard survival regulation was that the rations were not to be touched for the first twenty-four hours. The Argentine sailors settled down in their little communities to pass the night. It is believed that only one life-raft capsized, drowning the occupants, but some injured men died in other life-rafts. Servicemen usually remember the humorous things. Petty Officer Nicanor Roldán describes conditions in his life-raft:

There were thirty-two of us; it was very crowded and almost impossible to get everyone in. We could not close the doors of the canopy properly, so we had to take off our shoelaces and made a long string of them to tie up the opening. One of the men had disobeyed orders and brought his steel helmet into the life-raft with him. We were pleased he did this; it came in very useful bailing water and for the obvious other purposes. That helmet turned out to be the most important thing in the life-raft.

A major search was soon organized; it was co-ordinated by Captain Héctor Martini, the Search and Rescue Commander at Río Grande. Neptune and F-28 Fokker Fellowship aircraft went out at first light. The two destroyers which had been with the *Belgrano* were also searching, but the cruiser had been sunk in a remote part of the South Atlantic, and there were few other ships nearby. The only other Argentine ships within reach were the ocean-going tug *Francisco de Gurruchaga*, which eventually saved many men, and the patrol ship *Comodoro Somellara*, which was further north and would play little part in the rescue operation. There was a Chilean naval vessel in the area, the Antarctic transport ship *Piloto Pardo*, and its services were offered. There was some hesitation over accepting the offer, because of the hostility between the two countries, and the decision was left to Vice-Admiral Lombardo, who 'accepted the offer at once for two reasons – it would improve relations with Chile, and the British would be less likely to interfere in the operation if a Chilean ship was present'.

It took until 1.00 p.m. on 3 May for the first life-rafts to be spotted by one of the Neptune aircraft, but the rescue ships were soon on the scene, and most of the survivors were picked up before dark, with the remainder being found and rescued the following morning. HMS *Conqueror* returned that next morning and observed 'two destroyers and a merchant ship', but her captain was under strict orders not to attack any rescue ships. Captain Bonzo was in the last life-raft to be found, being picked up by the *Francisco de Gurruchaga*.

An early report that 368 men were lost in the *Belgrano* sinking persisted for a long time, often being quoted by those who wished to deepen the controversy over the incident, even after a lower figure became available. The actual figure was 321 navy men and two civilians lost in the ship, drowned or died of wounds, the majority, as has been described, being killed by the after torpedo explosion. This is a breakdown of the naval deaths:

| | Men on board | Men died | (Percentage died) |
|---|---|---|---|
| Officers | 56 | 3 | (5.4 per cent) |
| Petty officers and regular seamen | 629 | 216 | (34.3 per cent) |
| Conscripts | 408 | 102 | (25.0 per cent) |
| Total | 1,093 | 321 | (29.4 per cent) |

The only three officers to die were all *guardiamarinas* – midshipmen. None of them died in the *Belgrano* itself. One was in a life-raft which was punctured and started to sink; he was drowned when the occupants transferred to another life-raft. Another was in a further life-raft which was punctured and became flooded; all the occupants died, the midshipman being reported as having perished through exposure while on top of the life-raft trying to attract help with a torch. The last midshipman is believed to have been in the life-raft which capsized and he was never found. Of the 102 young conscripts who died, 82 were in the Class of 1962 and 20 were in the newly joined 1963 Class.

There was some criticism, particularly in Britain, over the torpedoing of the *Belgrano*. This was based on the fact that the cruiser was outside the exclusion zone and was steaming westwards, but the British had given clear warning that ships in or out of that zone might be attacked if considered to pose a danger to British forces, and earlier quotations have shown that the Argentine naval commanders fully understood the implications of that message. Moreover, the *Belgrano* group was not steaming back to port, but only to an intermediate point to await further developments. It must also be clear that the commander of the British task force, on the basis of the incomplete knowledge that he had of the various Argentine movements, could reasonably expect to be attacked from several directions on the day after the sinking if the *Belgrano* group – which was far from lacking in hitting power – was not attacked and if it reversed course and came in over the shallow Burdwood Bank. In my first book about the Falklands War, I described criticism of the attack on the *Belgrano* as 'humbug'; I have not changed that opinion. I heard not one word of criticism while I was in Argentina. Let the last words here on this subject come from Rear-Admiral Allara, who was in command of the Task Force 79 operations, and from Captain Bonzo of the *Belgrano* itself. Allara says: 'After that message of 23 April, the entire South Atlantic was an operational theatre for both sides. We, as professionals, said it was just too bad that we lost the *Belgrano*.'

Captain Bonzo says:

By no means do I have any feelings of anger. If I was in the company of the captain of the *Conqueror* we should be discussing tactics in the same way that you and I are discussing them now. I realized from the outset that the 200-mile limit had nothing to do with the mission I had to accomplish. The limit did not exclude danger or risks; it was all the same in or out. I would like to be quite precise that, as far as I was concerned, the 200-mile limit was valid until 1 May, that is while diplomatic negotiations were taking place and/or until a real act of war took place, and that had happened on 1 May.

After the sinking of the *Belgrano*, the other units of Task Force 79 were ordered into the shallow waters of the mainland to escape further submarine danger. This withdrawal of the Argentine warships from the open sea marks the end of the dramatic first phase of the main conflict. The British task force had arrived, commenced operations and survived unscathed from a major attempt by the Argentine Navy to join battle. The Argentines had suffered a series of minor setbacks in the 1 May operations around Stanley and had now lost their second largest naval unit. All this had happened in just forty-eight hours.

# 10 · The Vigil

The first two days of May were followed by eighteen days of less hectic action. The British needed time to complete the assembly of the landing force at Ascension Island and sail that force to the Falklands. They intended to use the interval to continue the preparatory actions of wearing down the Falkland garrison and of carrying out reconnaissance work. The Argentines quickly realized that no immediate landings were to take place and they instituted a policy of conservation for their air and naval units, keeping these back on the mainland for future use. The troops on the islands had to endure the British shelling and bombing, but the effects of these were not serious. The scene was thus set for a time of relative quiet. There was always the chance that action would flare up, and there certainly were sudden bursts of activity as minor units of one side or another managed to strike a blow, but the main feature of this period would be the complete absence of contact between the main forces of the two sides. Some Argentines later called this waiting period 'the vigil'.

A convenient way to cover the spasmodic actions of that period is to present them in date order. I hope that this treatment may manage to convey the general tenor of that time.

## Night of 2–3 May

This night found the Argentine naval vessel *Alférez Sobral* about 100 nautical miles north of the Falklands, searching for the ditched crew of the Canberra bomber shot down on 1 May. The ship was the 860-ton ex-American patrol vessel USS *Catawbe*, built in 1945, sold to Argentina in 1972 and now classed as an ocean-going tug/patrol vessel. The *Alférez Sobral* and its sister ship the *Comodoro Somellara* were grouped for operational purposes as Task Force 50. They were the only ships in the force, and their duties were air-sea rescue, the *Alférez Sobral* on the Comodoro Rivadavia–Falklands route and the *Comodoro Somellara* further south, covering the routes from Río Gallegos and Río Grande airfields. The British assumed that the two ships were together, probably because of signals to 'Task Force 50', but the *Comodoro Somellara* was at least 200 miles away from the incident about to be described.

Just before midnight, the *Alférez Sobral*'s crew observed a large helicopter which hovered over the ship for a few seconds and then flew off. The captain, Lieutenant-Commander Sergio Gómez Roca, believed his ship was in danger of attack so he ordered a northerly course, an increase of speed and all lights to be doused. Forty-one minutes later, at twenty-six minutes past midnight, the crew saw the outline of another helicopter and opened fire with a 20-mm cannon. The helicopter was not hit and it flew away again. It was a British Sea King, still searching for the submarine *San Luis*. The Sea King reported its contact with a hostile ship, and two smaller Lynx helicopters from H M S *Coventry* and H M S *Glasgow* were ordered to attack. The Sea King first guided in *Coventry*'s Lynx, which fired two Sea Skua missiles, aimed and guided by radar at a range of eight miles. Explosions were seen; the radar echo of the target ship seemed to disappear, and the British believed the ship was sunk. Both helicopters then closed the scene of action to look for survivors, but the radar echo of what was believed to be a second ship was detected. *Glasgow*'s Lynx fired its two missiles at this supposed new target and claimed further hits.

This is the description from the Argentine side, provided by Lieutenant Sergio Bazán, the *Alférez Sobral*'s second-in-command. He starts with the sight of the first two missiles approaching:

The signalman spotted lights in the distance on the starboard side. The Captain went to the side and could see two lights approaching; he realized they were the exhausts of missile rockets. Almost at once, one missile hit us on the ship's fibreglass motor boat. The other missile passed over the bridge, just above my head, without hitting us. The one that did hit us

injured the crew of the 20-mm gun, one of them being badly
injured in the stomach and also with a piece of metal in his
bottom. The gun crew on the other side opened fire on the
other missile as it flew off but they did not hit it. The Captain
then ordered the 40-mm gun on the bow to open fire to starboard. After only a few shots, he ordered 'cease fire' because
there was no target to be seen.

We started looking after the wounded and sorting the ship
out. There were no serious problems, but we could not com-
municate with Puerto Argentino because the radio aerials had
been destroyed. Then came the second attack with some hits
on the bridge, possibly with two missiles; it is difficult to say
but I believe both of them hit us. I was on my way up to the
bridge at the time; the doctor wanted me to see a man there
who was wounded in the leg from the first attack. There was a
huge explosion. I could even see the paint blown off the super-
structure. I think I remember hearing two explosions, one on
top of the other, and then a thud which I think was the mast
falling. That is why I think both missiles hit the bridge.

I tried to get up back to the bridge. I had to wait a little
because there was a wounded man trying to get down. When I
reached the radio room I found there was a casualty there,
badly wounded – an exposed fracture of the right arm and
splinters all over his body – but he survived. I helped to get
him down to the doctor. But there were four men dead in the
radio room – Midshipman Olivieri, the officer of the watch
who was also the communications officer and had probably
been sent by the Captain down to the radio room to deal with
our communications problem, and three radio petty officers.
When I went up to the bridge I found it completely destroyed
and a fire building up on the starboard side. The Captain and a
seaman were dead; it had been a direct hit, and there were parts
of bodies all over the bridge. Two other men were killed by
splinters in other parts of the ship. Eight men were injured.

Lieutenant Bazán, who was suffering from two injuries himself,
took over command. The fire was extinguished and the wounded
treated. The hull was intact, and the ship could steam, but its radio

and gyro compass were destroyed. Course was maintained by observing the motion of the waves. It was not until more than twenty-four hours later that a signal from the hand-cranked emergency radio on a life-raft was heard on the mainland, and it was the morning of 5 May before a naval helicopter spotted the ship. The coast was in sight by then, and the *Alférez Sobral*'s surviving crew members were very proud that they had reached the mainland unaided. At noon that day, two and a half days after the attack, this gallant little ship came into Puerto Deseado, escorted by a destroyer and a Coast Guard vessel, and was given a fine reception by a large crowd.

The British heard of the arrival of the damaged ship and, still thinking the helicopters had attacked two ships, assumed the *Comodoro Somellara* was sunk, a belief that was not corrected for several years.

### Afternoon of 3 May

Two Aeromacchis of the 1st Naval Attack Squadron, based at Stanley airfield, were dispatched to investigate a ship out at sea. Nothing was found, and the two aircraft returned, but one pilot, Sub-Lieutenant Carlos Benítez, made a mistake in bad weather and was too low on his final approach. His aircraft struck some rocks just off shore, tore off its wing and crashed into Cape Pembroke just over two miles from the runway. Benítez was killed.

### Early Morning, 4 May

An RAF Vulcan bomber flew from Ascension Island and dropped twenty-one 1,000-lb bombs on Stanley airfield, the stick of bombs just missing the western end of the runway. No serious damage was caused, but two Argentines – a conscript from the Marine Anti-Aircraft Battalion and another conscript from the 10th Logistic Battalion – are believed to have been killed. These two men were both buried in Stanley cemetery the following day; the anti-aircraft gunner was definitely a victim of the Vulcan's bombs, and the logistic man probably was.

## Mid-Morning, 4 May

One of the most modern and powerful weapons in the Argentine armoury was the naval squadron of Super Étendard aircraft and their Exocet missiles, both French built, designed purely for attack against surface ships, the ideal weapon for use against the British task force. Unfortunately for the Argentines, the premature starting of the war found the squadron only partially equipped, with five aircraft and only five Exocets. There were ten fully trained pilots, but the ground technicians for this sophisticated weapons system had not completed their training; a French team due to arrive in Argentina on 12 April for the completion of the technicians' training had their visit cancelled because of the EEC embargo on help and trade for Argentina. By mid-April, however, the completion of the 127 separate pre-flight checks had been resolved, and it was believed that the system could be used, though no missiles could be spared for a trial firing. The successful preparation was a considerable achievement, and the British suspected that the French may have surreptitiously broken the embargo and given advice. I asked about this when I visited the Super Étendard unit; the answer was that the work was all done by Argentine technicians but that a French communications team which had been in Argentina for some time on other work had given general advice, though they were not Exocet specialists. There was also much work to be done on the aircraft's vital Inertial Navigation System. The set intended for the Super Étendard had not arrived when the embargo came down, and an older model, designed for the Mirage fighter, had to be adapted.

The Super Étendards were intended to operate from the Argentine aircraft-carrier, but this was not yet possible. A plan to base them at Stanley airfield was abandoned when the runway there was found to be not quite long enough. The squadron was sent instead to the extreme southern mainland base of Río Grande from where, with the assistance of Hercules tanker aircraft, the Super Étendards could operate well out to sea. The ten available pilots were graded in order of experience; the squadron commander was Number One and the most junior pilot Number Ten. It was agreed that each operation would be flown by two aircraft; Number One pilot would fly with Number Ten as the first pair, Number Two with Number Nine as the second pair, and so on. It was also agreed that once a pair had taken off on an operation, that pair would go to the bottom of the roster, even if their operation had to be abandoned.

The squadron had been anxious to attack the British task force as soon as the British ships arrived, but two attempts to do so during the first days failed. The squadron commander and pilot Number Ten had taken off on 2 May, but the in-flight refuelling of the commander's aircraft failed, the fuel draining out as fast as it flowed in because of a faulty valve. The operation was abandoned, and the two pilots went to the bottom of the roster. Two more Super Étendards were waiting at Río Grande to take the place of the returning aircraft, but the tanker aircraft reported that it would not have sufficient fuel to replenish them, so the two reserve aircraft did not take off. The Neptune reconnaissance aircraft which was tracking the British ships as a preliminary to each operation reported a further contact the next day, and a mission was nearly launched, the Super Étendards actually being at the end of the runway ready to take off. But this operation was cancelled either because the Neptune reports were not sufficiently detailed or because the tanker aircraft operation could not be co-ordinated in time. The second pair of pilots thus remained at the top of the roster.

Those two pilots — the squadron second-in-command, Lieutenant-Commander Augusto Bedacarratz, and Sub-Lieutenant Armando Mayora — had their patience rewarded when, soon after 7.00 a.m. on 4 May, a report came in that a Neptune had made firm radar contact with British ships south of the Falklands. The pilot of the Neptune was Lieutenant-Commander Ernesto Leston, and his work and that of his crew should be recognized in the day's success. The dangerously slow Neptune remained in contact with the British ships for more than three hours, cleverly altering its position to give British radar operators the impression that it was searching for survivors from the *General Belgrano*, but periodically popping back up to take bearings on the British radar emissions. It established that there were four British ships, all moving eastwards. Three of these ships were probably the *Coventry*, *Glasgow* and *Sheffield*, and the fourth ship may have been a smaller warship returning from landing special forces on the Falklands coast or a ship which had been carrying out a bombardment the previous night. The Neptune was thus in contact with the British outer screen, not the main task force; the easterly course was a general retirement from the Falklands after the night's operations. It took more than two hours to prepare the complicated Super Étendard mission, but Bedacarratz and Mayora were able to take off at 9.45 a.m. The Neptune provided a final report forty minutes later, giving the positions of the two contacts which would be the most suitable for attack. The refuelling with the Hercules tanker aircraft was successfully completed, and the world's first air-borne Exocet mission was on its way. Sub-Lieutenant Mayora provides this description:

We refuelled 260 miles from the contacts and flew on towards where the Neptune had given their latest position; we had been told there was one large and one small contact. We descended at 130 miles out. The weather was bad – visibility about one mile and a ceiling of 300 feet with squalls. Those were favour-able conditions for us. Our worst danger was considered to be the Sea Harrier patrols, not ships' missiles. The nature of Super Étendard operations was to go in low and fast and turn away early; the Exocet range exceeds that of ships' missiles. That was the whole reasoning behind the development of the Super Étendard–Exocet system. The only way to stop us was to get us before launching our missiles and that was very difficult. If you English had had early-warning aircraft, then you might have caught us.

We passed south of Isla Beauchêne [45 miles south of the Falklands]. When it was time, the commander broke radio silence and told me he would attack the larger contact, the one reported by the Neptune as being on the right, leaving me to go for the smaller one. We climbed to 2,000 feet when we were 50 miles out and switched our radars on for three seconds. Neither of us found anything. We went down again and flew on another 20 miles before coming up again. This time Bedacar-ratz's radar showed a large contact on the right and a small one further away on the left; I only saw the large contact on the right. We thought it was an aircraft-carrier with two escorts. He ordered that we should both attack the right-hand contact; we would have a better chance with it being larger and closer.

And that was what we did. We went to maximum speed –
500 knots – through more rain squalls. We knew that we were
well within range. I made all the necessary adjustments to
activate my missile. Everything up to now had been practised,
but not from here on. At 20 miles out, Bedacarratz ordered
'launch'. I was in a squall at the time, and he was out of sight
but in the clear. As soon as he saw his Exocet flying under his
aircraft, he told me and ordered me to launch mine. It was
exactly 11.04. Both missiles ran parallel; we were not able to
follow them by eye for long because they went into the mist or
some cloud. We turned away to the right and got out of the
area as fast as possible.

We did not need to refuel on the return flight. There were
no problems, and we came home without difficulty. There was
a lot of excitement at Río Grande and a lot of interest in how
the Exocets behaved, whether we had hit anything and, if so,
which ship. That evening the British announced that it was the
*Sheffield*. Our reaction? We didn't feel that it was a retaliation
for the *Belgrano* – the operation was never for that – but we felt
that we had proved that we had the ability to sink one of theirs
too. We were never able to discover which of our missiles hit the
*Sheffield*; that is something we shall never know.

The Exocet caused severe damage to the *Sheffield* and a large fire.
Twenty British sailors were killed; 236 survived. The ship sank
while under tow a few days later. This was a clear success for the
Argentine cause, the first since the occupation of the Falklands and
South Georgia just over a month earlier. The attack would cause
Rear-Admiral Woodward to be more cautious in the use of his ships,
forcing his task force to keep further from the Exocet threat and also
further from the Falklands. There were only three more Exocets
left, but as long as these were in existence they would considerably
inhibit the British freedom of action.


### Afternoon of 4 May

Three Sea Harriers from HMS *Hermes* were dispatched to carry out
a bombing attack on the airfield at Goose Green, but an Argentine

radar controller at Stanley detected the raid coming in and warned Goose Green. The anti-aircraft detachment at Goose Green was alerted, and its Skyguard radar picked up the Sea Harriers ten miles out at sea over the Choiseul Sound. Two of the Sea Harriers came straight in from that south-east direction while the third wheeled round to attack from the south-west. One of the first two was hit by cannon shells fired by a 35-mm Oerlikon. The Sea Harrier immediately caught fire and crashed just short of the airfield. The other two aircraft dropped their bombs and flew away pursued by Argentine fire. The bombs caused further damage to two Pucarás which had been hit in the raid three days earlier and blew some craters in the grass airfield. The Argentines were pleased at their success at shooting down the Sea Harrier and claimed that a second Harrier was so badly damaged that it would soon crash. The diary of a sergeant of the 12th Regiment – Sargento Primero Guillermo J. Potocsnyak – tells how he was one of a party of men sent by helicopter to search for the pilot of the second shot-down aircraft; they were unsuccessful but were later told that the pilot had been found in the sea. This was another example of overclaiming; the two other Sea Harriers were not hit by the Argentine fire.

First Lieutenant Carlos Esteban was the first to reach the wreck of the Sea Harrier:

It was in pieces along the airfield. The pilot was dead, still in his seat, with his parachute partially open. I think he died on impact. His body appeared to be quite intact externally, and his flying helmet was OK. I had a camera, but out of respect I decided not to take a photograph. I found a piece of paper near him with navigation notes showing the location of the task force. I think that was a big mistake.

The British pilot was Lieutenant Nicholas Taylor. The Argentines buried him with military honours near the graves of their own men killed on 1 May; this was in a nearby paddock which the local people used for pony riding and horse-racing before the war. The funeral was filmed and shown on television throughout the world. That Sea Harrier was the first one lost by the British task force.

### Morning of 6 May

Two Sea Harriers from HMS *Invincible* were on routine combat air patrol when they were ordered to investigate a possible ship contact. The weather was bad. The radar tracks of both aircraft were followed until they lost height, but nothing was ever seen either of the aircraft or the pilots after that. No Argentine ships or aircraft were in action, and the loss may have been due to a collison.

### Evening of 8 May

The Argentine submarine *San Luis*, still operating north of the Falklands, was lying stopped when it picked up a contact passing only 2,000 yards away. An anti-submarine torpedo was fired at the contact. It was heard to explode much later, either at the end of its run, or on hitting 'something biological' or the ocean floor. Commander Azcueta later believed that his contact was a whale, but he considered that the decision to fire the torpedo was a sound defensive move which, if there had been a British submarine present, might have saved the *San Luis* from attack.

### Morning of 9 May

Two Sea Harriers from HMS *Hermes* dispatched to bomb Stanley airfield abandoned this mission because of cloud over the target. On their return to the *Hermes* they detected a surface contact by radar which turned out to be the Argentine fishing trawler *Narwal*. The Sea Harriers attacked using bombs and cannon fire. One bomb struck the trawler but did not explode because it had been fused to be dropped from a higher altitude. Two further Sea Harriers arrived and also attacked with cannon fire. The ship was crippled. One seaman, Contramaestre Omar Rupp, was killed, and others were injured. A Sea King helicopter later arrived and let down a Royal Marine boarding party which took over the ship. The presence of an Argentine naval officer and of certain documents confirmed the ship's intelligence-gathering activity. The prisoners were returned to Argentina via Montevideo on 2 June.

## Afternoon of 9 May

For the first time since 1 May, mainland air units attempted bombing missions against British ships off the Falklands. The destroyer *Coventry* and the frigate *Broadsword* were operating near Stanley, ostensibly to bombard shore targets but in reality to entice Argentine aircraft into the combination of Sea Dart and Sea Wolf missiles with which the ships were equipped. The mainland air command responded, and the 4th Fighter Group at San Julián sent eighteen Skyhawks to attack the ships. Most of the Skyhawks turned back because of very bad weather conditions, but one formation of four aircraft pressed on and lost two aircraft and their pilots, one crashing into the cliffs of a small island and the second presumably crashing into the sea in the bad weather.

Later that afternoon, an army Puma helicopter from Stanley which was attempting to find and help the *Narwal* was engaged by *Coventry* and shot down into the sea by a Sea Dart, the first ever success for a Sea Dart missile. No trace was ever found of the helicopter or the three crew members. The pilot and co-pilot, Lieutenants Roberto Fiorito and Juan Buschiazzo, were the first Argentine army officers to be killed in the Falklands area.

## Night of 10–11 May

On the evening of 10 May, Rear-Admiral Woodward ordered the frigate *Alacrity* to attempt the first passage by a British warship of Falkland Sound, the 60-mile-long channel between the two main islands of the Falklands group. This mission was part of the continuing pressure being put on the Argentine garrison during this period and an attempt to extend the area over which the British were achieving naval superiority. Unknown to the British, there were five Argentine supply ships in various parts of the Falkland Sound that night. After the British Sea Harrier and naval bombardment of Stanley on 1 May, the Argentines had ordered three supply ships out of Stanley Harbour to be dispersed at various places in Falkland Sound. These three ships were the *Bahía Buen Suceso*, the *Isla de los Estados* and the *Río Carcaraña*. The small local ships *Forrest* and *Monsunen* were requisitioned and sent in a series of shuttle voyages

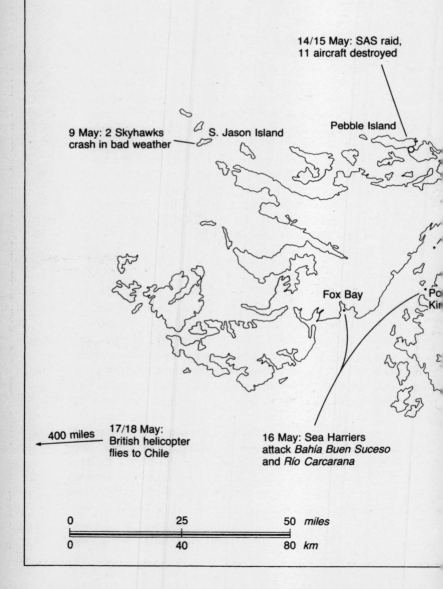

# Actions of Period 2 to 21 May 1982

14/15 May: SAS raid,
11 aircraft destroyed

Pebble Island

9 May: 2 Skyhawks
crash in bad weather

S. Jason Island

Fox Bay

Po
Kir

400 miles

17/18 May:
British helicopter
flies to Chile

16 May: Sea Harriers
attack *Bahía Buen Suceso*
and *Río Carcarana*

| 0 | 25 | 50 | *miles* |
|---|----|----|---------|
| 0 | 40 | 80 | *km* |

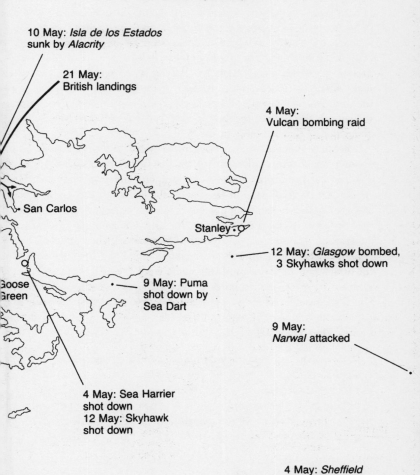

40 miles

2/3 May: *Alférez Sobral*
attacked by helicopters

10 May: *Isla de los Estados*
sunk by *Alacrity*

21 May:
British landings

4 May:
Vulcan bombing raid

• San Carlos

Stanley

12 May: *Glasgow* bombed,
3 Skyhawks shot down

Goose
Green

9 May: Puma
shot down by
Sea Dart

9 May:
*Narwal* attacked

4 May: Sea Harrier
shot down
12 May: Skyhawk
shot down

4 May: *Sheffield*
hit by Exocet

to carry the larger ships' cargoes to Stanley or to the other Argentine garrisons. All of these ships were in Falkland Sound when *Alacrity* steamed through that night.

The frigate entered the sound from the south and was about halfway through when her radar detected a ship six miles ahead. *Alacrity* increased speed to close the gap and then fired a star-shell in an attempt to identify the contact, then twelve rounds of air-burst shells in the hope of persuading the ship to stop. This did not happen, so, after a pause of two minutes, high-explosive shells were fired. The whole engagement was carried out by radar on a dark night with heavy rain falling. At least three hits were seen through the rain. *Alacrity* left the scene of action and continued her dash up the sound; she needed to be well clear and on her way back to the protection of the task force by dawn.

The ship attacked was the Argentine naval transport *Isla de los Estados*. She had brought army stores and fuel to the Falklands, but only part of her cargo – mainly the weapons and ammunition of B Battery, 101st Anti-Aircraft Regiment, the last army unit to be sent to the Falklands – had been unloaded, leaving on board the battery's vehicles and 325,000 litres of fuel for army helicopters and radar generators. The ship was steaming to San Carlos when attacked by *Alacrity*. The ship's officers were taken completely by surprise by the attack and believed the firing came from the army unit at Port Howard which was seven miles away; the *Forrest*, which was at Port Howard, was contacted in an attempt to stop the firing. Lieutenant-Commander Alois Payarola, the naval liaison officer on board, describes what happened: [1]

We were hit on the starboard side twenty seconds after the shelling started. I contacted the *Forrest* again, reporting hits under the waterline. The ship developed a list, and there was a big fire in the fuel, a large amount of which was in both holds. I continued in touch with the *Forrest* until an explosion destroyed the bridge area. Everything around me was gone. Of the eight

[1] Lieutenant-Commander Payarola's account is contained in a report provided by Lieutenant-Colonel Jorge Monge, who in 1982 was the battery commander whose guns and vehicles were brought to the Falklands in the *Isla de los Estados*. Monge had been on the ship a few hours earlier, overseeing the transfer of his unit's material and also meeting Captain Marcelo Novoa, an old friend who was the officer in charge of the army cargo on the ship.

or so people who had been there, I only saw Captain Panigadi, who was on the floor until he stood up and came over to the starboard side of the bridge.

The ship was now listing 35 degrees. Then the last shell-hit I can remember took place, followed by a great explosion of JP 1 fuel. The ship went over to 90 degrees. The engines were still running, and the ship kept moving ahead on its starboard side but plunging down below the waves front first.

I jumped into the sea from the stern of the boat, into the wake from the propellers. I watched the ship slowly sinking. I was afloat without any life-jacket, just with underwear, pullover and an Antarctic diving-jacket. I only had socks and service boots on my feet. I could hear other people in the water, some were shouting and screaming for help. A 'Sea Lynx' flew overhead twice, only about fifty metres up. That was when I realized we had been sunk by a British warship.

The ship sank. It was the only surface ship action between the two sides during the war. The local Argentine authorities did not know what had happened, and other Argentine ships were asked to give reports. The *Río Carcaraña*, which had entertained the officers of the *Isla de los Estados* to dinner the previous evening, had only heard a frantic radio message: 'Tell the bastards to stop firing.' An extensive search took place, but only Lieutenant-Commander Payarola and an unnamed seaman were found by *Forrest* on a small island five days later. Twenty-one men died: fifteen merchant service and three naval personnel, one Coast Guard man, the army officer Captain Novoa (son of a general) and an NCO from the anti-aircraft battery who had been left on the ship to look after his unit's vehicles. The body of one officer was recovered and buried in the cemetery at Stanley, where it was identified as 'Captain of Cargo Ship'; this was probably Captain Tulio Panigadi, the ship's captain, to whom Lieutenant-Commander Payarola refers in his description of the explosion which destroyed the ship's bridge.

*Alacrity* completed her passage of Falkland Sound and was met at the northern entrance by her sister ship *Arrow*. The two ships turned east and made off at high speed, zigzagging hard, about five miles apart and making 30 knots. The two ships were actually steaming straight at the Argentine submarine *San Luis*. Commander Azcueta showed me the detailed notes of the encounter, together with a neat diagram showing every move made by the two frigates. Acoustic conditions were very good. His passive telemetry sonar detected the *Arrow* waiting, and then *Alacrity* emerging from the sound. He called *Alacrity* 'Blanco A' and *Arrow* 'Blanco B'. The submarine was ideally placed midway between the oncoming paths of the two ships. Azcueta stopped the *San Luis* and allowed the two ships to come up to him. He selected *Alacrity* for attack, because the coast was behind that ship and there was thus less room for the target to manoeuvre. His torpedo-firing computer was still not functioning, so the submarine's bow was kept turning on to *Alacrity*'s path ready for the manual firing of the two AEG SST-4 torpedoes in the bow tubes. The first torpedo refused to fire, and only the second left its tube (at 1.42 a.m.). But, as in its first attack on British ships on 1 May, the wire guide of the torpedo broke, and it missed *Alacrity* and was heard to detonate either against the coast or on the sea bottom. The two ships did not know that they had been so close to danger; their high speed precluded the use of their various detection devices, but it was that same speed and the zigzagging which gave the Argentine torpedo little chance of a hit.

Commander Azcueta soon reported his technical difficulties to his headquarters and two days later was ordered to return to base at Mar del Plata. The *San Luis* had fired three torpedoes in two attacks on British ships and one torpedo at a suspected submarine contact. It is probable that none of her attacks seriously endangered the target ships, but a considerable British effort had been tied down in attempts to locate the *San Luis*. The technical problems experienced by the only member of Argentina's submarine service to be dispatched against the British task force were a source of embarrassment to the naval commanders. When I asked Vice-Admiral Lombardo about the submarine's voyage, he just said: 'Ah, yes, the *San Luis*', and shrugged his shoulders. The comparison between the *San Luis*'s poor technical condition and, for example, *Alacrity*'s swift and effective radar destruction of the *Isla de los Estados* an hour or so earlier, or *Conqueror*'s smooth torpedo sinking of the *Belgrano*, illustrates the difference in performance between the two navies in the war. The *Conqueror* was two years older than the *San Luis*!

## Early Afternoon, 12 May

The British ships *Glasgow* and *Brilliant* had replaced *Coventry* and *Broadsword* off Stanley and were bombarding land positions, again hoping to draw Argentine aircraft out from the mainland and engage them with missiles. The authorities at Stanley reported the bombardment and requested help from the mainland air units. The 5th Fighter Group at Río Gallegos was ordered to dispatch two flights, each of four Skyhawks; all of the pilots were flying their first war missions.

The first formation attacked just before 2.00 p.m., making a timed run from Fitzroy Settlement to the position where the two ships had been reported. The ships were ready. *Glasgow*'s Sea Dart system failed to engage, but *Brilliant*'s Sea Wolfs scored a spectacular success, destroying two of the Skyhawks and causing a third to crash, either because it hit fragments of the first two Skyhawks or because it crashed into the sea trying to avoid the missiles. The fourth Skyhawk pilot, a young ensign, failed to hit the ships but managed to escape unharmed. The other three pilots were all killed.

The second formation of Skyhawks came in soon afterwards, unaware of the fate of the first flight. Captain Zelaya, the leader, provides this description:[2]

We flew on from Fitzroy, just on top of the sea. The pilots on either side of me were flying even lower than I was, which was understandable as I had to take a safer level to check my navigation chart. Within myself, I didn't really want to find the target – not so much for fear of dying (although I did feel that) but more for fear of the unknown, the things I had never experienced. I felt fine physically, except for perspiring well beyond the normal.

I had planned to maintain my heading and speed for about three minutes, 15 kilometres per minute, and I would turn back if I didn't find the target in that time. But it was not necessary to take that decision, for soon I saw the two ships in front of me, moving fast south-south-east. I could tell the speed by their foaming bows. They were obviously escaping from the first attack.

[2] From the unpublished English translation of *Dios y los Halcones*.

There was no need to tell my pilots anything; everything had been arranged at the pre-flight briefing. The lead section was supposed to attack the ship placed to the north, while the second section took the one to the south. I was the only one who made a mistake, attacking the ship to the south which was nearer in my sight; this was why three planes attacked the leading ship and only one the rear one.

What I most clearly remember before the attack is that they started shooting when we were a few kilometres from the target. I didn't see any missiles but I could hear the explosions of the anti-aircraft shells. All I could concentrate on was my aim and target. I didn't see any sailors or helicopters, and it was just the immense radar scope constantly rotating that remained in my memory.

We turned homewards after the attack, hearing the joyful shouts of the others in my headphones. Lieutenant Arraras said: 'Thank God we all made it!' First Lieutenant Gavazzi shouted: 'Viva la Patria! I hit it; I am sure I hit it!' 'Piano' – Ensign Dellepiane – was swearing.

The four Skyhawks all survived, the missile systems of both ships having failed to function. Gavazzi had hit the *Glasgow* with a bomb which went straight through the ship without exploding, but the damage was serious enough to prevent *Glasgow* from taking much further part in the war. This, together with the recent loss of the *Sheffield*, marked a considerable reduction in the British task force's air defence capability and would endanger future British operations. The British had succeeded in drawing out Argentine aircraft from the mainland and inflicting losses, but it was decided that daylight operations by ships so close to Stanley were now too dangerous, and these were abandoned for the time being.

But tragedy was still to strike. On the return flight, First Lieutenant Gavazzi took a route near Goose Green which was prohibited to Argentine aircraft and was engaged by the local anti-aircraft unit, which shot the Skyhawk down with a 35-mm Oerlikon. Gavazzi was killed. The anti-aircraft gunners were most distressed, some in tears, when the men who went out to examine the wreckage of the shot-down aircraft reported that it was one of their own planes. This

Argentine air sortie thus damaged one British ship but at a cost of four of the eight aircraft and pilots involved; two of the surviving pilots would die later in the war.

Captain Zelaya was shaving next morning when he heard a radio report claiming that HMS *Brilliant* had been sunk and HMS *Broadsword* pierced by a bomb. The *Gaceta Argentina* at Stanley which was published on 14 May reported the action, only admitting one Skyhawk shot down by the ships, not the three actually lost, but it did record the shooting down of the Skyhawk by Argentine gunners at Goose Green. The next edition of the paper, published on 17 May, printed the deliberate lie that the British had confirmed that HMS *Brilliant* had been sunk in the air attack. There had been no such British statement; indeed the *Brilliant* was not present at the 12 May air action. The newspaper also stated that the aircraft-carrier *Hermes* had 'fled from the theatre of operations seriously damaged' and was 'in search of a port for effecting repairs', which was equally untrue.

The British task force lost a Sea King anti-submarine helicopter in an accident on this day; the crew members were saved.


## 13 and 14 May

There were no major events on these days.


## Night of 14–15 May

The aircraft-carrier *Hermes* and the destroyer *Glamorgan* left the main British task force and came round the north of the Falklands to launch a raid by SAS men on the airfield at Pebble Island Settlement, on the north coast of West Falkland. A small Argentine naval air base had been established on the grass airfield here. This was officially known as Base Aérea Naval Calderón, after Puerto Calderón which was the Argentine name for the settlement, but most Argentines call the base 'Borbón' after Isla de Borbón, their name for the whole of the 18-mile-long Pebble Island. The four Turbo-Mentors of the 4th Naval Attack Squadron had operated from here ever since their arrival from the mainland but they had recently been joined by six Pucarás dispersed for safety reasons from Goose Green after the Sea Harrier raids there, and there was also a Coast Guard Skyvan light transport aircraft present on this night.

Two Sea King helicopters left *Hermes* carrying forty-five SAS men and a small artillery observation team; *Glamorgan* gave covering shellfire. The protective garrison for the airfield was provided by a marine infantry platoon, but it had suffered much sickness, and there was only a small guard in a hut on the edge of the airfield on this wet and windy night when the SAS men and the shell fire both arrived without warning. The SAS men placed demolition charges on most of the parked aircraft and fired bursts of bullets into others. A large crater was also blown at the intersection of the two grass runways. There was an exchange of fire between the Argentine marines and the SAS; some men were wounded on both sides, but there were no deaths. All eleven Argentine aircraft present were put out of action and never flew again; ten of them were valuable ground-attack aircraft which could have operated against the British forces about to land in the Falklands. Helicopters recovered the SAS men, and the two British warships were safely away from the danger of air attack by dawn.

The Argentines never attempted to use this airfield again. Some of the 'dismounted' pilots were formed into teams and placed on local mountain tops to observe and report air activity. Comodoro Mendiberri, an air force officer involved in the collection of intelligence at Stanley, says that the stories of sophisticated tracking by radar of British air activity are exaggerated and that most of the information on British air patrols came from 'men on the tops of hills with binoculars and radios'; these observers were nearly all Mentor and Pucará pilots who lost their aircraft at Pebble Island. (Two of the ten aircraft put out of action at Pebble Island still survive. Pucará A-529 was taken to Stanley after the war and will be housed in a local museum. Turbo-Mentor 0729 was saved from souvenir hunters by the people of Pebble Island, mainly the children, and that aircraft was later brought to England where it is an exhibit at the Fleet Air Arm Museum at Yeovilton.)

### Afternoon of 16 May

Two Sea Harriers from HMS *Hermes* carrying out a reconnaissance flight over Falkland Sound spotted two Argentine merchant ships, one alongside the small jetty at Fox Bay West Settlement and the other in Port King which was an uninhabited bay. Both ships were photographed, and it was decided that they should be attacked.

The ship at Fox Bay West was the naval transport *Bahía Buen Suceso*, which had been involved in the first events of the war when she took the scrap-metal workers to South Georgia. She was one of the ships sent away from Stanley for safety purposes and had since covered 600 nautical miles in various local voyages. When I met Captain Niella, he studied my Falklands map nostalgically and said how wonderful it would have been to make those voyages in peace-time. He had put into Fox Bay West only to collect some fresh water. He saw the Sea Harrier reconnaissance aircraft and realized that an attack was possible. This is his account; the two Sea Harriers which made the attack were only armed with cannons because the ship was so close to the civilian settlement:

> I told the crew to disembark; I remember that I gave the order exactly eighteen minutes before the actual attack. We were lucky. It is something marvellous I shall never forget, that I gave that order at that time. Only three of us were still aboard, getting our sleeping equipment together, when we heard the planes and the sound of the cannon shells. There were several hits, some near me – too many! On the second or third attack, the cannon shells exploded while I was trying to reach the bridge, and I got some splinters in my face, fortunately just missing my eye. I also received a bad wound in my leg. I was later given a bit of that shell as a souvenir by the army doctor at Fox Bay. One of the other men was also wounded, but by the grace of God no one was killed. The ship was badly damaged and remained there at Fox Bay. The wind later broke it loose from the moorings, and it beached itself on the nearby rocks. We tried to get it off, but it could only have been salved with tugs.

A fuel dump on the shore near the *Bahía Buen Suceso* was set alight by the cannon shells and burned furiously, but there were no casualties ashore. The ship never sailed under her own steam again. She was towed out to sea after the war and sank after being used as target practice by Sea Harriers.

The ship at Port King was the E L M A ship *Río Carcaraña* (8,482 tons), which had managed to discharge her cargo of military stores – and television sets – a week earlier but had been prevented from sailing back to the mainland by an order enforced by a naval officer and two armed seamen. Because there were no civilians nearby, the two Sea Harriers sent to attack this ship were armed with bombs as well as cannons. Captain Dell'Elicine describes what happened. He is an avid reader of war books, which explains his correct anticipation of the direction from which the attack came:

It was a lovely day – a Sunday. There was a light wind and a cloudless blue sky, a lovely day for sailing; one of the crew suggested getting a little sailing in with one of the lifeboats. I remember saying to him that it would also be a good day for flying and I refused permission. We received a warning from the *Bahía Buen Suceso* by V H F that she had spotted two aircraft. A few minutes later it was full Red Alert from Fox Bay, and a few minutes after that I saw smoke coming from the south-south-west, obviously from Fox Bay. I realized we were in a dangerous situation. I briefed the crew about taking shelter. I estimated that we would be attacked from the starboard side, that is out of the sun, the classic pilot's tactic. I told the men to pack small bags with their belongings, particularly warm clothes, blankets and some drinking water, and I ordered them to keep awake, to keep a sharp watch and not to take a siesta.

It was exactly 13.50 when the look-out on the bridge shouted, 'Aircraft!' I was in the chart room and ordered everyone to take cover and then dashed downstairs, so I never saw the Harriers myself. They made four passes, the first was bombing, two separate aircraft dropping a bomb each. The ship shuddered, but we were not hit; I think the bombs fell about twenty metres away. Then they made about three more attacks with cannon fire. The noise was terrific. I think they were using armour-piercing shells, making small holes, and explosive shells, making big ones. The attacks all came from the starboard side, and none of the cannon shells went more than halfway through the ship, so we were all safe on the port side. It was a good job for us that those pilots carried out their attacks by the book.

When the noise of the jets died away I ordered 'abandon ship' immediately. There was no critical damage, but I expected another attack, and it was no use running away; the islands offered no shelter for a big ship like mine. We lit two smoke flares to deceive them into thinking that we were on fire. We were all gone in ten minutes – forty-four crew members and a few naval personnel. There was no panic. We got away in two lifeboats and a raft from the port side; the starboard-side boats were all destroyed. We had only got 150 metres away when two more Harriers came over. They made two passes but did not fire; I don't think they were the same planes.

We landed on the shore just under a mile away. It was cold, and some of the crew got the shakes. I told them to take it easy; I joked with them: 'We are going to make a new settlement on the islands; we can call it Villa Carcaraña.' We waited until dark, when some of us went back to the ship to fetch sheets and timber to make a shelter and some more food.

The *Río Carcaraña*'s crew spent only one night on that isolated coast; they were picked up next day by the *Forrest* and taken to join the crew of the *Bahía Buen Suceso* at Fox Bay, where the two crews were a considerable drain on the local army unit's food supply. Captain Dell'Elicine returned in a fishing vessel to his ship, which was still afloat, to salvage some of the plentiful food supply left aboard, but the ship had been set on fire in a later missile attack by a British helicopter. The *Río Carcaraña* would still remain afloat for some time and attract attacks from at least two Argentine aircraft before she eventually sank. The merchant navy members of the two crews were later evacuated to Argentina on the hospital ship *Bahía Paraíso*. Captain Dell'Elicine reached Ezeiza International Airport on 7 June, being able to telephone his wife with the first news of him for six weeks. The taxi driver gave him a free ride home.

### Night of 17–18 May

A Sea King helicopter flew from the British task force and, after a long flight near the mainland air base of Río Grande, crash-landed near Punta Arenas in Chile. What happened during that flight re-

mains a mystery, the British still not having released details when
this was written. Perhaps S A S men were landed to observe the take-
offs of Argentine aircraft. Perhaps electronic devices were dropped
by parachute or placed on the ground to transmit warnings of take-
offs. Perhaps the operation was a failure. Perhaps the whole flight
was a bluff, with the Sea King deliberately coming down and being
reported at Punta Arenas to lead the Argentines to think that S A S
men were on the mainland preparing to mount another airfield raid,
particularly on the Super Étendards, thus hoping to frighten the
Argentines into withdrawing those aircraft to airfields further north
and putting them out of range when the amphibious landings took
place in four days' time.

I hoped to solve this mystery when I went to Argentina, but the
only answers to my questions were negative ones, which tends to
support the possibilities of a failed operation or a bluff. There were
two Argentine destroyers – *Piedra Buena* and *Hipólito Bouchard* – on
radar watch off the coast and both reported the passage of the
helicopter, but a considerable land search discovered nothing. The
Super Étendards had already been removed from the airfield to
sandbagged emplacements along Highway 3 – the main coastal road
– for protection against possible air or land attack. It is clear, however,
that the ability of the S A S was highly respected, and a considerable
effort by all three Argentine services would continue to be devoted
to airfield and coastal protection on the mainland.

### Early Morning, 18 May

The ships carrying the British landing force joined the warships of
the task force off the Falklands.

### Night of 18–19 May

A further anti-submarine Sea King of the British task force was lost
in an accident; the crew were rescued.

### Afternoon of 19 May

A Sea King transhipping troops of the landing force crashed in the
sea; twenty-one men, most from the S A S, died.

## Evening of 19 May

After a postponement of twenty-four hours because of bad weather, twelve ships carrying British military units and an escort of seven warships set sail for the landing area.

So ended what was for the British the softening-up and reconnaissance period. Some of their objectives had been achieved. The Argentine fleet had been forced back to the mainland; the sea blockade was partially effective, and even the waters immediately around the Falklands were becoming unsafe for Argentine shipping. The preliminary reconnaissance work had also been completed with not a single one of the SAS and SBS parties landed being detected. But the softening-up of the land garrisons had achieved only limited successes. The naval shelling and the Sea Harrier and Vulcan raids had achieved little after the successes of the first day when the Stanley runway was holed, three Pucarás were put out of action at Goose Green, and twelve men were killed by shelling or bombing. The names of all the Argentine servicemen killed in the Falklands are known but not all the dates of death. It seems, however, that the deaths of only three men can with certainty be attributed to the combined air attack and naval shelling effort during the period 2 to 20 May. Fatal casualties are not the only yardstick of success, but there are no reports of any serious material damage being caused or of large numbers of wounded during this period. The reason for this was that the Argentine air defences at Stanley and Goose Green had forced the Sea Harriers to operate at high level after the initial raids, and the naval shelling was usually 'by the map', with no artillery observation officers yet ashore, and with daylight bombardment with helicopter spotters found to be too vulnerable to air attack. The British aim to draw the Argentine air units on the mainland into serious action was also largely unfulfilled, and the demonstration of the effectiveness of the Super Étendard–Exocet combination in the attack on the *Sheffield* was severely restricting the ability of the British task force to approach the islands. On the air side, however, the SAS raid on Pebble Island had caused serious casualties to the locally based air units.

What was the state of the Argentine garrison in the Falklands on the eve of the British landings? The Argentine commanders were ready. Their men easily outnumbered the potential British landing force in total numbers, but the Argentine units were basically static, in fixed defences. If the British landed at Stanley, then the opposing forces would be of approximately equal strength, but if the landings were elsewhere, the British would have local superiority but would face the major task of moving to 'Fortress Stanley', which would be a formidable obstacle to British success. The mainland air units were almost intact and ready to carry out determined attacks on any ships attempting to put ashore a landing force.

There had been only little increase in the Argentine forces in the Falklands since 1 May. The last unit to arrive, B Battery of the 101st Anti-Aircraft Regiment, had collected its guns from the *Isla de los Estados* before that ship was sunk, and the battery was now deployed along Cortley Hill ridge, the northern arm of Stanley Harbour. This completed the ring of anti-aircraft defences in the Stanley area. There were now sixty-one anti-aircraft guns and seven missile-launch units preventing the Sea Harriers from making low-level raids inside that defended area. The Argentine field artillery was also reinforced. When three British warships had appeared off Stanley on 1 May and started shelling without the Argentine artillery being able to reply, a call went out for the means to do so. Two 155-mm guns belonging to the 101st Artillery Regiment were brought across by air and, with their range of 15 miles, were able to force the British bombardment ships to remain further out to sea with a corresponding reduction in accuracy. Two more of these guns would be flown in later. The main worry of the Argentine commanders was a continuing shortage of food. The sea blockade had stopped all recent sailings, and the scale of rations issued to units had to be reduced. Brigadier-General Menéndez purchased every sheep in the Stanley area, but it was still not enough to provide more than one cooked meal a day for the Argentine troops. There was very little reserve of food other than this sheep meat.

The Argentine Air Force did what it could to help the Falklands garrison. Twelve more Pucarás were flown across from the mainland, the transfer starting the day after the Pebble Island raid. This more than replaced all the Pucará losses incurred so far. The 'Air Bridge' which had been discontinued on 29 April was resumed on 6 May

after it became clear that a British landing at Stanley was not imminent. But the presence of Sea Harrier patrols by day restricted
flights to the night hours, and the damaged runway meant that the
Air Force would only use its rugged Hercules transport aircraft. The
Navy, having to make its own arrangements, also dispatched an
occasional Electra flight. But the average nightly airlift fell to about
one-tenth of the large April effort, and only essential cargoes – like
the 155-mm guns – were carried. In an attempt to conceal the new
flights, Vicecomodoro Vinals organized a party of men of the Air
Force's 1st Construction Group at Stanley airfield to make dummy
bomb craters out of mud on the runway to make it appear unusable.

There had been no major redeployment of Argentine troops
during the last three weeks, but one minor move of great importance.
Until 15 May there had been no troops stationed near the extensive
bay called San Carlos Water. At the mouth of the bay was a huge,
towering headland called Fanning Head which rose almost sheer
from the sea to a height of nearly 800 feet. This headland dominated
not only the narrow entrance to San Carlos Water but also the
northern entrance to Falkland Sound, which was only three miles
wide at that point. It was decided that Fanning Head should be
manned, and the Argentine garrison at Goose Green, 25 miles away,
was ordered to send a small force. So 'Eagle Detachment' (Equipo
de Combate Aguila) was formed, with sixty-two men from the 12th
and 25th Regiments, under the command of First Lieutenant Esteban, who had been the original commander at Goose Green before a
larger garrison arrived there. Esteban was given three tasks: to provide early warning of any landing in that area; to control the nearby
Port San Carlos Settlement; and to control the northern entrance to
the Falkland Sound. It was actually HMS *Alacrity*'s dash through
the sound and the sinking of the *Isla de los Estados* three nights
earlier which led to the dispatch of the force. The weapons installed
on Fanning Head were two 105-mm anti-tank guns and two 81-mm
mortars. It was realized that these provided hardly enough firepower
to control the surrounding waters, but that was all that could be
spared. Eagle Detachment installed itself at Port San Carlos Settlement, providing a rotation of men to man the post of Fanning Head
which was much exposed to the Falklands weather; the civilian
settlement manager helped transport by Land-Rover from the

headland several men suffering from exposure as an act of mercy. The importance of the small garrison sent to this area was that the British intended to send their amphibious ships through the northern entrance to Falkland Sound and then right under the noses of the Argentines on Fanning Head to make their landing in San Carlos Water.

The Argentine commanders did not realize that the landings would be at that place, nor did they know that the landings were imminent, though they could not be delayed much longer. Once again, the nature of the war was to be violently changed, and a completely new phase was about to start. The mantle of combat was about to pass, firstly to the air units on the mainland and then to the Argentine army units in the Falklands. The Argentine Navy, which had started off the whole Falklands venture, did not feel able to risk the threat of British submarines and would remain within a 12-mile mainland coastal limit imposed by the British on 7 May.

# 11 · D-Day and 'Death Valley'

After a delay of twenty-four hours, the British amphibious ships steamed undetected into the northern end of Falkland Sound during the night of 20–21 May. It is difficult to say exactly where the first shots were fired because preliminary operations by British special forces started during the night at two places, on Fanning Head and near Goose Green. It will be convenient to deal with what happened at Goose Green first.

This operation was a diversion, intended to contain the large garrison at Goose Green and prevent Argentine troops moving towards the main landing area. A party of forty SAS men were landed by helicopter north of Darwin during the night. The frigate HMS *Ardent*, 11 miles away, was to give covering fire with her 4.5-inch gun. But part of the plan went amiss. A forward artillery observation officer who had been on Sussex Mountain for three days protected by an SBS team was unable to direct the naval bombardment, probably because his codes had been rendered out of date by the postponement of the landing, and *Ardent* could not carry out her bombardment. The SAS party produced a demonstration of fire-power, but without actually attacking the main Argentine positions. The commander of A Company of the 12th Regiment, First Lieutenant Jorge Manresa, reported the firing to his commander, Lieutenant-Colonel Italo Piaggi. Piaggi, who kept copious notes of everything he and his unit did during the war, says that the firing was not very impressive, but he did bring his troops to maximum alert and reported the incident to Stanley.

It was not until daylight that *Ardent* was able to commence her bombardment. The Argentines say that the shelling was all just north of the airfield, believing that the airfield surface was to be kept intact for later British use, but the true reason was probably to ensure that the shells fell well away from the civilian settlement. The Argentines suffered no casualties, but a 20-mm anti-aircraft gun was damaged. The personal diary of Sergeant Guillermo Potoscnyak contains an entry referring to the shelling: '09.30 – An intense bombardment by five English frigates began. I was really frightened. We were defenceless against the shells, which rained down on us for an hour.' He goes on to describe how three of his fellow sergeants were sent out on patrol in a civilian Land-Rover that afternoon to find out if British troops were still present north of Goose Green: 'I am afraid for them because they are not front-line soldiers. Magiarate makes me sad because, before leaving, he gives me a letter for his mother. Tonight, before going to bed, I will pray to God for them.' But no British were found; the SAS had melted away.

A far more serious action was taking place 25 miles further north, where First Lieutenant Esteban's 'Eagle Detachment' was the only Argentine force standing between the British commanders and an unopposed landing. Second Lieutenant Roberto Reyes, four NCOs and fifteen conscripts were manning the position on Fanning Head; the remainder of the detachment were at Port San Carlos. A party of thirty-five SBS men, together with an artillery observation officer and a Spanish-speaking officer, were landed by helicopter during the night to the east of Fanning Head. The bombardment of HMS *Antrim*'s two 4.5-inch guns opened on time and drove the Argentines out of their positions on the headland and towards the SBS who were equipped with a 'thermal imager' which could detect movement in the dark. The SBS men formed a line and opened fire, and then the Spanish-speaking officer called on the Argentines to surrender to save bloodshed. After a brief little action, six Argentines gave themselves up, and three more were found lying wounded in the grass. The remainder, under Second Lieutenant Reyes, escaped in the dark.

Five miles away at Port San Carlos, First Lieutenant Esteban heard the shelling but not the small-arms fire. For more than three hours he tried to make contact with Second Lieutenant Reyes and hoped that a runner would come and report what was happening, but no one came. At dawn he sent a look-out with binoculars to the high ground behind the settlement. At first nothing could be seen because of early-morning mist, but at 8.10 a.m. the look-out was amazed to see the shape of a large white liner – the *Canberra* – steaming into San Carlos Water three miles away. Soon afterwards the mist cleared sufficiently for three warships to be seen, and then, almost immediately, a landing craft full of troops was observed leaving the white ship. The mist finally cleared; landing craft could be seen 'travelling in all directions', and then 'English troops advancing in single file' were seen moving towards Port San Carlos itself.[1]

Esteban reported all this information by radio to Goose Green and requested an air attack; that was the last contact with him that day. Esteban then withdrew his force of forty-two men from the settlement to a position in open ground to the east, not wishing to fight near the civilians. As the Argentines left the settlement the civilians made 'catcalls and rude signs' and then pointed out to the British troops the way his party had gone.

A succession of British helicopters then approached Esteban's new position. The first two were a Sea King carrying an underslung load of mortar ammunition and an escorting rocket-equipped Gazelle. The helicopters flew too far inland and were engaged by Esteban's men. The Sea King jettisoned its load and swung away; Esteban believed that it was damaged, but it was not. The Gazelle, however, was hit by six bullets at a range of only sixty or seventy metres, the fire damaging the tail rotor and the engine area and injuring a crewman who later died. The Argentine troops watched the helicopter come down gently into the water and the two crew members emerge. Esteban shouted to his men to stop firing, but some continued to fire on the men in the water, a regrettable incident which Esteban explains:

> The men who were firing were some distance away and did not hear my order. You must understand that they were only conscripts with forty-five days' service and knew nothing of the Geneva Convention. They stopped firing when the kelpers put out in a boat to help the men in the water. Instruction on the Geneva Convention is now part of the basic training of our conscripts because of this incident.

[1] These details come from First Lieutenant Esteban's after-action report; the British troops here were men of 3 Para.

We moved our position then, to get up on to higher ground. The British troops opened fire but did not hit us. Then another Sea King, escorted by a smaller helicopter, appeared. The small one nearly came over us; it was only about thirty or forty metres away. We opened fire and it was hit at once. It crashed only ten metres from me. It didn't burn but was badly crushed. I could see that both of the crew had died at once. Then another Gazelle came in. We opened fire at that one, and it got out quickly.

I had always thought that a helicopter would have a shock-paralysing effect upon troops – like a tank – but I found that my men easily stood and fought. When I first saw all those men with red berets landing, I didn't think that I would survive, but after the fight with the helicopters and after watching the cautious manner in which the British troops moved I became much more sure of myself and started to think that I would survive.

Esteban now withdrew his party eastwards, into the interior, pursued by small-arms and mortar fire and, so he thinks, naval shelling, all of which he describes as inaccurate. He and his men slipped away without incurring any casualties. After four days of cross-country trekking they reached Douglas Settlement 18 miles away. From there they helicoptered to Stanley and later back to Goose Green, arriving just in time for the battle there. Second Lieutenant Reyes and the men who escaped from Fanning Head also slipped away safely. Both officers were decorated for their actions that day.

These actions on Fanning Head and at Port San Carlos were the only clashes of the day between the opposing ground forces. The withdrawal of Esteban's men left a vacuum into which the British units could continue their landings and start to consolidate. In one of the most important days of the war, the sixty-two men of Eagle Detachment were the only Argentine army participants; nine were prisoners, three of them wounded. The three Gazelle helicopter crewmen were the only fatal British casualties in what might be termed the 'ground action' part of D-Day.

It became a very fine day after the early-morning mist cleared –

perfect flying weather, not what the British wanted before their anti-aircraft defences were established in the landing area. But it was the British who took first advantage of the good weather. The task force had recently received a reinforcement of six RAF Harriers, aircraft which were specifically intended for ground attack and reconnaissance work. (These were Harrier GR3s but it will be convenient to describe them here as 'RAF Harriers' as distinct from the navy's Sea Harriers. The RAF Harriers were flying from HMS *Hermes*.) An SAS observation team near Stanley had been watching the movements of the Argentine helicopter force. By day, the helicopters worked from Stanley, but they were flown inland each evening to a position just north of Mount Kent, 12 miles from Stanley. The SAS advised that an air attack at first light would catch the helicopters before they flew back to the protection of the Stanley air defences.

Two RAF Harriers took off and found the helicopter site. There were fourteen helicopters of the 601st Combat Aviation Battalion and the unit's tents and fuel dumps. The Harriers dropped cluster bombs, which caused no damage, but later passes with 30-mm cannon fire hit a Chinook, a Puma and a Huey. Greater damage would have been caused if the colour schemes of the helicopters had not merged so well with the terrain; the Harrier pilots did not see most of the helicopters. A description of the attack comes from First Lieutenant Ignacio Gorriti, commander of the infantry company (B Company, 12th Regiment) which was guarding the helicopter site:

We heard the Harriers coming. Our pilots ran to their helicopters and tried to start them between the attacks, but the engines were all cold. The Huey was the only one warmed up. It was going to take me to the farm at Estancia House; I wanted to get a battery off a tractor or one of the other vehicles for my radio. We had just got airborne when the two Harriers made their first pass.

I heard the bombs falling on another part of the helicopter area, and then they were on top of us, hitting us with cannon fire. The pilot landed, and we jumped out. It was the first time I had seen war action; it was like a film – not a pleasant experience. The noise was terrific – horrible. My family moved to a new house near a hill after the war, and when the trucks had to change gear going up the hill I used to wake up thinking those Harriers were on top of me again.

The large Chinook was completely burnt out, and two smaller helicopters were damaged. There were no casualties among the troops.

War often consists of blow followed by swift counter-blow, and this is what happened now when an Argentine soldier of the 601st Commando Company at Port Howard shot down an RAF Harrier into the sea with a Blowpipe missile. The pilot managed to eject and was rescued from the sea by the Argentines. He was badly wounded but was well treated by his captors and eventually transferred to the mainland where he had a long stay in hospital.

At about the same time as the RAF Harrier was being shot down – approximately 9.30 a.m. – the first Argentine flights were taking place. That time coincides almost exactly with the time that First Lieutenant Esteban's small party was withdrawing from contact with the British troops at Port San Carlos. The Falklands War – as wars often do – passed through a series of distinct phases. Looking at the war from the Argentine side, it had started with a flurry of action by their marines in the April occupation of the Falklands and South Georgia, but most of the action since then had been at sea, with the Argentine fleet losing the *Belgrano* and with Argentine merchant ships being attacked. Now the emphasis would change. On that morning of 21 May, when the British were pouring troops ashore and Carlos Esteban's men were disappearing inland, the mantle of combat would pass almost exclusively to the pilots of the Argentine air units for the next week of frantic and often deadly action. With their fleet confined to mainland waters and their army mainly concentrated 50 miles away at Stanley, there was no one else who could stop the British landing on the beloved Malvinas. The whole world would come to admire the gallantry shown by the Argentine pilots during that week.

The first flights of the day were made by the locally based units. Six Pucarás were ordered to take off from Goose Green airfield, but only one was able to take off before HMS *Ardent* started her shelling there. The Pucará pilot, Captain Jorge Benítez, did not yet know that landings were taking place at San Carlos and he set off to carry out a routine patrol of an inland area. It was only later that he strayed into the San Carlos area and spotted British ships and troops. Before he could make an attack, however, his Pucará was hit by a Stinger missile fired by a member of the SAS party which was withdrawing from its diversionary action at Goose Green. Benítez ejected safely and spent the rest of the day walking the ten miles back to Goose Green.

The second local flight was also a solo one. Carlos Esteban's news of the landings in the San Carlos area eventually reached Stanley, and a naval pilot, Lieutenant Guillermo Crippa, was ordered to investigate. He took off in his Aeromacchi, flew round to the north of San Carlos and ran into the area with the sun behind him for better visibility. He was about to attack the easy target of a Lynx helicopter when he saw a warship further ahead. This was the frigate *Argonaut*, the most northerly of the 'gun line' of British warships which would be stationed in Falkland Sound throughout that day to provide air defence for the amphibious ships. In a brave action, Crippa attacked the *Argonaut* with cannons and rockets. Some damage was caused to the ship's upperworks, and two sailors were injured; it was a foretaste of the determination to be shown by the Argentine pilots. Crippa then banked and flew at low level over San Carlos Water, being fired at by many missiles and guns but not hit. Realizing the importance of what was happening below, he turned again, gained height and flew carefully back along the bay, counting the British ships. On returning to Stanley, he reported personally to Menéndez and was congratulated for the detailed nature of his report. He was later awarded the Cruz-La Nación Argentina al Heroico Valor en Combate for the flight, the only pilot of the war to win that high decoration.

Two more Pucarás from Goose Green were able to take off later in the morning but they had the bad luck to meet two Sea Harriers. The Argentine pilots tried to escape by hugging the ground and flying along narrow valleys, but the aircraft of Major Carlos Tomba was eventually shot down by cannon fire; he ejected and survived. The efforts of the local air units had caused little damage to the British, and two Pucarás had been lost, but clear details of what was happening at San Carlos were now known to the Argentine command.

*

The air units on the mainland had been standing by for action for many days, conserving their strength since the false start on 1 May and absorbing the lessons learnt on that day. Some changes in policy had been made, and the full strength of the units available would not be committed in this new phase. The Canberras of the 2nd Bomber Group were now considered to be too vulnerable in daylight operations and were kept back for night work. The 8th Fighter Group, which only had eight Mirages left after the combats with Sea Harriers on 1 May, would also be kept back to defend the mainland air bases; their all-weather capability would enable them to intercept British air raids if these were mounted against mainland targets.

These changes left the Argentine Air Force with an estimated 62 available strike aircraft – 39 Skyhawks of the 4th and 5th Fighter Groups and 23 Daggers of the 6th Fighter Group. A small reinforcement of eight Skyhawks had arrived at Río Grande in the form of the 3rd Naval Fighter and Attack Squadron, which had been disembarked from the aircraft-carrier *Veinticinco de Mayo* now that the Argentine fleet was confined to coastal waters. The pilots of this unit were well trained in ship–attack tactics. The Super Étendard unit at Río Grande still had three Exocets remaining but this unit was only suitable for open sea work and it would not be used in the coming offensive against the landing area. The Argentine pilots destined for that battle would have to operate under most unfavourable conditions. They would have to carry out low-level bomb and cannon attacks, which would have to be pressed right home to be effective. They would have to operate over the sea, at maximum range from their own bases, without fighter escort and having to run the gauntlet of the Sea Harriers, which had already proved their effectiveness in combat, as well as the mass of missiles and gunfire put up by the British ships and ground forces. It would be a daunting task.

The attacks carried out by those Argentine pilots during the San Carlos landing period have been subjected to intense analysis – though not always with conclusive results – and have been described in detail several times. I do not intend to republish yet another step-by-step account but will confine my contribution to giving an overall view and providing personal accounts from some of the Argentine pilots who survived. In doing this, I would like to acknowledge the hard work done by specialist aviation writers on whose work I have drawn.[2]

The main air attacks were spread over a period lasting nearly five hours, from about 10.30 a.m. until nearly 3.30 p.m. There were three distinct waves, each containing between fourteen and seventeen aircraft. The first wave consisted of eight Daggers from the 6th Fighter Group flying from San Julián and Río Grande and six Skyhawks of the 5th Fighter Group from Río Gallegos. A personal account from this phase is available from First Lieutenant Filippini, who was leading a combined Skyhawk flight of five aircraft after his fellow flight leader had to turn back with technical trouble. Filippini describes his attack on the frigate *Argonaut* in the northern entrance to Falkland Sound, just under Fanning Head:

When the Falkland Sound was in sight, one of my wingmen shouted over the radio: 'To the right!' It sounded like an order to me, so I banked and caught sight of a frigate. The ship detected us at the same time and headed rapidly towards a high cliff, looking for shelter, hoping to force us to climb to avoid crashing into the headland. Then we began to attract their anti-aircraft fire, which we could distinguish as a curtain of small red light beams formed by their tracer ammunition. The quiet island soon became hell. As we got nearer we could see this fire in the air in front of us and then passing over our cockpits, so we were forced to descend even lower to get into their blind cannon area, where we aimed to drop our bombs a little before reaching the target.

We concentrated on aiming. The ship, protected by the cliff 200 metres high, was in my sight, so I dropped one of the bombs which would cause its destruction. I felt like destroying the enemy, thinking of my comrades shot down by them on 12 May. I pulled my control stick backwards in a climbing turn, trying to pull over the headland. I felt a violent blow under my plane; an auxiliary fuel tank hanging under one of the wings had crashed against the mast of the frigate. Then I dived to

[2] I have used in particular Rodney A. Burden *et al.*, *Falklands – The Air War* (Arms & Armour Press, 1986), and Jeffrey Ethell and Alfred Price, *Air War South Atlantic* (Sidgwick & Jackson, 1983). For the personal accounts of pilots, I have used the unpublished translation of Pablo Carballo's *Dios y los Halcones*, and my own interviews with naval pilots.

escape by staying as close to the ground as possible and eventually I took refuge behind some hills. We reached the sea and then headed to our base at low altitude. As we flew past the northern mouth of the Sound, we could see the frigate we had attacked. A dense column of black smoke was coming out of its side; our bombs had hit it, and we saw the colour of the ship's structure starting to change from light grey to reddish brown.

Very excited at this victory over our enemies, we broke radio silence with joyful shouts. Once the euphoria was over, I checked my wingmen apprehensively to make sure they were all there and safe. That was the happiest moment after the attack; thank God, the five planes which had entered the target area were all present.

Two bombs had hit *Argonaut*, but neither exploded because the Skyhawks were flying too low and this did not give the bomb fuses time to arm themselves after leaving the aircraft. But one of the bombs set off an explosion in the Sea Cat magazine, and it was the smoke from this which Filippini saw as he passed the entrance to Falkland Sound after the attack. Two seamen were killed in the ship.

The Daggers operating at this time caused cannon-fire damage to various ships and also put a bomb into the destroyer *Antrim*; but this bomb did not explode, and one Dagger was shot down, probably by a Sea Wolf fired by HMS *Broadsword*. Its pilot was killed.

The next wave of attacks came in two and a half hours later. Fourteen Skyhawks from three units were dispatched, but the six naval Skyhawks flying from Río Grande met difficult weather conditions, had their orders altered in mid-flight and were forced to turn back before reaching the islands. One of the other formations also suffered two early returns, leaving just four aircraft of the 4th Fighter Group and two of the 5th Fighter Group to carry on. The attacks were not successful. Sea Harriers caught the 4th Fighter Group flight, shooting down two Skyhawks and damaging a third and preventing any of these aircraft from reaching the landing area. The two shot-down pilots were both killed. The pair of Skyhawks of the 5th Fighter Group, led by Captain Pablo Carballo, flew up Falkland Sound from the south-west and observed what they believed to be one of the British landing ships. Carballo's wingman dropped his bombs on the ship, but Carballo held his back at the last moment because he thought something was wrong. He was correct; this was the abandoned Argentine ship *Río Carcaraña*. Carballo then pressed on alone towards the landing area and finally encountered the *Ardent*, which was still in its solitary bombardment position north of Goose Green. Carballo describes his attack:

The effect produced by the compression of the air between my plane and the sea caused a constant beating on the bottom of the plane when flying so low, almost skimming the waves. It was much the same as the vibration one feels when driving a car over a cattle grid or a level crossing. In those endless two or three minutes leading up to the attack, I heard something on the radio that froze my blood. It sounded like the breathing of a person in agony, and I wondered how this mournful breathing could have entered my VHF until I suddenly realized that it was my own breathing. I looked at my chest, expecting to see it heaving up and down, but it looked quite normal.

Soon I entered a quiet area where I was no longer being fired at and I concentrated on the gunsight. When I saw the huge steel structure of the ship filling the sight, I pressed the trigger and felt the plane climb a few metres when the bomb released. I was kind of stupefied and dizzy, and this could have cost me my life. Suddenly, right in front of me, I saw the two pillars of the pointed masts against which I was about to crash. Instinctively hitting my control stick, I banked the plane and dived in between them, seeing one of them flash past my cockpit. Then I recovered my balance and started a slight turn left, mentally counting the seconds for the bomb to explode. When time was up and nothing happened, just as I was saying 'I have failed', I saw a dark cloud of smoke rising up to the height of the masts of the ship and pieces falling into the sea. I can't really say for sure whether the smoke was caused by an explosion or by the launching of a missile, but I believe that kind of frigate doesn't carry missiles.

I began to shout happily and levelled off. I had a very unpleasant surprise when I met another frigate, but it didn't open fire. Only God knows why.

Then I made for the 'sun route' as we called it in our squadron, leaving the islands behind, heading west, with the tremendous satisfaction of being able to say we had fulfilled our duty and were still alive. I felt really well; I had fought against a fearful enemy with my veteran plane under the protection of Our Lord Jesus Christ. On landing, I was surprised to meet my supreme chief, Brigadier-General Lami Dozo, Commander-in-Chief of the Air Force, who had come to the south to see how we were doing. I remember he told me that we had to grit our teeth, as there was still a long way to go. How right he was!

Pablo Carballo had made a brave, solo attack but he was not successful. The evidence from *Ardent* is quite clear that his bomb fell into the sea alongside the ship. The second round of attacks thus ended with only this one Skyhawk reaching the British ships out of fourteen aircraft dispatched and at a cost of two Argentine aircraft lost.

The final burst of action, starting one and a half hours later, was the most effective of the day. Seventeen aircraft burst through to the landing area between 2.30 and 3.15 p.m. and in the savage action which followed, both sides suffered severely. Eleven Daggers and six naval Skyhawks had taken off, and all but one reached the landing area, flying in small tactical groups of three or two aircraft. Captain Robles was leading one of the Dagger pairs. Passing over West Falkland, he was unaware that his wingman was shot down by a Sea Harrier; he thought that the pilot — First Lieutenant Luna — had flown into a hill. Robles now joined another pair of Daggers and soon sighted the still solitary *Ardent*:

We carried on, swallowing our sadness at 'Negro' Luna's accident. On the other side of Falkland Sound, over Grantham Sound, we saw a frigate close to the coast. As we started the attack we thought: 'This will be for Luna.' They started firing at us as we skimmed over the water. Captain Mir González bravely flew straight towards the masts of the ship, a path forming in front of his plane from his cannon shells. His bomb struck ten metres short, and up flew a mass of water which practically covered the ship; the bomb then bounced off the water and I believe it entered the hull.

Then Lieutenant Bernhardt dropped his bomb, which hit the upper and front part of the ship. When I was within range I dropped my bomb and, while passing over the ship, I saw a large piece of the rectangular antenna (which had been constantly rotating when we started the attack) go past my cockpit, whirling in the air. A missile aimed at one of the other planes went past on my right. I shouted at him to make an abrupt turn; he did so, very near me, and disappeared in the sky. As we were leaving, banking away to the right, the frigate was enveloped in an enormous cloud of smoke. That burning ship was worth far more than the plane and pilot we had lost. We didn't know if Lieutenant Luna was alive, but I'm sure he would have exchanged his life for the success of our mission.

One of the bombs – the one dropped by Lieutenant Bernhardt – had struck the stern of the ship, not the forepart; the 'rotating antenna' blown into the air which Captain Robles nearly hit was probably *Ardent*'s Sea Cat launcher, which was blown into the air by Bernhardt's bomb.

The six other Daggers in action at this time suffered contrasting fortunes. One flight of three aircraft attacked various British ships, though without inflicting serious damage, and returned safely to their base. But the final formation of three Daggers was wiped out, all shot down by Sea Harriers, though all three pilots ejected and survived.

The very last attacks of the day were carried out by six naval Skyhawk pilots, flying in two formations of three aircraft. Both formations flew up Falkland Sound from the south; both were ordered to attack the solitary British ship reported north of Goose Green – *Ardent* again, though that damaged ship was now nearing the protection of the main group of British ships further up Falkland Sound. Lieutenant-Commander Alberto Philippi was leading the first flight:

Our primary duty was to get that picket ship; if we could hit that, it would enable other aircraft to come in and attack the landing area. Our navigation was good, and we came in and made a good landfall. We descended from 27,000 feet down to

100 feet, closing up the formation because the weather was deteriorating, with low cloud and rain; the ceiling was 500 feet, and visibility was one mile. That was very dangerous for us, because if there was a picket ship at the southern end of Falkland Sound it would have picked us up by radar at fifteen to twenty miles' range and launch missiles at five miles. Those missiles would have been in the air for four miles before we could see them. We had no radar; the Skyhawk was a very simple, old aircraft.

There was supposed to be one of our Tracker reconnaissance aircraft in the area. We were supposed to call him, and he should have told us where the ship was and directed us in. I called him twice but got no reply. The Tracker pilot told me afterwards that he was there but he couldn't make contact. We went up the eastern side of the Sound – over lots of islands and bays. We ran into some clearer weather, and both myself and Lieutenant Arca saw two masts behind some rocks about eighteen kilómetres ahead.

I told the flight to commence the attack, but the ship started to move, quite fast, from behind the rocks; I assume that he was getting away from the coast to gain sea room and be able to manoeuvre at speed. This move meant that we lost the chance to be covered by the rocks in our approach. So I swung right in order to follow the coast, hoping that his radar would lose me in the echoes of the land behind us. If I had been on a freelance mission I could have jumped over that narrow neck of land and attacked the large ships in San Carlos Water, but I had been ordered to go for that picket ship, and we carried on. I could see that it was a Type 21.

We turned and, by the time we were ready to attack, we were in a good position because he was crossing in front of us and I could come in from his port quarter. I dropped my four 500-lb bombs – Mark 82 Snakeyes, each with metal plates to retard them. My number Three shouted out: 'Bien, señor!' – 'Well done, sir!' Then, a little later, he said: 'Otra en la popa' – 'Another hit on the stern'; that told me that another bomb had hit, one of Arca's. We could not tell whether Márquez was successful; there was no one behind to report his attack.

The second naval Skyhawk flight was led by Lieutenant Benito Rotolo:

Our orders to get the picket ship were changed during the flight, and we were told to go for San Carlos Water; a Tracker aircraft had said that there was no ship in the south end of the Sound now. We went on in radio silence, listening to the conversations in Philippi's flight; we were very interested in what they were saying about the islands, seeing them for the first time. We were still at high level; we couldn't hear it all but we could follow their route. I heard them saying they had found a ship and were attacking. Then I heard them talking about Sea Harrier action. I heard Philippi say: 'I'm O K. I am ejecting.'

Then we made our descent and started our approach. After hearing about the Sea Harriers, I went further inland over East Falkland to get among more hilly ground, intending to go over the Sussex Mountains into the anchorage at San Carlos. But I found that I was having to cross an open bay and was too far to the west. I couldn't go to my right now, because of our air defences at Goose Green, so I broke radio silence and told my wingmen to be prepared to attack the first ship we met. They acknowledged.

Then we saw two or three ships and prepared to attack. I banked left to approach one of them from the starboard side. The two wingmen checked that they could also see it; it was about four miles away and it seemed to me that it was a Type 21; the other pilots say the same. It opened fire with its guns; I didn't see any missiles. Its fire was opened very early; I saw the shots falling in the water in front of me. It also increased speed. So I used the tactics we had practised with our Type 42s – continually banking during the final stages of the attack. I was not hit. Then I climbed up to 250 feet and dropped my bombs. As I passed over the ship, I saw men running on the deck; others were firing with machine-guns lashed to the ship, not part of its proper equipment.

I went down fast – 250 feet was very high for that day; you feel very exposed. Our plan was to escape south down Falkland Sound, but I saw a County Class ship right in front of me,

shooting off everything he had. We came upon it suddenly
when we broke out into a clear patch, and it was all lit up by
the sun. I veered sharply away to the right, then had to climb
hard to get over the hills in the west island. I alerted the others,
and fortunately they understood my short message and were
able to turn away as well. So we all escaped, flying low level
through the mountains all the way across the island. It was bad
weather, but it was good to get away from the ships and all that
fire. We were lucky.

Rotolo and his wingmen all returned safely, though the wingmen's
aircraft were both damaged by the blast of bomb explosions. These
pilots had at least, like well-trained naval pilots, attacked from sufficient altitude to enable their bombs to explode, even if they had not
allowed the recommended twenty-seconds interval between aircraft
in order to escape the bomb blast damage to their aircraft.

When I met Benito Rotolo more than five years after the war, he
was still disappointed that the good attack carried out by his flight
had not been recognized in the popular post-war publications, unlike
his squadron colleague, Alberto Philippi, whose flight was credited
with inflicting the main damage on the *Ardent* which resulted in that
ship sinking later in the day. One aspect of many of the accounts by
Argentine pilots is a desire to be associated with attacks on the
*Ardent*, the only ship to sink on that day. There was also an element
of inter-service rivalry between the Air Force and the Navy to secure
the credit for the sinking. The attack of Rotolo's flight was squeezed
out in the crush of these claims. Some accounts say that he attacked
before Philippi and that his bombs all missed or that he attacked
another ship, not *Ardent*. But Rotolo's evidence is quite clear. He
heard Philippi's flight attacking on the radio and then being intercepted by Sea Harriers. He identified his target as a Type 21
frigate; *Ardent* was the only such ship in the landing area that day.
He describes his attack as coming in from the ship's starboard side.
The captain of the *Ardent* described one attack from astern (I
believe Philippi's) which scored two hits and then a final attack
being made by three light-coloured Skyhawks coming in one after
the other *from the starboard side*, with bombs from the first and
second of these aircraft scoring direct hits. I believe that Rotolo's

flight scored these final hits on *Ardent* and sealed the fate of the ship, which was soon abandoned and sank that night.

But these last successful attacks by the naval pilots were not achieved without serious loss. Rotolo's flight returned safely to the mainland, but Philippi's were all lost. That made seven aircraft destroyed out of the sixteen which reached the operational area in that final phase of the day's action. One of Philippi's flight – Sub-Lieutenant Marcelo Márquez – was killed when his Skyhawk was shot down by a Sea Harrier. A second aircraft, that of Lieutenant José Arca, came to a bizarre end. After being damaged by a Sea Harrier it was still flyable but would not be able to reach the mainland. Arca flew to Stanley and reported his difficulty. Major Iannariello, an air force officer there, describes what happened:

A Skyhawk approached the base with some damage to the hydraulic system which feeds such things as the controls, the landing gear, the flaps and the hook, and its fuselage was riddled with holes. We analysed the damage and decided that it would be too dangerous for him to land; the plane would break up and the pilot be killed. So we ordered him to eject over the sea and not on the land where there might be some minefields. We saw him go out, tumbling around in the air like a little puppet until his parachute opened.

To our surprise, the plane seemed to become alive and ready to play a nasty joke on us. For some moments it flew towards the pilot, as if to crash into him, then towards the town, then to the airfield in a lively and playful flight. It looked as if it were happy to be free from its master. Considering the damage it might cause, we ordered our guns to destroy it, but surprisingly enough and in spite of the aim of our gunners, it went on flying without being touched, as if the shells refused to hit a friendly plane. Finally it landed by itself on the beach and was smashed against the rocks with all the dignity of an A-4 Skyhawk. Its pilot was rescued.

Lieutenant-Commander Philippi describes what happened to him:

We tried to escape by flying back down Falkland Sound, weaving a little, hoping to avoid any missiles fired at us from behind, knowing that there were no English ships in front of us. Then, maybe one or two minutes later, I started to relax, engine still at full throttle, thinking that we were clear, when I heard Márquez shouting: 'Harrier! Harrier!'

My first reaction was to order tanks and bomb racks to be jettisoned and to start evasive action at high G, trying to see where they were. While doing that, while only in the second or third turn, I felt a violent explosion in the tail. The whole plane shuddered and started to climb. I pushed on the stick with both hands but could not get the nose down; there was no response. I looked around, and the Harrier appeared on my right side about 150 to 200 metres away; I think he was coming in for the kill. So I told my wingmen that I was hit, but I was OK and must eject. I tried to shut down the engine, but it did not respond. I opened the air-brakes, but they did not work. I pulled the ejection handle between my legs with my left hand; I didn't use my right hand to pull the hood release because, as aircraft-carrier pilots, we always keep lateral control; that is why I kept my right hand on the stick. If you lose the stick, the plane may start to turn, and if you eject when banking you go straight into the sea when you are low – so a naval pilot never leaves go of the stick. There was a huge explosion, and I was thrown out at 500 knots. I lost consciousness. When I opened my eyes I was falling near the edge of Falkland Sound, quite close to where the abandoned *Río Carcaraña* was. I saw a splash – either my own or Márquez's aircraft going in. I swam the 200 metres to land but was so tired that I could only crawl up the beach.

I was out there for four days, the first night in the open, the second and third in a building called Congo House. On the fourth day I was walking to Wreck House when I saw some men working near the coast. They had a Land-Rover. I thought they were Argentine troops and I signalled with a mirror, but it was Mr Tony Blake from North Arm Settlement. He was very polite, introduced himself and gave me my first food – sandwiches, cakes and chocolate. We went to North Arm, where I met the family and had a bath. He was a very nice person, one

1 Mass on board the landing ship *Cabo San Antonio*, Sunday, 28 March 1982.

2 Raising the Argentine flag at Stanley.

3 Rear Admiral Büsser, General García and Rear Admiral Allara in Stanley on 2 April

4 Argentine officer with captured Royal Marine officers, Majors Noott and Norman, on 2 April. Amtrac in rear.

5  Captured Royal Marines and sailors.

6  Argentine Amphibious Commandos at Government House.

7 An Amtrac patrols the streets of Stanley, 2 April.

8 Argentine trucks, Amtracs and infantry on the outskirts of Stanley, 4 April.

9 Commander Pedro Giachino

10 Funeral service at the Stella Maris Church at Puerto Belgrano naval base for the 2 April hero Lieutenant-Commander Giachino, who was killed in the attack on Government House, Stanley. At least one of the six officers acting as pall bearers, Lieutenant-Commander Menghini (second row, left), would later serve in the Falklands as O.C. of the Marine Amphibious Engineers Company. Junta member and Navy Commander-in-Chief Admiral Anaya, the driving force behind the Falklands invasion, is in the congregation on the extreme left.

11   Argentine president General Leopoldo Galtieri gets an effusive greeting from a youngster in Buenos Aires. The president's popularity increased markedly immediately after the Argentine invasion.

12  Excited soldiers, possibly recalled reservists, off to the war

13  Jubilant Argentines wave the national flag and cheer in Buenos Aires after the Government's announcement that the armed forces had occupied the Falklands.

14   First view of the 'Malvinas' by troop transport aircraft.

15   A confident army unit just after landing at Stanley airfield.

16 Argentine Air Force officers, probably Pucará pilots, map reading at their base on the Falklands.

17 Argentine troops at an encampment somewhere in the Falklands pose for this photograph, which was taken on 27 April.

18　The aircraft carrier *Veinticinco de Mayo*.

19　Neptune aircraft which guided in the Super Étendards which attacked HMS *Sheffield* on 4 May.

20 The standard Argentine naval attack aircraft, the Skyhawk A-4Q. Skyhawks were also flown by the Argentine Air Force and were responsible for many of the raids on British ships in the San Carlos anchorage.

21 Tracker recce aircraft which discovered the location of the British task force when it commenced operations off the Falklands on 1 May (see map on page 85).

22 The cruiser *General Belgrano*.

23 Captain Hector Bonzo, captain of the *Belgrano*.

24 The Argentinian cruiser *General Belgrano* sinks in the South Atlantic on 2 May. This Photograph was taken by a survivor from his lifeboat.

25 Return home of a *Belgrano* survivor.

26　Argentine troops man their 20-mm Rheinmetall anti-aircraft gun near Stanley on 4 May following a British bombing attack.

27　Soldiers (probably from the 25th Regiment) walk around craters after Squadron Leader Reeve's Vulcan crew's raid on the airfield at Stanley on 4 May.

28  The capture of the intelligence-gathering trawler *Narwal* on 9 May.

29  Sea Harrier cannon-shell holes in *Rio Carcaraña*, 16 May.

30 *Rio Carcaraña's* crew coming ashore after abandoning the ship.

31 *Rio Carcaraña* after being abandoned by its crew. The crew left smoke floats burning to mislead the British into thinking the ship was on fire.

32 Demolition charges on the runway at Pebble Island and destroyed aircraft after the SAS raid, 15 May.

33 In Argentine Headquarters at Stanley: *left*, Vice Admiral Otero, Naval Commander; *centre*, Brigadier-General Jofre, Army Commander Stanley Area; *right*, *sitting*, Brigadier-General Menéndez, Governor and Commander-in-Chief.

34, 35  The naval Skyhawk pilots who were mainly responsible for the sinking of HMS *Ardent* on 21 May. First, Lieutenant-Commander Alberto Philippi, who was shot down by a Sea Harrier immediately after he attacked *Ardent*. Second, the three members of the flight which finished off the *Ardent*, from left to right: Lieutenants Rotolo, Sylvester and Lecour; they are photographed against a Super Étendard which has now replaced the old Skyhawk as the Argentine Navy's main strike aircraft (see Chapter 11).

36  Air Force Commander-in-Chief and Argentine junta member Basilio Lami Dozo (on the right) shaking hands with an Argentine pilot in the southern base at Rio Gallegos after the pilot had made a raid on British ships on 21 May, the first day of the British landings.

37  Pucará aircraft.

38  Battered Stanley airport at the end of the war.

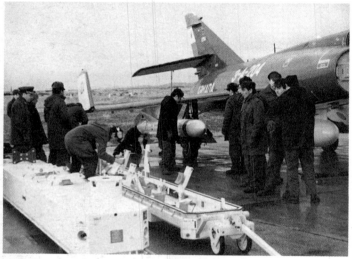

39 Sub-Lieutenant Armando Mayora, who was one of the Super Étendard pilots who carried out the Exocet attack on HMS *Sheffield*. He is standing beside a Super Étendard which took part in the so-called *Invincible* attack on 30 May and which still shows the success silhouette of HMS *Invincible* five years later.

40 An Exocet missile being loaded on to a Super Étendard before the successful attack on the *Atlantic Conveyor* on 25 May (see late in Chapter 11).

41 Brave Argentine marine officer, Lieutenant-Commander Camiletti, captured after observing the San Carlos landing area.

42 Argentine dead awaiting burial at Goose Green.

43 Argentine prisoners drawing water at Goose Green.

44 The so-called *Invincible* attack; the two Super Étendards *en route* to the target area on 30 May (see Chapter 13).

45 Press conference of Air Force pilots after the 30 May attack.

46 Argentine soldiers on hill positions outside Stanley photographed by a very low-flying RAF Harrier.

47 Stanley - the capital of the Falklands and the key to a huge area of the South Atlantic.

48  Argentine anti-aircraft gun and ammunition abandoned at Stanley.

49  Argentine prisoners at end of war.

hundred per cent. We informed Puerto Argentino next day, and I was taken by helicopter to Goose Green.

The last personal account of this day's action comes from First Lieutenant Luna, the Dagger pilot whose friends thought he had flown into a hill. But Luna had been shot down by a Sea Harrier when the flight of four aircraft flew in single file through a valley when forced down by low cloud. Luna was in the last aircraft:

On entering the valley, I saw a shadow passing over me to my left. Almost simultaneously there was a flash in the mirrors and the impact of a missile on my plane; it became uncontrollable. I tried to gain altitude, but the plane was nose down and inverted. I thought I was going to die. Releasing the stick, I desperately searched for the upper ejection handle. That is when I found that I was right side upward again, because the ejection was normal. I heard the explosion, felt a jerk, and the parachute opened almost at the same time as I hit the ground. I broke a bone in my shoulder and dislocated an arm and a knee.

It was getting dark, and I knew I wouldn't be found just yet, so I fixed my knee and gathered together all the means of survival. After inflating the dinghy, I dragged it towards me with the aid of its retaining rope, got myself inside it and prepared a bed with part of my equipment and the parachute. Then I drank a litre of water from a plastic container and swallowed seven analgesic pills one by one to soothe the terrible pain I was in. During that terrible night, half awake, I heard the noise of an engine so I fired a flare, but this brought no response. Clenching my teeth, for it was really cold, I fell asleep until about nine the following morning.

When I woke up I found myself in a valley surrounded by mountains, about 20 kilometres west of Port Howard. I looked for useful pieces of my plane and with the aid of my knife turned them into a metal splint for my leg; I must have looked like a modern pirate. Putting all the useful things into the dinghy, which I dragged with a rope, I set off. I can only imagine my odd appearance with my metal leg and my load behind. By 12.30 I could drag the dinghy no further so I abandoned it. I kept on walking, with great difficulty because of my leg, following the direction of the noise I had heard during the night. About 15.15 I came across a man and a woman in a Land-Rover followed by three more people riding motor cycles. I signalled to them desperately, but they continued on their way without a word, leaving me alone. My leg hurt terribly, and my shoulder was numb. Hobbling along with my metal leg, I followed the vehicle tracks. It became more and more difficult, but coming round a hill I came across a house with the vehicles parked in front of it. The people watched my approach. I thought they might kill me or hand me over to the enemy, yet I was aware that I would not be able to get anywhere in the wretched condition I was in. They came to me in the Land-Rover when I was about 400 metres from the house. At first they were unwilling to help me; one of them in particular objected vehemently.

I realized they were anxiously looking at my survival equipment, so I gave them my knife, the flight gloves and the torch. This obviously had a calming effect on them, and they agreed to carry me to the house of a man with a radio. This man turned out to be a true 'English gentleman'; he looked after me and said he would help me to get back to my people. We contacted Puerto Argentino. After this he provided me with pain-killing tablets every three hours for two days until our people came to get me.

(I tried to find the name of the 'true English gentleman' who helped Luna but was unable to do so.)

So ended the 21 May air attacks. The number of aircraft dispatched from the mainland totalled 45 – 26 Skyhawks and 19 Daggers; 36 of these reached the Falklands and 26 carried out attacks on British ships. The *Ardent* was sinking; *Antrim* and *Argonaut* were temporarily out of action with unexploded bombs inside them; *Brilliant* and *Broadsword* had been damaged by cannon fire. Thirty-two British sailors were dead and more than twenty others were injured. The Argentine pilots had pressed home their attacks with great courage, but two important mistakes had been made. The emphasis on attacking the warships in Falkland Sound allowed the landing ships in San Carlos Water to carry on discharging troops, guns and stores in relative safety at a time when the ground missile defences were not yet established. The importance of this error cannot be overemphasized; the Argentine pilots would never again find the transport ships in San Carlos Water so vulnerable to air attack. The second mistake was that most of the air force pilots flew too low, with the result that their bombs did not explode. This is only a muted comment because attacks at altitudes any higher than the 'on the deck' approaches made by so many Argentine pilots would have brought them a higher casualty rate – but more success. The cost had been grievous enough. Ten Argentine aircraft – five Daggers and five Skyhawks – failed to return to the mainland, all but one shot down or hit by Sea Harriers; this was more than a quarter of the Argentine aircraft which reached the scene of action.

Nightfall came and brought relief from action and danger. The work of unloading the British ships progressed sufficiently to allow the *Canberra* and three other large ships to be released, and these were sent back to the comparative safety of the task force out at sea. The damaged destroyer *Antrim* also departed as their escort. The sailings of these ships provided room in San Carlos Water for the warships which had been left out in Falkland Sound exposed to air attack the previous day. In less than twenty-four hours the British landed all of their fighting units – more than 3,000 infantry, 24 field guns, 8 light tanks and a battery of Rapier anti-aircraft missile launchers.

The Argentine commanders at Stanley had discussed the possibility that the British might land well away from Stanley and had recognized that a direct attack against such a British move would be difficult to accomplish. Brigadier-General Menéndez's first action was to request air attack from the mainland, and this had clearly been granted. Menéndez and his staff had always believed that the first forty-eight hours after a landing would be critical; after that the British would be too well established ashore for an attack to have any chance of success. The big question to be decided at Stanley was whether this was the main British landing or only a diversion. There were no Argentine troops in contact with the beach-head or even observing it from a distance. Future air flights over the area would have little chance of obtaining reliable details of how many British troops were ashore.

Menéndez ordered two immediate staff studies, the first a combined one by his own staff and that of Brigadier-General Parada – because the landing had taken place in Parada's area – and the second by Brigadier-General Jofre's staff, who, being responsible for the Stanley area, were not directly involved but whose separate opinion might be useful. A final joint conference then took place under Colonel Cervo, Menéndez's chief intelligence officer. The conclusion reached was that the British had landed less than a brigade of troops at San Carlos and that most of a second brigade was still available for a further landing elsewhere. It was decided not to launch the helicopter-borne reserve; the single company of infantry available would have had a tough time anyway against so substantial a landing. The only direct move ordered was that some 105-mm guns would be sent by sea to Goose Green; the garrison there had no artillery. Two guns of the 4th Air Mobile Regiment were dismantled and loaded on to the Coast Guard vessel *Río Iguazú*, which sailed from Stanley at 4.00 a.m. the next day.

But the next morning, 22 May, started with an immediate Argentine setback. Because of its late sailing, the *Río Iguazú* was at sea when daylight came, still 13 miles from its destination. In an example of sheer bad luck for the Argentines, the first two Sea Harriers of the day to take off from *Hermes* passed right over the ship, and one of them came down and seriously damaged it with cannon fire. Two Coast Guard seamen were injured, and one of them later died. The ship ran aground, but a mission was later mounted from Goose Green to salvage the two guns and other stores. A helicopter lowered an air force officer, a young army officer and several men on to the boat, and these men went into the flooded cargo hold and reclaimed the guns, which were taken to Goose Green in time for the battle there; one of the guns was damaged, but the other was made serviceable. The young army officer will be met again. His name was Second Lieutenant Juan Gómez Centurión.

The fatally wounded Coast Guard man was the only person to die on 22 May. The remainder of that day was an anticlimax. Bad weather in mainland Argentina prevented air operations from the bases there for most of the day. Only two Skyhawks reached the landing area in the evening; their bombs caused no damage, and they returned safely to their base.

The next two days – 23 and 24 May – constituted another period of sundry blow and counter-blow. These started with the small coaster *Monsunen* (230 tons) being attacked. This was one of two local ships taken over by the Argentines. The British had learned – probably from radio intercepts – that she was sailing by night from Goose Green to Stanley, and two Lynx helicopters caught her in the early hours of 23 May. The crew of the *Monsunen* defended themselves well with machine-guns, but the ship was eventually forced ashore. She was later towed back to Goose Green but she would be out of use until the British captured Goose Green and set the ship working again for their side. The loss to Argentine service of the *Monsunen* now made a total of five ships used by the Argentines for local supply work put out of action by British naval ships or aircraft: *Isla de los Estados*, *Bahía Buen Suceso*, *Río Carcaraña*, *Río Iguazú* and *Monsunen*. This left only the large and unwieldy *Formosa* and the tiny ships *Forrest*, *Islas Malvinas* and *Yehuin* to carry on the hazardous work of transporting supplies to outlying garrisons. In fact there was not much further movement, and those minor operations by the Royal Navy were a major cause of the chronic lack of manoeuvrability suffered by the Argentine forces in the Falklands in the last weeks of the war.

The damaging of the *Monsunen* was followed immediately by another blow to Argentine mobility. Two Sea Harriers on patrol over West Falkland spotted a group of four Argentine army helicopters – three Pumas and an Augusta – which were carrying ammunition to the Port Howard garrison. The Harriers attacked with cannon fire, and two Pumas and the Augusta were destroyed, though amazingly no one was killed. The Argentine army's helicopter force in the Falklands was now reduced to ten serviceable aircraft, out of the nineteen originally available.

But the main focus of attention during those two days continued to be on the San Carlos area, where the build-up of the British beach-head was interrupted by many Argentine air attacks. These raids all came from the mainland; the locally based air units were down to very low numbers of serviceable aircraft, and these were not risked against the now strongly defended area. The dangerous task of attacking the British landings was left to the Skyhawks and Daggers of the 4th, 5th and 6th Fighter Groups with a little help from the few remaining naval Skyhawk pilots. It is not known how many sorties were dispatched from the mainland during those two days but it is believed that only thirty-three reached the San Carlos area. The Argentine attacks became more ragged now under the constant pressure and strain of operations; more aircraft became unserviceable; link-ups with the refuelling Hercules tankers did not always succeed. But the Argentine pilots showed no lack of courage and pressed home their attacks as valiantly as ever. Four ships were hit by bombs during these two days; again the attacks were from too low an altitude, and not one of the bombs exploded on hitting the ships. But the frigate *Antelope*, hit by two bombs dropped by Skyhawks of the 5th Fighter Group on 23 May, blew up the night after the attack while attempts were being made to defuse one of the bombs. Most of the ship's crew had already been evacuated, and only two men died, but *Antelope* sank later, the first major success for the Argentine Air Force. The bombs in the other three ships which were hit were all removed safely, and they were not out of action for long.

For these successes, the Argentines lost six more aircraft – four Daggers and two Skyhawks – though the British ships and ground defences claimed many more. The Argentines named the area 'Death Valley'; the British called it 'Bomb Alley'. Four of the six shot-down pilots died. The 3rd Naval Fighter and Attack Squadron had to be withdrawn from action after 23 May. It dispatched four Skyhawks on that day; two were damaged over San Carlos, and a third suffered a calamity on its return to Río Grande. The four 500-lb bombs had 'hung up' over San Carlos, and the pilot, Lieutenant-Commander Carlos Zubizarreta, could not shake them off. A stiff crosswind at Río Grande's only runway caused the Skyhawk to swerve during the landing. Probably fearing the explosion of the bombs, Zubizarreta ejected, but the Skyhawk was tilting and he was not thrown clear enough for the parachute to open and he died. The bombs did not explode, and the Skyhawk was later repaired, but the casualties on this day left this small unit with only one serviceable aircraft from the eight available three days earlier, and the squadron was temporarily withdrawn from offensive operations. This was a major setback to the Argentine air effort because these naval pilots were the best qualified for ship attack.

Lieutenant-Commander Zubizarreta's death brought the number

of Argentine pilots to die in those two days to five. Only two other Argentines lost their lives at that time. A conscript of the 12th Regiment at Goose Green died of illness; the diary of a member of his unit mentions malnutrition, but it was probably the privations of open-air campaigning which caused the young man's illness and death. The other death was at Stanley airfield, where an anti-aircraft gunner had the misfortune to be hit on the head by a piece of rock when a delayed action bomb exploded just as he was walking from his foxhole to the field kitchen for lunch; he died at once.

The British deaths during the two days were two men on HMS *Antelope* and a Sea Harrier pilot who died when his aircraft exploded and crashed into the sea soon after taking off from HMS *Hermes* on the evening of 23 May.

Tuesday 25 May was Argentina's National Day, and a combination of chance circumstance together with the skill of Argentine pilots would make it one of the best days of the war for their cause, a day of glory comparable only to 2 April when they occupied the Falklands.

The early action of the day stemmed from Rear-Admiral Woodward's decision to risk two of his air defence ships in an exposed forward position in order to give relief from air attack to the ships and land units in the San Carlos area. The two ships were *Coventry*, equipped with Sea Dart, and *Broadsword*, which was equipped with Sea Wolf. Working from an open sea position off Pebble Island, 40 miles north-west of San Carlos, the primary role of the ships was to give early warning of incoming raids to the San Carlos defences. But the combination of missiles and radars in the ships could directly engage Argentine aircraft at ranges of up to 12 miles and vector Sea Harriers on to other aircraft at greater ranges. The plan was working well. Sea Harriers had been vectored on to one raid the previous day, and three Argentine aircraft had been shot down. But the ships were clearly detectable by the Argentine radars on Pebble Island and could even be seen visually by the 'air watchers' on the hills there. The Argentine air command decided to attack these ships.

The first opportunity to strike at the ships was given to the 5th Fighter Group at Río Gallegos. Careful preparations were made. The take-off of the four Skyhawks involved was before dawn, and the aircraft were all refuelled by a Hercules tanker, also during darkness, to allow them ample time to set up their attack in the combat area. Another Hercules made a preliminary reconnaissance, established by radar the exact location of the two ships and radioed this information to the Skyhawk flight. But this well-prepared operation ended in disaster for the Argentine side. The Skyhawk flight probably left its descent to sea level too late, and *Coventry* detected the planes and fired a Sea Dart which hit the Skyhawk of the flight leader, Captain Hugo del Valle Palaver. The Skyhawk crashed; the pilot was killed, and the three remaining aircraft decided to abandon the operation. (An early post-war version, that Captain Palaver's Skyhawk was shot down in error by Argentine anti-aircraft gunners at Goose Green, was incorrect.)

Another raid against the beach-head area followed soon afterwards. Four Skyhawks of the 4th Fighter Group from San Julián made a good, indirect approach overland but when they attacked the anchorage the bombs of two aircraft failed to release and the attacks of the other Skyhawks failed to score any hits. The aircraft of Lieutenant Ricardo Lucero was shot down, but Lucero managed to eject and was rescued from the water by the British. His friends back at San Julián saw his injuries being treated on HMS *Fearless* in a television news programme that night. He was the only pilot from a mainland air unit to be taken prisoner by the British during the war. The formation's ill fortune continued when the aircraft of the flight leader, Captain Jorge García, was shot down by another of *Coventry*'s Sea Darts; this was the second formation leader *Coventry* shot down that day. No one saw García's Skyhawk crash, but he must have ejected and survived temporarily, because his body was found in a dinghy on a remote beach on West Falkland more than a year later. The remaining two Skyhawks reached their base, though one of them was badly damaged and losing fuel all the way home. Some extravagant claims were later made on this flight's behalf. One of the returning aircraft had the symbol of a Type 21 frigate and the day's date painted on its nose, and the dead Captain García was wrongly credited with forcing a pursuing Sea Harrier to fly into the ground on his way into the target area.

That afternoon a further raid was mounted against the two ships off Pebble Island which were causing so much trouble. Two flights of three Skyhawks of the 5th Fighter Group were prepared, but one aircraft was withdrawn before take-off, and another had to return early. So just two pairs of Skyhawks proceeded. They were helped in their final approach by various interesting means. They were in touch with two senior Skyhawk pilots flying as passengers in a support plane, probably a Hercules, which was keeping distant radar surveillance on the British ships. They were also in touch with the Stanley air control, which was in turn receiving information from Pebble Island where a naval pilot, Sub-Lieutenant Daniel Manzella, was perched on a hilltop with a pair of binoculars and could see both ships and the local Sea Harrier patrols on this clear day. A Spanish-speaking officer on HMS *Coventry* was actually listening to the Argentine reports. The four Skyhawks approached in radio silence, taking in all the information broadcast for their benefit.

For once, the fortunes of war swung in the Argentines' favour. The two pairs of Skyhawks came in almost simultaneously but from different directions. They were detected by the ships' radars, but some malfunctions in the missile equipment and some tactical mishandling of the ships themselves prevented *Coventry*'s early Sea Darts from being launched and also stopped *Broadsword* from launching any of her close-defence Sea Wolf missiles at all. Worse still, two Sea Harriers which had been in perfect position to intercept were warned to break off and keep away to allow the ships' missile systems freedom of action. *Coventry* only managed to fire one Sea Dart, but it was at too close a range for that type of missile, and the incoming Skyhawks cleverly avoided it. The gunfire of the two ships also failed to stop the incoming attack.

Captain Pablo Carballo's pair came in first. Carballo had had an adventurous but frustrating war so far. On his first mission, on 1 May, he had attacked an Argentine merchant ship by mistake. On 21 May his wingmen had attacked another Argentine ship, leaving Carballo to carry on and make a solo attack on HMS *Ardent*, but his bomb narrowly missed that ship. Two days later another of his wingmen had dropped the bombs which were responsible for *Antelope*'s subsequent explosion and loss. Now Carballo was facing British fire again, his third close attack on a British warship in five days, hampered this time by a film of salt which had formed on the front of his cockpit canopy. An air force biochemist had developed a special anti-salt solution for this low-flying work, but an overhelpful

groundcrew man had polished Carballo's cockpit canopy so vigorously that morning that the solution had all been removed. Carballo
and his wingman, Lieutenant Carlos Rinke, commenced their attack
run, low down on the water, running in fast. This is Carballo's
account:[3]

> The two imposing warships were surrounded by a slight mist,
> silhouetted against the horizon, far from the coast. I said to
> myself, 'Things are going to be difficult, for we will be exposed
> to their fire for a long time.' I applied full power, pressed the
> push-button of my VHF equipment, shouted: 'Viva la Patria!'
> and began my final run in to attack. I remember how small I
> felt when, with my solitary but sturdy wingman, I began to
> attack those huge steel structures. In order to deter us, they
> began shooting as soon as we let down over the water, long
> before we came within range.
>    Their shots fell well ahead of us at first, the shells forming
> tracers in the air and the water splashing, while the ships them-
> selves were covered with smoke with every shot fired. For a
> moment I thought I was living through a film of one of those
> old naval battles. I could never have dreamed, three months
> before, that I would be undergoing such a terrible yet fascinat-
> ing experience. The curtain of fire was really dense, for both
> ships gave us everything they had. I couldn't see how close
> their fire was because I had to look through the side of the wind-
> shield.
>    My wingman asked me: 'Which one shall we tackle?' 'The
> rear one; it is less well protected,' I replied. The two ships had
> begun to move fast, heading east, sailing roughly 200 metres
> one from the other. When I could see the huge ship I was
> attacking through both sides of my partly covered windshield, I
> pressed the bomb release switch, probably taking a little longer
> than usual due to the difficulty I had in seeing. I remember
> that when I dropped my bombs, the other ship was still firing
> at me. I immediately asked: 'Are you there, Number Two?'
> and with deep joy heard him shout: 'Yes, sir. Right behind you.
> I can see you.' Almost at the same time, I heard another voice

[3] From the unpublished English translation of his own book, *Dios y los Halcones*.

on the frequency saying: 'My target is in sight, and I am going in.' That was the other two pilots starting their attack.

Carballo and his wingman had made a good attack but again he was to be unlucky. One of the bombs skipped off the sea and came *up* through the side of *Broadsword*, out through the deck, removing the nose of the ship's Lynx helicopter, and dropped back into the sea again without exploding. This was extremely bad luck because a new type of nose fuse was fitted to the bombs being used that day, and if the bomb had hit anything substantial it would have exploded, at the very least causing serious damage to the British ship.

The second pair of Skyhawks was flown by First Lieutenant Mariano Velasco, who was also seeking some success after several disappointing sorties, and young Ensign Jorge Barrionuevo, who was probably on his first war mission. These pilots flew unscathed through the British fire. Barrionuevo's bombs failed to release, but, in one of the best ship attacks of the war, Velasco put all of his three bombs into *Coventry*. They plunged deep into the ship, exploded and caused the ship to sink. The four Skyhawks returned safely to the mainland and to a big celebratory dinner. The unit had sunk one ship, damaged another and removed that British presence off Pebble Island which had been causing the Argentines so much trouble. The only pilot of the unit lost on an earlier raid in the day, Captain del Valle Palaver, was believed by his comrades to have had a good chance of ejecting safely over land, so his absence did not mar the celebration. His friends did not know that he was dead.

The story of the second major Argentine success of the day can be told more quickly, because there was no close contact between the opposing forces and because no personal account is available from the Argentine side; but it was just as important as the sinking of the *Coventry,* probably more so. The Super Étendard squadron had been waiting patiently at Río Grande for the firm intelligence which would allow it to carry out another Exocet attack. That morning the air command at Stanley detected the location of the main British task force about 100 miles north-east of Stanley; the task force had been forced to come in closer than before because of the need to support the landing force under air attack at San Carlos. Lieutenant-Commander Roberto Curilovic and Lieutenant Julio Barraza were at the head of the roster and took off in mid-afternoon. In a perfectly executed operation, the two Super Étendards were refuelled and then approached the task force from the north. They detected the British ships at their first attempt, launched their Exocets and turned away, hoping as always that the British aircraft-carriers would be hit. One Exocet found a target when the large container ship *Atlantic Conveyor* was struck on its port side. The missile penetrated deep into the ship, exploded and started a fierce fire. The Argentine pilots had come closer to hitting an aircraft-carrier than they knew. The task force was always deployed in such a way that other ships were positioned between the vital aircraft-carriers and the likely approach of Exocets. *Atlantic Conveyor* was in the last row of those protective ships, and if she had not attracted the missile it might have run on into the aircraft-carrier area.

Thus ended a most successful Argentine National Day. At a cost of three aircraft lost, with two pilots dead and one a prisoner of war, the Argentine units had sunk the destroyer *Coventry*, damaged the *Broadsword* and caused the total loss through fire of the *Atlantic Conveyor* with its hugely valuable cargo of military stores and helicopters. Nineteen British sailors died in *Coventry* and twelve in *Atlantic Conveyor*.

But the successes of 25 May would prove to be the high watermark of the Argentine air effort. There were only two further small raids against the San Carlos landing area, by six Skyhawks on 27 May and by four Daggers two days later. The first raid caused seven deaths and some injuries to British troops when shore positions were bombed for the first time. Mariano Velasco, the pilot who had sunk *Coventry* two days earlier, was shot down on this raid but he ejected and survived. No success was achieved on the second raid, but another aircraft was lost. This time the pilot was killed; he was Lieutenant Juan Bernhardt, the man who had put the first bomb into HMS *Ardent* on 21 May.

Those raids concluded the mainland air effort against the British landing area. In nine days of intensive operations, approximately 120 sorties had been launched, of which about 90 reached the operational area. Three warships – *Ardent*, *Antelope* and *Coventry* – had been sunk in or near the landing area. Three more warships and three amphibious ships had been hit by bombs which failed to explode. Other ships had suffered superficial damage by cannon fire. Casualties had been inflicted to land units in one raid. In addition, the Super Étendards had destroyed the *Atlantic Conveyor*. The pilots of the Argentine Air Force and Navy had done their best and were willing to continue the attacks, but the British defences were now so well established that there was no longer any prospect of achieving a decisive success that would influence the outcome of the war. The British had been severely shaken by the air attacks but they were now firmly established ashore and ready to move out from the beach-head. The Argentine losses had been appalling. Twenty-one aircraft had been shot down, nearly a quarter of those which reached the operational area. Twelve of the aircraft were shot down by Sea Harriers, eight by ships' or shore units' weapons and one by a combination of all three causes.

Unfortunately the Argentine propaganda service sullied the efforts of the air units by publishing outrageous claims on their behalf. The *Gaceta Argentina* at Stanley no doubt reflected the Buenos Aires line when it published a supposed list of all Argentine successes up to 25 May: 5 warships sunk (the actual figure was 3); 3 transport ships including *Canberra* sunk (*Atlantic Conveyor* was the only loss); 14 Sea Harriers destroyed (only 2 actually shot down plus 3 more lost accidentally); 12 helicopters destroyed (only 3 plus some accidents); many ships 'seriously damaged' including H M S *Hermes* (which had not been scratched). The *Gaceta* concluded: 'All of these details refer only to proven claims and not to estimated or unproven claims.'

Air attack had been the only real threat to the success of the British landings. The Argentine Navy did not put in an appearance, though its Skyhawks and Super Étendard air squadrons had performed courageously and effectively. The powerful army garrison in the Falklands did not interfere in the landings in any way, not even with commando operations. After First Lieutenant Esteban and his men withdrew from Port San Carlos on the first morning, there was not a single contact between British and Argentine troops until 27 May when Royal Marines captured an Argentine marine officer who had installed himself on high ground overlooking San Carlos and was presumably reporting British movements by radio back to Stanley. The name of this brave man was Lieutenant-Commander Dante Camiletti.

The Argentine commanders in the Falklands had faced a dilemma. As the days passed, it had become obvious to them that the landing was more than a diversion. Several possible courses of action were considered. The helicopter force at Stanley could have brought forward troops from the large garrison there. The 12th Regiment at Goose Green – 17 miles from San Carlos – could have mounted a land attack. The 5th and 8th Regiments at Port Howard and Fox Bay could have been helicoptered or sailed across Falkland Sound to attack San Carlos. The British tried to discourage these last possibilities by bombarding both places with naval gunfire at night. The Argentine units there lost five men killed and others injured in the shelling. It was even suggested that a parachute unit from the mainland might be flown to Goose Green airfield and attack the beachhead from there; a regiment of IV Air Mobile Brigade at Córdoba was standing by for this possibility. But nothing was done for two reasons. The previously agreed plan was that Stanley was regarded as the key to the Falklands. If the British landed elsewhere, then they must be forced to come to Stanley and fight in front of the defences there. The second reason was that any move out from Stanley or the other garrisons or the dispatch of the parachute unit from the mainland would face enormous transportation difficulties as well as great danger from the British air superiority. President Galtieri protested to Menéndez that nothing was being done to attack the beach-head but was reminded by Menéndez that he was sticking to a policy which Galtieri had previously approved. The only changes made were the dispatch of some guns to Goose Green (already mentioned) and the strengthening of the positions in that sector of the Stanley defences which could be expected to face a British approach from San Carlos. It was not even certain that the British would move out from the beach-head. Forty miles of seemingly impassable terrain lay between San Carlos and the edge of the Stanley defences. It was thought that perhaps the British would consolidate their landings and reopen political negotiations. This was not so. The British were now about to move forward, and the whole character of the war was about to change again. The Argentine Army, almost alone, would now have to fight and attempt to hold the 'Malvinas' for Argentina in what would prove to be the final phase of the war.

## 12 · The Battle of Goose Green

(The British soldiers of 2 Para prefer to call it the
Battle of Darwin-Goose Green)

The British move out of their beach-head started in the evening of
26 May when men of 2 Para left their positions on the Sussex
Mountains above San Carlos and marched southwards to a deserted
shepherd's house called Camilla Creek House which was within
three miles of the outer Argentine defences covering Goose Green.
The task of 2 Para was to attack and capture Goose Green. It was
not a popular operation with Brigadier Julian Thompson, the British
land commander at that time. Goose Green, with its airfield and
army garrison, was situated south of the route the British units must
eventually take from San Carlos to Stanley, but Thompson would
have preferred to mask it with a smaller force than the complete
battalion – one-fifth of his total infantry at that time – which was
now being deployed. But London had urged that an early success
should be obtained, and so this major operation against Goose Green
was being mounted.

The sheep-farming settlement at Goose Green was the second
largest civilian community in the Falklands. Together with the much
smaller place called Darwin – which was only a few houses about a
mile away – there were about 120 civilians, who had been confined
to the community hall since the evening of 1 May. The settlement
was near the southern end of the distinctive neck of land which
joined the main island of East Falkland with the large sub-island of
Lafonia. This isthmus, five miles long and two miles wide, would be
the scene of the first major land battle of the war.

The first garrison at Goose Green had been Carlos Esteban's C
Company of the 25th Regiment, but there had been many changes
since then. The Argentine army force now present was known as
Task Force *Mercedes*. The main unit was the 12th Regiment, whose

home base in Argentina was at Mercedes in Corrientes Province, hence the name of the task force. The regimental commander was Lieutenant-Colonel Italo Piaggi, a tall officer whose shaven head and hearty nature gave him the appearance of the television detective Kojak. The first of Piaggi's many burdens was that the whole of his B Company was not present, it having been retained near Stanley as the helicopter-borne reserve there. Part of Esteban's company and a platoon of Piaggi's own A Company had then been sent to provide the Fanning Head–Port San Carlos detachment which had been in action on the day of the landings. However, an isolated platoon of the 8th Regiment had somehow found its way to Goose Green, and Piaggi had also created a further platoon from what a British unit would call the 'spare details' or 'odds and sods' of his regiment. So Piaggi had the nominal strength of a full regiment under his command, but that strength came from three different regiments. At the start of the battle there were actually eleven Argentine rifle platoons, which were almost matched by 2 Para's strength of ten rifle platoons. Piaggi's total infantry strength was 554 men.

There were many other Argentine servicemen at Goose Green. Part of A Battery of the 4th Air Mobile Artillery Regiment had recently arrived with four 105-mm guns, two salvaged from the *Río Iguazú* and two flown in later by helicopter. One gun from the *Río Iguazú* was damaged and was not capable of firing. There were 1,800 rounds of ammunition for these guns, compared to the 840 rounds which were available at the three British guns supporting 2 Para; 2 Para also had the support of the frigate *Arrow* with its quick-firing 4.5-inch gun, and some RAF ground-attack Harriers would also be available. But conditions during the battle would be such that the artillery of neither side would be very effective, and it would mainly be an infantryman's battle. Together with a handful of engineers, some air force anti-aircraft gunners and a large contingent of other air force personnel, there were approximately 1,500 Argentines at Goose Green. There were no flyable aircraft at the airfield; all the airworthy Pucarás had been withdrawn to Stanley. The army and air force commanders were of equal rank, with Vicecomodoro Pedroza, the air force commander, being slightly more senior in service, but it would be Lieutenant-Colonel Piaggi's responsibility to handle the coming battle. Piaggi says that he was on good terms with Pedroza, and there was no friction between the two services. Brigadier-General Parada carried the overall responsibility for this area and should have been at Goose Green; he had been ordered to move his headquarters out of Stanley but had not yet done so. Parada would later be officially criticized for this failure.

Lieutenant-Colonel Piaggi was one of the most helpful of the officers I met in Argentina; we had two long sessions with the documents and maps of the battle he had carefully compiled. He kept stressing the deficiencies of his command. His regiment was part of III Brigade, the last to be sent to the Falklands, and much of his heavy equipment never arrived. The process of recalling reservists had not been completed, and many of his men were from the 1963 Class of conscripts who had been in the army for less than four months when sent to the Falklands. Then, passing through Stanley, several key officers and some of his men had been detained there for various duties, besides the complete B Company kept back with the helicopters. Piaggi gave me some examples of his equipment shortages. He only had two radios out with his companies; both were in Land-Rovers taken from the civilians at Goose Green. There were no other vehicles. His regiment should have possessed twenty-five 7.62-mm machine-guns; there were only eleven. Out of ten 81-mm and four 120-mm mortars, he had two 81-mm mortars and a 120-mm which could only fire at one set range because it was welded to its base plate. Instead of thirteen 105-mm recoilless rifles, he only had one – without a sight. He summed up the general shortages of his command by saying that 'Task Force *Mercedes* would have to meet the British in its shirt-sleeves.'

Shortages of weapons and men were not Piaggi's only difficulty. His original task – to protect the two settlements and the airfield – entailed a defence perimeter of 17 kilometres, *with the main emphasis on countering a landing from the sea*. But, after the British landings at San Carlos, Brigadier-General Parada ordered Piaggi to extend his defences further northwards and to be prepared to face a land attack from San Carlos. Piaggi's men, who had earlier constructed a strong defence line approximately halfway up the isthmus protected by minefields out in front, now had to move beyond the minefields and

construct new defences. His new perimeter was 31 kilometres long!
'Those changes', says Piaggi, 'caused us a lot of problems.'

The men of 2 Para marched to Camilla Creek House during the
night of 26–27 May. The Argentine guns recently installed at Goose
Green carried out a harassing shoot during the march, not sure
whether the British were advancing but shelling an area of likely
approach. A Royal Artillery officer was able to recognize that three
105-mm guns were in action, the first indication to the British that
Goose Green had been reinforced with artillery. Something extra-
ordinary happened early the next morning. The BBC World
Service announced in one of its news broadcasts that British parachute troops were approaching Darwin. It was mainly speculation on
the BBC's part but based on strong hints from the Ministry of
Defence, which was anxious to show that the troops landed at San
Carlos were now getting on with the war. The broadcast was heard
by the men of 2 Para – who were furious at what they saw was a
stupid and dangerous disclosure – and also by the Argentines both at
Stanley and at Goose Green. Contrary to British beliefs, however,
no reinforcements of any kind were sent to Goose Green as a result
of that radio broadcast. Most Argentines believed it was a bluff.
Lieutenant-Colonel Piaggi's reaction was: 'I did not take it too seriously; I thought it was more a psychological action because it would
be crazy for them to announce an actual move. I made no changes
because of that broadcast.'

Two observation parties of paras went forward during the day of
the 27th to carry out a careful examination of the ground over which
the battalion would attack that night. Some of the new trenches
recently dug were seen. Two RAF Harriers arrived and were guided
in to make a cluster-bomb attack, hoping to put the Argentine artillery out of action, but little or no damage was caused, and no Argentine soldiers were hurt. A second run by the Harriers strafed
positions of the 12th Regiment's A Company with cannon fire, but
again there were no casualties. One of the Harrier pilots decided to
make a third run, and this time a 35-mm anti-aircraft gun shot it
down; the Harrier pilot ejected several miles away and was eventually
rescued by a British helicopter.

The para observation parties were detected by Argentine troops and were fired upon by a machine-gun, but they too were not hit. Lieutenant-Colonel Piaggi ordered his Reconnaissance Platoon to find out what was happening to the north, and the platoon commander, Lieutenant Carlos Morales, and three men went out in a commandeered civilian Land-Rover. That was the last that Piaggi heard of them because the vehicle was ambushed by the para patrols and all four men were captured, two of them being wounded. Also lost with the Land-Rover was one of the only two radio sets available in the northern sector of the Argentine defences. Its loss would cause Lieutenant-Colonel Piaggi major problems during the battle. He sighed deeply when describing this and said: 'It makes my blood boil every time I think of it. Most of the communications I had with my forward company in that sector during the battle were by young soldiers on foot!'

So the Argentines at Goose Green braced themselves for a possible battle. Piaggi sums up his feelings:

From midday onwards I knew from various sources – particularly the disappearance of the Land-Rover – that an attack was imminent. I did not think that we could hold out for long, particularly because of my reading of British military history, which showed that they would attack with skill and with at least the necessary strength – and probably more. I had read all about that in books on the Second World War.

The battle started at 3.55 a.m. on Friday 28 May, the British showing that they preferred to attack by night and use their superior tactical training to overcome the dangers of operating in the bare Falklands terrain. It was the hope of the British commander that his troops could overcome most of the Argentine defences in the ground north of the settlement before daylight came. The first shots were fired when a supposedly Argentine-occupied building known as Burntside House was attacked. But there were no Argentines in the house, although a patrol had been there the previous evening. Four Falklands civilians in the house were very fortunate not to become the first casualties of the battle when the paras' fire riddled their home.

A general British advance down the mile-wide neck of the isthmus now commenced. This was the area in which the Argentines had been ordered to extend their defence positions a few days earlier.

The sector was defended by A Company of the 12th Regiment, which only had two platoons present. The company commander was First Lieutenant Jorge Manresa, and his strength was three other officers, fourteen NCOs and about one hundred conscripts, together with a few men from the Reconnaissance Platoon who were occupying outposts. The supporting weapons available to Manresa were the 120-mm mortar fixed to its base plate, either one or two 81-mm mortars and only two 7.62-mm machine-guns. The newly dug positions were about a mile and a half north of the much better constructed main line across the isthmus behind A Company.

The initial fighting was confused. The paras passed by some of the forward Argentine positions without seeing them in the dark. It started raining, and the whole battle would be fought in raw, wet, windy weather conditions. More general fighting broke out as the British advance continued, and soon most of the Argentine company was involved. It was the first proper action between formed units of the two adversaries, a fight between one of the most aggressive and skilful battalions of the British army and a typical Argentine unit based on the conscript system. Some of the Argentine posts fought well and inflicted casualties on the paras, but British accounts also show that some of the frightened conscripts curled themselves up in the bottom of their trenches and allowed themselves to be taken prisoner without a fight. 'They were just like little children,' said one of the British officers. It was too dark for either side to call down close artillery support. The British made some mistakes, for it was their first battle too, and no amount of training replaces experience; but their advance continued. One by one, the Argentine posts were eliminated or the defenders fell back, despite Lieutenant-Colonel Piaggi's urging that the positions be held. The action here lasted until first light, and Manresa's men did at least stop the British advance from reaching Goose Green by daylight, which, when it came, found the British still nearly two miles north of the settlement.

A series of very important moves now took place and these should be examined carefully. The next phase of the action would take place at the one-mile-long line of positions across the isthmus which had been carefully constructed in the weeks before the British landed at San Carlos. The ground here consisted of a series of low rises

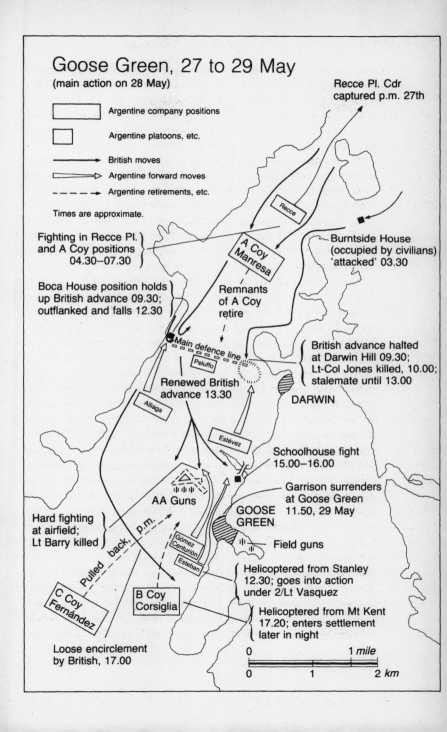

# Goose Green, 27 to 29 May
(main action on 28 May)

☐ Argentine company positions

☐ Argentine platoons, etc.

——▶ British moves

⟹ Argentine forward moves

- - -▶ Argentine retirements, etc.

Times are approximate.

Recce Pl. Cdr
captured p.m. 27th

Recce

A Coy
Manresa

Burntside House
(occupied by civilians)
'attacked' 03.30

Fighting in Recce Pl.
and A Coy positions
04.30–07.30

Boca House position holds
up British advance 09.30;
outflanked and falls 12.30

Remnants
of A Coy
retire

Main defence line

Peluffo

British advance halted
at Darwin Hill 09.30;
Lt-Col Jones killed, 10.00;
stalemate until 13.00

Renewed British
advance 13.30

Alliaga

DARWIN

Estévez

Schoolhouse fight
15.00–16.00

AA Guns

Garrison surrenders
at Goose Green
11.50, 29 May

GOOSE
GREEN

Hard fighting
at airfield;
Lt Barry killed

p.m.

Gómez
Centurión

Field guns

Esteban

Pulled back,

C Coy
Fernández

B Coy
Corsiglia

Helicoptered from Stanley
12.30; goes into action
under 2/Lt Vasquez

Helicoptered from Mt Kent
17.20; enters settlement
later in night

Loose encirclement
by British, 17.00

0        1 mile
0      1        2 km

interspersed with re-entrants; there was a long gorse hedge behind the Argentine trenches but mostly open ground in front, with a minefield in the central part which would divert the British advance to the flanks. The line of weapons trenches was well constructed, some with overhead cover. For convenience, we can call this the 'main Argentine line'.

The Argentines had been forced to vacate these positions when ordered to extend their defence perimeter to the north. When this battle opened they were only manned by a scratch platoon of the 12th Regiment's administrative personnel present under the command of Second Lieutenant Ernesto Peluffo. But before the British troops reached the defence line, two fresh platoons were sent up from the rear. On the Argentine left, a platoon of the 8th Regiment (No. 3 Platoon of C Company) under a newly commissioned officer, Second Lieutenant Guillermo Aliaga, had been defending a beach position to the south, in case of a sea-borne landing, but was now moved in to the left end of the main line, occupying trenches around the tumbled ruins of a long-abandoned building called Boca House. Another reinforcement also came up on the right. This was one of the platoons of C Company, 25th Regiment, which were being held back at the settlement as a central reserve. Lieutenant-Colonel Piaggi ordered the platoon commander, Lieutenant Roberto Estévez, to move up and counter-attack to relieve the pressure on A Company and to recover the positions earlier lost by A Company. It did not take long for Estévez to move his men past the airfield and up to the main defence line. He is believed to have occupied the positions at the eastern end of the line, on and around the small rise known as Darwin Hill. This platoon was probably the most effective of the three platoons now manning the line. It had its full complement of weapons and possessed some internal radio communications; its commander was an older and more experienced soldier than the other two platoon commanders.

Estévez's orders to counter-attack and regain the positions further forward could not be carried out because his arrival at this position coincided with the withdrawal to the line of the remnants of First Lieutenant Manresa's company and also the arrival of the first British troops. When this next clash took place, therefore, the main line of defences would be held by three platoons which had not yet been in action and a possible further thirty or forty men who had fallen back from the earlier fighting. There would be no immediate artillery support for these Argentines; the three guns at Goose Green had fired off all their ready-use ammunition, and the local mortars had also expended their supply of bombs. The advancing British would also have little artillery or mortar support. The frigate *Arrow* had departed, having fired off most of its ammunition earlier and needing to return to the safety of the San Carlos anti-aircraft defences. The three British artillery guns back at Camilla Creek House were now at near extreme range and were unable to fire too close to their own men because of the fierce gusts of wind which made the fall of shot uncertain. The coming fight would thus be a purely light-infantry weapon clash.

The fighting which broke out here was fierce and bloody and resulted in a reverse for the British. The company of 2 Para involved (A Company) had not yet seen any fighting, having moved along the eastern coast of the isthmus, skirting the scene of the earlier action. The company was moving fast over open ground in the belief that the main Argentine positions had already been penetrated. The paras were intending to deploy on Darwin Hill and then attack the little group of houses in nearby Darwin Settlement. But it was on Darwin Hill that Lieutenant Estévez had just established part of his platoon. The oncoming British saw men on the rise ahead, apparently waving them on. These were Argentine soldiers, probably assuming that the troops approaching were other Argentines falling back from the earlier fighting. The paras thought that these men might be local civilians telling them that it was safe to continue their forward move. They continued to advance over the open. But then some more Argentines in the main defence line opened fire. The paras were caught exposed, suffered several casualties and went to ground in whatever cover they could find. They attempted an attack on the hill, but the Argentines had the ground well covered, and three paras – including two officers – were killed at once.

Lieutenant-Colonel Jones, the commanding officer of 2 Para, now came up and attempted to initiate a further attack round his right-hand side of the hill, but he too was shot while attempting an individual assault on one of the Argentine trenches. He was dragged back, seriously wounded, and would die later in the morning. He

was awarded a posthumous Victoria Cross, one of only two awarded
to British troops in the Falklands War. Who killed Colonel Jones? It
is impossible to say. No Argentine made a specific report; to them he
was just another British soldier. The Argentine responsible was probably a member of Lieutenant Estévez's platoon but it could have
been a man from one of the other units manning that end of the
main defence line.

While this was happening, the British advance at the other end of
the line was being held up by the defence of young Second Lieutenant Aliaga and his platoon at the Boca House position. The British
suffered casualties here as well, and the paras were forced to pull
back.

These British repulses occurred between 9.00 and 10.00 a.m. It
would take about two hours for the second-in-command of 2 Para to
come forward and to reorganize the attack, and this is a convenient
time for other events to be described. Lieutenant-Colonel Piaggi was
reporting the progress of the battle to Brigadier-General Parada at
Stanley and urgently asking for support. Parada replied that a series
of air attacks would take place, to be flown by the Pucarás and
Aeromacchis based at Stanley. This type of close ground support
was exactly the purpose of these aircraft's presence in the Falklands.
But it would not be an easy task for the Argentine pilots; the low
cloud was making flying conditions difficult, and the aircraft would
be vulnerable to ground fire. Three Pucarás made the first raid, at
about 9.00 a.m., attacking British troops some distance north of the
area of close contact. The Pucarás' rocket attacks caused no British
casualties, and they were lucky to escape from several Blowpipe
missiles and the bursts of fire put up by the British troops. Two more
Pucarás returned later in the morning and this time they achieved
more success, catching two Scout helicopters which were bringing
ammunition forward and evacuating wounded. One of the helicopters
was actually flying south, following an urgent call to pick up the
seriously wounded Lieutenant-Colonel Jones, when a Pucará attacked it and shot it down by cannon fire. The helicopter pilot was
killed and his crewman seriously injured, losing a leg. The second
helicopter evaded the attack and was unharmed, despite Argentine
claims to the contrary.

But the Argentine pilot who shot down the helicopter did not survive his success for long. His partner saw him flying up into the clouds, his aircraft possibly damaged by ground fire but not seriously disabled. The pilot – Lieutenant Miguel Giménez – made one more radio contact with the Goose Green air base, but after that neither he nor his aircraft was ever seen again. The second Pucará pilot involved in this sortie – Lieutenant 'Chino' Cimbaro – made his escape at such low level that the front of his cockpit canopy became covered by mud thrown up by what he describes as the 'compression wave' of his aircraft. The Scout helicopter shot down by Lieutenant Giménez was the only firm success achieved by the Pucará unit during the whole of the Falklands War.

Brigadier-General Parada also dispatched some troop reinforcements. Eighty-four men of the 12th and 25th Regiments were gathered together at Stanley under the command of First Lieutenant Esteban (another note says there were 106 men). Some of these men had been with Esteban at Fanning Head and Port San Carlos and had made their way back to Stanley; others were oddments who had been performing various duties at Stanley but were now sent to Goose Green. They were loaded into eleven helicopters, were flown in one mass lift along the coast, up Choiseul Sound, and were landed south of Goose Green, the bad weather protecting them from British air attack. It took only twenty minutes for Esteban to form up his men, march them into the settlement and report to Lieutenant-Colonel Piaggi for orders.

The respite in the action also gave First Lieutenant Manresa the opportunity to come by Land-Rover from the main defence line, tell Piaggi what was happening, collect more ammunition and return to the remnants of his company. Meanwhile, the Argentine artillery guns were replenished with ammunition. These guns were located very close to the houses of the civilian settlement and were causing the British some trouble; the British had not yet been able to locate their position.

The only other incident at this time was that Piaggi drew in the company which was manning the defences south of Goose Green. This was the 12th Regiment's C Company, commanded by First Lieutenant Ramón Fernández. One platoon had been sent off to the south by helicopter to investigate a report of British troops landing from the sea, a report which turned out to be false. The helicopter was needed elsewhere; the platoon had no radio and would be out of contact for the rest of the day. The remainder of C Company moved nearer to Goose Green; this, together with the earlier British advance in the north, now signified a distinct shrinking of the area held by the Argentine garrison.

It was almost noon before the fighting resumed. The British company held up in front of Darwin Hill eventually worked round to the right (from the British side) of the Argentine position there. This was achieved by an NCO with a 66-mm anti-tank rocket launcher who put a round through the firing slit of one of the covered Argentine trenches. From this start, the paras then 'took out' one trench after the other, but it was slow work and hard fighting. The 25th Regiment platoon of Lieutenant Estévez fought well. Estévez himself was hit three times – in the leg, the arm and the left eye – and died. His radio operator, Private Fabrico Carrascul, then continued to direct the defence until he too was killed. Both men received posthumous awards for bravery. Roberto Estévez was the only Argentine army officer to be killed at Goose Green; only three or four men from his platoon escaped back to the settlement.

A similar situation occurred at the Boca House position, which was at the other end of the main defence line. One of the para companies (D Company) outflanked the position by following a footpath right at the edge of the sea. These troops fired into the flank of the Boca House trenches from the path – which was so narrow that the rising tide came up around their feet – while more paras in the front of the position put down a hail of fire. One Argentine NCO and four conscripts were killed, and many more were wounded, including Second Lieutenant Aliaga, the young platoon commander who had been a cadet only a few weeks previously. The Argentines surrendered. The scratch platoon holding the middle of the main line then fell back, carrying its commander, Second Lieutenant Peluffo, who was injured in the head.

These British successes forced the Argentines back to the defences around the airfield, the last positions covering Goose Green itself. To counter this British advance, Lieutenant-Colonel Piaggi sent forward the remainder of the reserve being held at the settlement.

This was the 25th Regiment platoon of Second Lieutenant Juan Gómez Centurión and the recently arrived 12th Regiment men sent from Stanley by helicopter and commanded by Second Lieutenant José Vásquez. First Lieutenant Esteban should have been commanding this combined force of about eighty men but he was called away at that moment to take command of two hundred air force men who were being prepared for action. Gómez Centurión and Vásquez moved off to the north but had gone no more than a mile before they saw British troops sweeping down on to the airfield from the north. The Argentines took up position, and fighting broke out again. The time was early afternoon, between 1.00 and 2.00 p.m.

It was during this engagement that an unusual incident occurred. The British troops involved in it were the ones who had recently taken the surrender of the Boca House position. A British platoon commander, Lieutenant James Barry, radioed his company commander and asked if he could go forward and attempt to negotiate another Argentine surrender. He judged that the battle was now going so badly for the Argentine troops that they might be willing to agree. The company commander gave permission and arranged for his men to hold their fire while the attempt took place. Lieutenant Barry and two NCOs then went forward, with weapons held above their heads to signify that they were not attacking. They were met by Second Lieutenant Gómez Centurión, who spoke perfect English, his father once having been Military Attaché in Washington. Gómez Centurión, a vigorous officer whose platoon had only just come into action, thought that the British were coming forward to surrender and was amazed when he found that it was his surrender that was being requested. He gave a firm refusal and allowed the British two minutes to return to their own positions, after which the Argentine troops would open fire again. Lieutenant Barry and the two NCOs turned and started walking back.

It was at this moment that a British machine-gunner opened fire, and several of the Argentine troops were hit. This machine-gun was one of several on the higher ground of Darwin Hill from which 2 Para's Machine-Gun Platoon was providing general support for the British advance. Those machine-gunners were nearly a mile to the north and were not aware of Lieutenant Barry's strictly local cease-fire; the machine-guns were firing at near extreme range. The Argentines did not know this and were enraged at the firing and the casualties they were suffering; several of them opened fire at Lieutenant Barry and his men, who were just climbing over a wire fence. All three British were killed instantly. It was an unfortunate incident in which no one had done anything dishonourable.

The incident did not end there, however. When it was afterwards found that Lieutenant-Colonel Jones, the commanding officer of 2 Para, had been killed in the battle, it was assumed that it was Jones who had come forward and parleyed with Second Lieutenant Gómez Centurión. It was believed that only a British officer of high rank would have acted in this way. Gómez Centurión was thus given, with much publicity in Argentina, the credit for killing Jones, thus contradicting the British account of how Lieutenant-Colonel Jones died. The story spread around the world after the war, causing much mystification to the men of 2 Para, many of whom had seen Jones fall in his lone attack at Darwin Hill. But after talking to Argentine officers involved – though I was not able to meet Gómez Centurión himself – it is clear that there were two separate incidents and that Lieutenant-Colonel Jones was killed at least three and probably four hours earlier and at a location a mile away from where Lieutenant Barry was killed.

The British gradually gained the upper hand in the general fighting which followed near the airfield, but again it was a hard fight. The Argentine 35-mm anti-aircraft guns joined in, the vicious, flat trajectory firing being much hated by the British troops. Some air force men were probably in action here as well, and three of their conscripts were killed. The platoons of Second Lieutenants Gómez Centurión and Vásquez suffered casualties and were steadily pushed back, almost to the edge of the settlement. There was some slightly higher ground here and good fields of fire for the Argentines. It was the last possible line of defence. In withdrawing to this line, Gómez Centurión was forced to leave behind one of his corporals badly wounded. He promised to return and bring the man in later and was able to do so that night. For this, and for his earlier defence at the airfield, this young officer was awarded the Cruz-La Nación Argentina al Heroico Valor en Combate, his country's highest award and one of only four to be awarded to surviving army personnel during the war. He became one of the most celebrated Argentine soldiers of the Falklands War. [1]

There was further air action during the course of this afternoon fighting. The first sortie was by two naval Aeromacchis from Stanley, but the weather was so bad that the air force controller at Goose Green sent them back to Stanley. The same two aircraft came back later and this time were guided in to make rocket and cannon-fire attacks on the British troops near the airfield. Both aircraft were met by a hail of ground fire, and one of them was shot down by a Blowpipe missile. It crashed spectacularly on the airfield, and its pilot, Sub-Lieutenant Daniel Miguel, was killed instantly. Two Pucarás also carried out an attack on the same area, one dropping napalm. First Lieutenant Micheloud, whose aircraft was carrying the napalm bombs, gives this description of the Pucará attack: [2]

We came in over the sea, from the north-west against a head-wind, hoping the wind would cover the sound of our approach. When I was within range I opened fire on the enemy's positions, which were shooting at us fiercely. I had to overfly them in order to drop my bombs; it seemed an endless run – a grey afternoon tinged with smoke, burning ruins, human silhouettes disappearing on the ground, tracer ammunition coming from all directions. I released my bombs where I had previously picked my target. Feeling hits on my plane, I came even lower. I made a slight turn to observe the impact of my bombs, and the smoke columns were a proof that they were no longer with me.

The second Pucará was shot down, but the pilot, Lieutenant Cruzado, managed to eject. His plane broke in half, and when his parachute opened he watched the rear half of his plane sliding under him to go on and crash. He came down among British troops and was taken prisoner. These costly air attacks caused no British casualties, but Lieutenant-Colonel Piaggi says that they were a great morale booster for his men, although he admits the Argentine pilots were 'almost killing themselves with those suicidal missions'.

The last air operation of the day was by three RAF Harriers which arrived in the late afternoon and attacked with cluster bombs

[1] Some accounts mistakenly state that Gómez Centurión was a member of a commando company at the time of the Goose Green battle. That is not correct; he became a commando after the war.
[2] From the unpublished English translation of *Dios y los Halcones*.

and rocket fire the Argentine anti-aircraft guns which had been causing the British troops so much trouble.

Lieutenant-Colonel Piaggi, on this most momentous day of his military career, was attempting to control the defence from his Command Post situated in one of the civilian houses in the settlement. He was in constant touch with Stanley. His requests for more ammunition to be sent in by helicopter had not been granted, but Stanley had sent a reinforcement of troops during the morning and several air sorties. Radio contact with Stanley was lost at one stage but was soon restored. Communications with his own companies were more difficult, usually depending upon runners or Land-Rover. Piaggi found, however, that the closer the British came the more easy it was for him to keep in contact with his officers. Soon after midday – at 12.25 p.m. according to Piaggi's notes – Brigadier-General Parada at Stanley ordered Piaggi to prepare his force to make an all-out counter-attack. This was after Piaggi had already committed his entire reserve:

> I was in a raving fury at that order. Counter-attack! With what? God help me. I remember that I picked up an aluminium mug and threw it at the wall. Normally I am a very placid character, but that order was impossible to carry out. I told him it was not possible and I told him why not – politely but firmly.

First Lieutenant Esteban, who visited the Command Post during the battle, says that Lieutenant-Colonel Piaggi seemed quite calm but that other officers were panicking.

The British were up to the very last defences around the settlement by 5.00 p.m., only about 400 yards away on both the northern and southern sides, with less close contact to the west. Piaggi ordered his artillery to stop firing in close support; the barrels of the guns had been almost vertical at the recent short range; only more distant targets were now to be engaged. The infantry fighting was slowly petering out. The British troops had all been in action for more than fourteen hours and had fought their way through three and a half miles of Argentine defences. More than a hundred Falkland civilians were somewhere in the settlement, and their lives must not be endangered. There had been enough fighting for one day.

It was soon after this – at 5.20 p.m. – that Argentine helicopters unexpectedly arrived and started landing troops at a position about three miles south of Goose Green, beyond the British troops who had recently encircled the settlement. These were men of Lieutenant-Colonel Piaggi's own B Company which had been held back as a helicopter reserve 40 miles away in the Mount Kent area for the past month. This was known as Task Group *Solari* and was under the overall command of Captain Eduardo Corsiglia, formerly S4 on Piaggi's staff. B Company's commander was First Lieutenant Ignacio Gorriti; his interesting description shows the confused nature of the company's dispatch to Goose Green:

I had been down to Estancia House to get some help for some men I had who were sick – frostbite and foot trouble mostly. I had to go on foot, with an escort, because my jeep could not be driven. I got back to the company position wet and exhausted. My second-in-command told me that helicopters were coming to take the whole company to Goose Green, where the regiment was fighting. The helicopters arrived at that very moment. I told him to take the first wave. I would stay, get changed and have just a little rest and come in on the second wave. I knew that I would be no good going into action in my condition. I had kept a bottle of red wine from Comodoro Rivadavia for a special occasion. I took it out, gave my officers a drink and cheered them on their way to join the rest of the regiment in battle.

Just as the helicopters were landing, I received an order on the radio from Brigade HQ, from Brigadier-General Parada I think, to cancel the helicopter move. I sent a soldier out to stop them, and he tried to bang on the side of the nearest helicopter, but it was too late. The pilot opened the window, but he saw that all the other helicopters were taking off so he took off too. I reported back to Stanley on the radio. I packed my own equipment, and the remaining forty men and I went down the hill to the pick-up point, but the helicopters never came back. I will tell you something sad. Those ten or so helicopters were nearly all we had. At the end of the war, when I was a prisoner of war, I saw seventy-five of your helicopters flying at one time when they were carrying out a particularly big job.

Soon afterwards I heard Colonel Piaggi on the radio asking to talk to Parada. Piaggi was surrendering. I started to cry, the first time I had cried since I was a child. I was crying because I had lost all of my regiment and nearly all of my company. My sergeant said: 'Please don't cry; we need you.' I told the soldiers what had happened and that we were all that remained of the 12th Regiment. It was a very moving moment. At that moment two Harriers appeared and bombed my Command Post – back to reality!

About 140 men under Captain Corsiglia were landed near Goose Green; their arrival came as a complete surprise to Lieutenant-Colonel Piaggi. It was getting dark, and lack of radios prevented Piaggi from making much use of these fresh troops. They found a gap in the British ring later in the night and came into the settlement.

The British were also bringing up reinforcements. When Brigadier Thompson heard about the arrival of the recent Argentine reinforcements, he realized that 2 Para would need help if the fighting resumed next morning. J Company of 42 Commando was helicoptered to a position three miles north of Goose Green. Some of the men in this company had been members of the Royal Marines detachment at Stanley when the Argentines occupied the Falklands exactly eight weeks to the day before this battle at Goose Green. Three more British field guns and fresh supplies of ammunition were also brought in.

But the senior British officer in 2 Para, Major Chris Keeble, tried that evening to persuade the Argentine garrison to surrender, or at least to allow a safe withdrawal of the civilians if the Argentines decided to continue fighting the next day. Major Keeble pointed out the hopelessness of the Argentine situation. They were surrounded and without hope of further support. A bombardment by ships and artillery would take place the next morning if they did not surrender. Major Keeble, a Catholic, pointed out this common faith to Lieutenant-Colonel Piaggi and appealed to his humanity to stop the bloodshed. Piaggi faced the dilemma that many commanders in war had faced in the past. He consulted Brigadier-General Parada at Stanley but was told that he must make his own decision. He held a meeting with Wilson Pedroza, the local air force commander, and with Lieutenant Canevari Gopcovich, the young Coast Guard captain of the *Río Iguazú* who represented the few navy men present. At the end of the meeting Piaggi announced that he had decided to surrender. He then called together his second-in-command and his company commanders and informed them of his decision. One officer cried; another burned the 12th Regiment's flag; another asked if he could break out from the settlement and link up with more troops which might be sent from Stanley by helicopter. Carlos Esteban left the meeting and went round his sector of the defence perimeter, telling his men of the decision – 'They were all very thoughtful and sad.'

Radio exchanges with the British continued until 1.20 a.m. the next morning. Initially the Argentines only agreed that there would be a temporary cease-fire, and a meeting was arranged at a little hut on the airfield at 9.30 a.m. to discuss the withdrawal of the civilians. Piaggi sent two English-speaking NCOs to that meeting with a written message, but they came back saying that the British insisted upon complete surrender, otherwise the bombardment would go ahead. A further meeting was arranged at 10.45 a.m.; this time Piaggi, Wilson Pedroza and the Coast Guard officer met Major Keeble, and terms for a surrender were agreed. Piaggi and Wilson Pedroza decided that it would be Wilson Pedroza, the senior in service, who would formally surrender the garrison one hour later. At 11.50 a.m. the British troops entered the settlement and encountered firstly the five hundred or so men of the air force contingent drawn up on parade and then, to their surprise, found a further parade of up to one thousand army personnel. Some of the Argentines were surprised to find that less than five hundred British soldiers had defeated them. There was an embarrassing moment when Major Keeble put out his hand to Lieutenant-Colonel Piaggi. Piaggi thought that he was being asked to shake hands and extended his hand in return, but Keeble was demanding his pistol to stress the formality of the surrender. The British interpreter, Captain Bell, quoted some details from the Geneva Convention to the Argentine troops. They were now prisoners of war and were to hand in their weapons; Lieutenant-Colonel Piaggi and Vicecomodoro Wilson Pedroza had ceased to be their commanders. Those two officers were immediately taken to San Carlos by helicopter. It was all a bitter event on what was Argentina's National Army Day. The first snow of winter fell that afternoon and quickly covered the torn battlefield.

Fifty-five Argentines lost their lives in the battle of Goose Green. These numbers were made up as follows:

| Unit | Officers | NCOs | Conscripts | Total |
|------|----------|------|------------|-------|
| 12th Regiment | — | 4 | 28 | 32 |
| C Coy, 25th Regt | 1 | 4 | 8 | 13 |
| Platoon, 8th Regt | — | 1 | 4 | 5 |
| Air Force | 1 (pilot) | — | 3 | 4 |
| Navy | 1 (pilot) | — | — | 1 |
| Total | 3 | 9 | 43 | 55 |

It would be the most costly of the set-piece land battles for the Argentines. The exact number of their wounded is not known, but Brigadier-General Menéndez later wrote that 131 army men were killed and wounded, so that might leave a figure of 86 army men wounded. Two of the wounded remained lying out on the battlefield until they were discovered three days later. The Argentine dead were buried in a grave on open ground north of Darwin Hill, the position which Lieutenant Roberto Estévez and his platoon had defended so stoutly. The British suffered 17 fatal casualties – 5 officers (including a helicopter pilot), 7 NCOs and 5 private soldiers; 33 men were wounded. Thanks to the timely Argentine surrender, no civilians were hurt. The number of Argentine prisoners is not known exactly but was at least 1,500. The first repatriation voyage of prisoners of war to Argentina on the ship *Norland* carried 1,536 men, almost all from Goose Green.

The Argentine authorities were severely shaken by the complete loss of the strong garrison and the air base at Goose Green in less than twenty-four hours of actual fighting. The news was not released on the mainland for some time, and then it was claimed that the surrender had only taken place after all the garrison's ammunition was exhausted. This conflicts with the British evidence of plenty of ammunition being found after the surrender. There was much bandying of figures. The Argentines objected to the British claim that less than 500 British troops had beaten 1,500 Argentines, pointing out that several hundred of the Argentines were air force men who were untrained for infantry fighting. In fact the numbers of trained infantry soldiers in the battle had been approximately 630 Argentines and 450 British, not counting reinforcements who arrived for both sides after the fighting ended.

The prisoners of war were kept at Goose Green for a few days, housed in sheep sheds and being required by their captors to help clear up some of the ammunition which remained. There was a tragic incident when four men of the 12th Regiment were made to clear some napalm containers. Something went wrong – the British suspected that it was a sprung booby-trap – and the napalm burst into flame. One unfortunate Argentine soldier was trapped in the middle of the fire, burning, in obvious agony and without any means of being rescued because of the intensity of the fire. His British guard shot him as an act of mercy. That incident caused a great deal of dissatisfaction among the Argentine prisoners. The wounded prisoners were transferred to the Argentine ship *Bahía Paraíso* – the ship which had taken Lieutenant Astiz and his men to South Georgia during the scrap-metal crisis in March; she was now a hospital ship, and the Goose Green wounded arrived home in Argentina less than a week after the battle. The remaining prisoners were eventually taken by helicopter to the San Carlos area, where they were put aboard a ship and returned to Argentina just before the war ended. Their homecoming will be described later.

Poor Lieutenant-Colonel Piaggi, who had the misfortune to be the first Argentine commander to meet the British and be beaten, found himself in trouble with the army on his return to Argentina after the war. He refused to consider voluntary retirement, so he was relieved of the command of the 12th Regiment and put under house arrest until February 1983, when he was compulsorily retired. In the following year he appeared before the first of several military and civilian tribunals at which he was alternately convicted and acquitted. When I met him in 1987 he was still fighting for reinstatement in the army and for the promotion which he would have received in the intervening years. He was the only regimental commander who fought in the Falklands to be so harshly treated. His second-in-command suffered the same treatment.

## 13 · The 'Invincible Attack' and Other Action

The battle of Goose Green was followed by another of those long periods of relative inaction – nearly two weeks during which there was no contact between the main bodies of ground forces. Once the beach-head at San Carlos was secure and their supplies built up, the British had intended moving most of their infantry and artillery up by helicopter to face the Argentine defences at Stanley, but the loss of helicopters on the *Atlantic Conveyor* prevented that plan being carried out. Instead, most of the British infantry had to trek across the intermediate 40 miles. It was this laborious and time-consuming task which caused this next interlude; as in the earlier pause, however, sporadic flare-ups of various kinds continued to occur.

Two of the British units – 3 Para and 45 Commando – commenced their march on 27 May, the day before the battle at Goose Green, and in the course of the next week they crossed most of East Falkland island. The only Argentine troops encountered were one sick soldier at Teal Inlet on 28 May and an air force observation party of three men captured two days later. The British unit involved in both cases was 3 Para. A swifter British move was made on the nights of 29 and 30 May, when sufficient helicopters were provided to move 42 Commando and three field guns directly from San Carlos to the foot of Mount Kent, a 36-mile leap forward. An Argentine company had earlier been located at Mount Kent, but most of the company had been helicoptered to Goose Green during the battle there, and the British move was unopposed. Only one Argentine soldier was found; he stated that he had been 'left behind by his officer'. The British guns brought forward to Mount Kent fired the first shots into the Stanley area on the morning of 31 May.

All of these British moves had been preceded by small special forces groups whose task it was to ensure that the way was clear for the advance of the British units, particularly of the vulnerable helicopter lifts. The SAS had several clashes with Argentine troops in the Mount Kent area. The Argentines were usually members of the 602nd Commando Company who were being used as outposts in this area to give early warning of any British approach and to harass the British when possible. There was much criticism by the commandos of the role allocated to them. They should, they said, have been used behind the British lines, not for this outpost duty, but the regular Argentine infantry units were not skilled enough to carry out this forward reconnaissance, and the commandos had to do it instead. The Argentines had the worst of the clashes. They had two men killed and one captured in an SAS ambush at Bluff Cove Peak in a night action on 30 May. First Lieutenant Rubén Márquez and Sergeant Oscar Blas were posthumously decorated for their part in this action. A larger fight took place on 31 May. A party of Argentines also from the 602nd Commando Company was spotted by the British in an isolated building, Top Malo House, which had been bypassed by the recent British advances. Nineteen Royal Marines were helicoptered there in daylight and attacked the house. During a fierce action the house was set on fire, and the Royal Marines later paid tribute to the stout resistance put up by the commandos, who suffered casualties of two killed and six wounded; there were only four unwounded prisoners. Two of the Argentines, Lieutenant Ernesto Espinosa and Sergeant Mateo Sbert, were posthumously awarded Argentina's highest decoration for bravery. The Argentines claimed that at least two British were killed; their comrades, they said, could be seen weeping over the bodies. But no Royal Marines were killed; what the Argentines saw were the British wounded being tended.

The only British death in this area was when an SAS patrol accidentally fired upon an SBS patrol in the early hours of 2 June and an SBS sergeant was killed. An SAS officer was killed by Argentine troops in this period, but this action took place on West Falkland. Captain John Hamilton and three other men were in the hills north of Port Howard observing Argentine positions around the settlement when they were detected and attacked by four men of the

601st Commando Company led by First Lieutenant José Duarte. The SAS group split into two pairs. Captain Hamilton and his signaller covered the escape of the second pair, but Hamilton was then killed trying to cover the escape of his signaller, who was taken prisoner, the only British soldier to be captured by Argentine forces during the main part of the war. Captain Hamilton also received a posthumous decoration.

There were other Argentine casualties not the result of direct action. On the morning of 30 May an army Puma helicopter was taking a party of Gendarmería Nacional men on a special mission when the helicopter crashed somewhere north of Mount Kent, killing seven of the passengers; the pilot and his crew survived. The cause of the crash was probably that the pilot was anxious about the danger of Harrier attack and flew too low, so that a rotor blade struck the ground. The embarrassed Argentines tried to blame the loss on a British missile.

The Argentines had the worst of these various special forces contacts and accidents, losing five killed and at least fourteen prisoners in action and seven more killed in the helicopter crash, compared to the British losses of two killed – one in action and one accidentally – and one prisoner. The last death to be described in these little actions was the sad loss of a young Argentine officer, Juan Abraham, who had been mobilized from the cadet academy a few weeks earlier and given an emergency second lieutenant's commission. He was now attached to the 181st Armoured Cavalry Reconnaissance Detachment and was sent by jeep to investigate a suspected coastal landing of a British special forces party, but was cut off by the rising tide and died of exposure.

Air action continued, but only spasmodically; the Argentine Air Force no longer had the capacity to carry out intensive operations. The Canberras of the 2nd Bomber Group recommenced operations, but only flying by night. Their first attack in this new phase, by two Canberras against British troop positions in the San Carlos area, took place on the night of 31 May. This night raid took the British by surprise, but only minor damage was caused, with one man slightly injured. The Canberras continued these night operations, most of the subsequent attacks being directed on the British positions in the Mount Kent area. The bombing was not very accurate but it did have a harassing effect on the British troops.

Two types of Argentine aircraft which had so far escaped loss suffered casualties during this time. The C-130 Hercules aircraft of the 1st Air Transport Group had been operating in a variety of ways, and one of these aircraft carried out a most unusual action on 29 May when it found a British tanker, the *British Wye*, on the supply route to the British task force operating area. The Hercules dropped eight bombs, but the only one to strike the tanker failed to explode. Another aircraft of the same unit was less fortunate when carrying out a reconnaissance flight north of the Falklands on 1 June and was intercepted by two Sea Harriers. After a missile and cannon attack, the large transport plane fell burning into the sea, killing all seven crew members. On 7 June one of four high-flying Learjets on photographic reconnaissance over the Falklands was hit by a Sea Dart missile fired by HMS *Exeter*. The tail of the Learjet was shot off, but the main body remained intact, with the five crewmen inside unable to escape. They were all killed when the remains of the plane fluttered slowly down to crash on Pebble Island. The loss of these two aircraft caused the Argentine Air Force its highest-ranking casualties in the war: Vicecomodoros (equivalent to Wing Commanders) Hugo Meisner in the Hercules and Rodolfo de la Colina in the Learjet.

The British suffered five aircraft casualties during this period. On 30 May an RAF Harrier was hit by ground fire while attacking positions well outside Stanley. The Harrier lost so much fuel that it crashed into the sea, but its pilot was rescued by a friendly helicopter. Two days later a Sea Harrier flying near Stanley was engaged by the Roland missile launcher, the most effective weapon in the Stanley anti-aircraft defences. The anti-aircraft units at Stanley had hardly been in action since 1 May; the defences were so powerful that British aircraft were usually kept at a safe altitude. This situation had given little opportunity for success to the anti-aircraft gunners but it had protected the airfield area and the military installations in the immediate vicinity of Stanley from low-level air attack for a month. But this Sea Harrier pilot came in a little too close, and a vigilant Roland missile operator engaged it. The initial launch was visually controlled, but the control radar was switched on during the flight of the missile, and a direct hit was scored. The pilot was able to eject and he came down into the sea by parachute. Argentine aircraft and helicopters searched for his dinghy, but it was a British helicopter which found it that night and rescued the pilot. This Sea Harrier was the only British aircraft shot down in the war by the anti-aircraft units around Stanley. The other British losses were accidental − a Sea Harrier sliding off the deck of the aircraft-carrier *Invincible* in rough weather, an RAF Harrier in a landing accident at a forward airstrip at Port San Carlos and an army Gazelle helicopter shot down in error by a Sea Dart missile launched by HMS *Cardiff*; four men were killed in the helicopter.

The most interesting − and most controversial − air action of the period took place on 30 May, a day which became known in Argentina as 'the day of the *Invincible* attack'. The Super Étendard unit at Río Grande only had one remaining Exocet and was determined to use that last missile effectively, if possible by scoring a hit on one of the two British aircraft-carriers. (An Argentine account which will be included later refers to an attack on 'the aircraft-carrier', and it is possible that the air units believed the Argentine propaganda that the *Hermes* had been put out of action.) Great care was taken in preparing this last Exocet mission. Two Super Étendards would take part; the second one would use its radar to help detect the target. In an interesting extension to the mission, four air force Skyhawks were added, each armed with two 500-lb bombs; these were to follow the Exocet in and bomb an aircraft-carrier if possible. Two Hercules tankers would complete the operation, refuelling all six aircraft twice on the outward flight and meeting them again on the return − if they all survived. The operation would require a long eastward flight from Río Grande and then a turn to the north-west, a total of 700 nautical miles, in the hope of catching the British task force partly from the rear, the best way to get at the well-escorted aircraft-carriers.

The air force unit taking part in this attack was the 4th Fighter Group at San Julián. Five Skyhawks were transferred to Río Grande on 29 May, and the operation was nearly flown that afternoon, but two of the Skyhawks became unserviceable and had to be replaced from San Julián, which was over 300 miles away. The Skyhawk pilots were far from enthusiastic to carry out this complicated mission. They would be flying from a strange base, in strange company with naval pilots, on a most unusual long-distance operation. For their part, the naval pilots would have preferred to carry out the attack on their own and they tried to have the air force involvement cancelled, but higher command was intent on creating the maximum opportunity to put a British aircraft-carrier out of action. A personal description of what happened is available, provided by the most junior pilot involved, Ensign Gerardo Isaac, one of the Skyhawk pilots: [1]

> The order arrived, and it was not a diversionary mission as had first been suggested; it was an attack mission. The situation was serious. We met for the briefing in order to plan the mission carefully. It was a point mission with the Super Étendards. Only one of them was carrying the Exocet missile; the other went as radar support. We were told that if either of the Super Étendards, or two of the Skyhawks, or one of the refuelling KC-130s had to turn back, we would all come back to the base. If we found radar pickets before reaching the target, we had to come back. If we could not find the target, we also had to come back. Everything had to be perfect.
>
> The Super Étendards took off five minutes before us. We said a Hail Mary together at the runway head and the four of us in our Skyhawks took off. We met at the rendezvous point. Seventy kilometres from the coast my gyro-horizon became unserviceable, and First Lieutenant Vásquez ordered me to return, but the controller on the ground ordered me to go ahead.
>
> I had already started back and had lost about fifty kilometres on the others, so I went alone to the refuelling. The Super Étendards refuelled at the forward Hércules, and we used the one at the back. It took us almost 200 kilometres flying over the sea, taking turns at the refuelling probes. We finally left the tankers behind, formed up and started our flight towards the blue immensity of the sea, feeling completely helpless. We

[1] From the unpublished English translation of *Dios y los Halcones*. On this occasion I have not edited the account but left it intact, so as not to be charged with altering the evidence in this controversial matter.

started the descent about 100 kilometres further on. The weather conditions were bad due to cumulo nimbus – strong wind, rain and a rough sea with clouds of foam emerging from it. We flew on at low altitude. After some time, the Super Étendards climbed up to check with their radar and then descended again. They repeated this movement several times. I kept on checking my navigation; I knew that at a certain time they would be releasing the Exocet. When my instruments indicated that point, I looked at the lead aircraft and saw the missile drop from his right wing. Its warhead was grey, and a steady flame from the propellant could be seen behind it. Once it was launched, the missile began to climb at an angle of 15 degrees but suddenly it descended with a dive of 30 degrees and seemed to be about to crash into the sea, but when it got near the water it levelled off. It flew away, leaving a neat trail of exhaust gases. Their mission had been carried out, so the Super Étendards returned to their base. We lost sight of the missile.

A minute later, I saw something in front of us, unmistakably enormous and majestic. We were approaching the stern of the *Invincible*. I called the flight leader. Until then, there had been total silence. 'The aircraft-carrier is in front of us!' We formed up for the attack. It was an astounding, impressive moment; a real struggle between feelings and science.

We began the attack, two from each side. As we were getting near, smoke began to come out from both sides of the tower, caused by the impact of the Exocet, and this became more and more dense. About thirteen kilometres out, I saw an explosion on my left; that was First Lieutenant Vásquez's plane shot down. First Lieutenant Ureta was now the leader, with First Lieutenant Castillo and me on each side. We were almost there – about two kilometres from the target – when another explosion hit First Lieutenant Castillo's plane; the shock wave shook my aircraft. First Lieutenant Castillo had been the Military Aviation Academy standard bearer when he was an aviation cadet in Córdoba and had been first in his class. I angrily pressed my gun button. When I reached the target, it was already covered in smoke. Its bulk covered everything in front of me; I pressed the bomb release and made a turn so as not to crash into the tower, which was still concealed by the smoke. The leader also released his bomb in front of me. I kept banking, pulling negative Gs and then positive Gs and inventing several other manoeuvres, trying to avoid the missiles which I knew they were firing at me. As I departed, the aircraft-carrier had completely lost its shape; it was just a cloud of smoke in the middle of the sea.

I was worried about the frigates and the Sea Harriers so I skimmed just over the sea for about 200 kilometres. It was terribly hot inside the cockpit, so I thought of lowering the temperature with the air regulator, but surprisingly my hands would not obey my brain and remained gripping the throttle control. I called on the radio, but nobody answered. Then I saw a small dot in front and thought it was an enemy aircraft. I was helpless, having fired the last rounds from my guns, but it was First Lieutenant Ureta. He saw me, so I went near and formed up at his side. I was able to identify him by his orange-coloured exposure suit. 'Let's go to the tanker,' he said. I relaxed then because I had found someone to take me home safely. Each of us went towards one KC-130. I found it difficult to connect with the refuelling drogue. Later I saw First Lieutenant Ureta sitting in his cockpit with his face down, probably wrapped up in his thoughts. I told him to watch out in case a frigate surprised us.

We went down through the clouds and the sea appeared below us. Then we reached the coast and landed. The runway was full of people – there were tears, congratulations, embraces, questions and more tears. Two brave Argentines would remain for ever in the immensity of our sea – First Lieutenant José Daniel Vásquez and First Lieutenant Omar Jesús Castillo.

The truth of what happened is well known among members of the British task force and has been described several times in British books. The Super Étendard approach, made without the benefit of up-to-date reconnaissance, was not far enough to the east and, instead of striking at the less protected rear of the task force where the aircraft-carriers were, came in amongst the outer Type 42 destroyer screen which was approximately thirty miles to the west of the carriers. The presence of the Super Étendard and the launch of the

Exocet were detected, and every ship in the task force took precautionary measures. These would normally consist of steaming as fast as possible *away* from the incoming Exocet, at the same time firing 'chaff' rockets, whose fluttering clouds of silver foil would hopefully attract the Exocet away from each ship. The task force had also received some special helicopters whose equipment was also designed to lure an Exocet from its target. One or other of these methods was successful, because the Exocet did not hit a ship and eventually ran out of fuel and fell into the sea.

But what of the smoke-wreathed '*Invincible*' which Ensign Isaac attacked? His target was actually the much smaller Type 21 frigate *Avenger*, which was only near the Type 42 screen because it was due to go into the Falklands that night to land an artillery observation officer and his team on the coast north of Stanley. Ironically, either the Exocet warning was wrongly broadcast or *Avenger* made a mistake, because instead of steaming hard away from the Exocet she was steaming hard *towards* it and straight at the four Skyhawks which were following the missile. It was the smoke from its 4.5-inch gun, firing furiously at the incoming aircraft, and the steam from its funnel that gave the ship the impression of being covered in smoke. Many members of *Avenger*'s crew saw the Skyhawks attack, and one of the shot-down Skyhawks actually crashed into the sea nearby; a small boat collected parts of it, and of the unfortunate pilot, together with some documents. *Avenger* was not hit; the evidence on this is quite incontrovertible. H M S *Invincible* was itself at least thirty miles away! The raid was a gallant failure.

But the Argentine authorities were anxious to announce a major success. The two surviving Skyhawk pilots were hurried to their debriefing as soon as they landed; the Super Étendard pilots could not help because they had turned away when the Exocet was released. I talked to Lieutenant-Commander Philippi, a naval pilot who attended the debriefing. Ensign Isaac has described the tension, emotion and tears on landing. Philippi says that the two pilots were still in tears at the debriefing. They were shown a recognition book of British warships. There was some doubt initially, says Philippi, but both pilots eventually and independently identified the *Invincible* as the ship they had attacked. And so an immediate public announcement was made that H M S *Invincible* had been hit and put out of action. Argentina rejoiced. That Argentine claim has never been retracted and it proves to be one of the most stubborn myths of the war. On the Argentine side there was never more than the evidence of two severely shaken and tired young pilots, who had seen two of their comrades shot down into the sea alongside them, who had flown under fire, at sea level, almost directly at a ship partially covered in smoke – not the best angle for identification purposes – and then flashed by that ship at jet speed, to be pressed on their return to identify the target. On the British side were 170 sailors on the *Avenger* who said they had been attacked by the Skyhawks and 1,100 on the *Invincible* who said they had not been attacked. The longer the Argentines stuck to their claim, the more difficult it became to correct the initial claim. And so the myth passed into their 'history' of the war. I have three post-war Argentine books in my office and the English translation of a fourth. Three of them persist with the *Invincible* story, claiming that the aircraft-carrier was taken somewhere secret to repair the damage and that this was the reason for its late return to England three months after the war ended. (*Invincible* was indeed late in returning from the war. The older *Hermes* was sent home first, and *Invincible* had to remain on station off the Falklands, during the period when Argentina refused to accept that hostilities were over, until relieved by her newly completed sister ship *Illustrious*. The Royal Navy had no other aircraft-carriers available.) When I was in Argentina five years after the war, most people I met still believed that the British had concealed the damage to *Invincible* from public knowledge, not accepting that it would have been quite impossible for the British to persuade the entire crews of the *Invincible* and the *Avenger*, and indeed of most of the other ships of the task force present on that day, to cover up a lie by the British Government.

The remaining air activities during that period are less controversial. In preparation for the imminent attack on the Stanley defences, a Vulcan bomber had been fitted with Shrike missiles which could home on to the emissions of Argentine radars. The main target was the Westinghouse ANTPS-44 'Alert' radar which could provide all-round surveillance within a radius of 200 miles from Stanley. The first of two anti-radar flights by the Vulcan took place on the night of 31 May. The task of the Vulcan crew was made difficult by the Argentines withdrawing the Westinghouse to a position among the civilian houses in Stanley and the operators either switching off the radar set when the Vulcan was overhead or reducing the signal, hoping to draw the Vulcan lower and into the range of the anti-aircraft defences. The Vulcan released two missiles on that first raid, but neither did any damage.

The Vulcan returned three nights later. Again the crew was unable to trap the Westinghouse, and two of the four missiles were eventually launched at a Skyguard radar attached to a pair of 35-mm Oerlikon guns. The 'dish' aerial of the radar was mounted on the top of a trailer which was well dug into a pit alongside the road between Stanley and the airfield, but one of the missiles penetrated the metal airstrip sheeting which was intended to provide overhead cover for the trailer and the crew, and the missile exploded between the trailer and the side of the pit. Four men were killed: an officer and an NCO inside the riddled trailer and two conscripts manning the communications equipment outside. The radar set was put out of action but it was not an important part of the Stanley defences, and these two Vulcan flights must be considered to have failed in their primary task. The interesting sequel to this flight was that the Vulcan was later forced to divert and land at Rio de Janeiro because of a failure by the Vulcan to take fuel from the tanker aircraft which met it on the return flight to Ascension Island.

Far away from the Falklands, two Argentine Canberras achieved a bizarre success when they attacked the Liberian supertanker *Hercules*, which was sailing in ballast down the Atlantic about 500 miles north-east of the Falklands *en route* to Alaska, intending to round Cape Horn. The tanker was spotted by an Argentine Hercules reconnaissance aircraft on 7 June. The ship's course – south-west – appeared to be taking it towards the British task force, and the Argentine aircrew believed that it might be carrying fuel for the British ships. They tried for two hours to contact the tanker by radio and persuade it to turn away, but the ship held its course. Two Canberras then appeared and aimed eight bombs at the ship. (Some books state that it was a Hercules aircraft which dropped the bombs, but this is not correct.) One direct hit was scored, but as so often before in the war the bomb failed to explode. The owners and insurers of the tanker later decided to scuttle the ship rather than risk the removal of the unexploded bomb. At 220,000 tons, the *Hercules* was four times heavier than the combined tonnage of all Argentine and British ships sunk in the war!

On land, the British units were steadily pressing forward, gradually closing up to the Argentine defences west of Stanley. The British received a major reinforcement at this time when the 5th Infantry Brigade – three battalions and supporting units – started to come ashore at San Carlos on 30 May. With them came Major-General Jeremy Moore, who would become the new British land forces commander. The British Government's decision to send this further brigade of troops was the direct result of the last Argentine reinforcement, when Brigadier-General Parada's III Brigade crossed to the Falklands during the last week in April; all that seemed a long time ago.

The first unit of the new British brigade to be given a task was the 1/7th Gurkhas, who were sent to Goose Green to clear up the battlefield there and to search outlying districts for any Argentine troops who might still be present in that area. This led to a small encounter at Egg Harbour House, another of those unoccupied shepherds' houses which often figured in the events of the war. This place was 16 miles from Goose Green but was nothing to do with the Argentine garrison which had been at Goose Green. A quantity of Russian SAM-7 Red Star small, hand-held anti-aircraft missiles had recently arrived in the Falklands together with the Argentine air force personnel who would operate them. Small missile parties were then distributed to various places. Ten missiles were taken to Egg Harbour House by Lieutenant Jaime Ugarte, being helicoptered there from Fox Bay. Ugarte's task was to hand over the missiles to a small army detachment so that they could engage any British aircraft flying up nearby Falkland Sound. Ugarte was supposed to be collected the following day, but the helicopter never returned, and it was a very hungry party of ten Argentines who had to wait for something to happen. Lieutenant Ugarte describes their difficulties: [2]

We ran out of food on the third day so we caught a bustard – a

---

[2]  From the unpublished English translation of *Dios y los Halcones*.

bird similar to the goose. As we feared being discovered if we made a fire, we heated up bits of its flesh with our cigarette lighters and ate them. We did the same with mussels and other sea food. We even ate a cabbage which we found in a deserted garden. It was so cold that one soldier began to show symptoms of gangrene in his foot; he was forced to stay in the refuge all day. I felt weaker each day but tried to appear confident so that my subordinates would not lose heart. At night, however, I used to walk some yards away to be alone. There I smoked a cigarette and then prayed while a few tears of helplessness ran down my face. This made me feel relieved and ready to face the struggle again. Being undernourished in such cold weather weakened us so much that we constantly felt dizzy, and our heads ached. We had enough food but it was unsuitable, the main problem being the impossibility of cooking it.

Our hopes vanished when we listened to the news on the radio of the British advance on Puerto Argentino. As days went by, we felt worse. The snow fell, there was a strong wind, and our weakness increased.

There was not much resistance when a party of Gurkhas appeared in helicopters, and the Argentines were taken prisoners without any casualties on either side. The Gurkhas who captured Lieutenant Ugarte and his party were destined by circumstances to be the only members of their unit who ever came into direct contact with Argentine troops before the end of the war. All stories published in Argentina about such events as drug-crazed Gurkhas being sent by the British through minefields, or Gurkhas infiltrating Argentine lines at night and cutting off the heads of Argentine soldiers with *kukri* knives, were pure fantasy.

# 14 · The Bombing of the *Sir Galahad*

The arrival of the new British brigade and its subsequent move up to the front led to the worst British setback of the war. A series of night transfers by sea caused two British ships – the *Sir Galahad* and the *Sir Tristram* – to be left exposed in daylight in an undefended inlet on the south coast of the Falklands on the morning of 7 June. The place was Port Pleasant, 'Bahía Agradable' to the Argentines. The persistent low cloud of the last few days had cleared, and it was a bright day of good visibility. The *Sir Tristram* was almost empty, but the newly arrived *Sir Galahad* was packed with troops, ammunition, fuel and vehicles. The arrangements for disembarking the troops and removing them from the danger of air attack failed, and most of them remained on board all through the morning.

The *Sir Tristram* had been observed from Argentine positions on Mount Harriet, 10 miles away, on the previous day, and now, on this morning, the second ship was also seen. The report reached the mainland, and a sizeable air effort was ordered. Eight Skyhawks and six Daggers of the 5th and 6th Fighter Groups were loaded with bombs and sent by a southerly route to attack the anchorage. A Learjet would lead in the attack flights and provide accurate navigation almost as far as the islands. Preceding the arrival of all these aircraft by a few minutes would be four Mirages of the 8th Fighter Group, which would be making their first appearance in the combat area since 1 May. They were to simulate a low-level attack along the north coast of the islands; but this was a decoy flight, and they were to turn away and return to base as soon as they attracted the attention of the Sea Harrier patrols. Vice-Admiral Lombardo mentions a further small element in the Argentine plans. He states that the Type 42 destroyer *Santísima Trinidad* was off the Argentine coast that day carrying out radio interference operations on the frequencies used by the British air controllers.

The Argentine aircraft took off in the late morning, but three Skyhawks – including both flight leaders – and a Dagger turned back because of various problems. The Mirage decoy flight was successful and temporarily attracted the attention of the Sea Harrier patrols. The five Daggers were the first of the attack aircraft to reach the islands, but their eastward flight to Port Pleasant was abandoned when one member of the flight spotted a solitary warship in Falkland Sound. The Daggers turned and made a very good attack on that ship – the frigate *Plymouth* – and hit it with four bombs. But once again none of these exploded, although the ship was damaged, and four of her crew were injured. Only one Dagger was slightly damaged by the ship's defensive fire, and they all returned safely to the mainland.

This left five Skyhawks to carry on and look for the two landing ships at Port Pleasant. The Mirage decoy flight and then the Dagger attack on the *Plymouth* left no Sea Harrier patrols available to intercept this raid, and the two ships they were seeking were almost defenceless. The earlier turning back of the two flight leaders left First Lieutenant Cachón, flying only his third war mission, to lead the now combined flight of five Skyhawks. Cachón provides an account which shows how the Skyhawks nearly missed their targets by being told that the ships were in Port Fitzroy, which was just north of Port Pleasant. Cachón's account starts with his taking over the leadership of the flight when his own leader had to turn back: [1]

I became flight leader. I had never had that responsibility before but now, suddenly and by chance, I found myself in charge not only of one flight but of *two*. Before he left, the Captain told me: 'Attack at one minute intervals, three aircraft ahead and two behind. . . . Take them to glory!' A very simple request, wasn't it? I felt a chill run up my spine but then I felt calmer, because the men who were following me were perfectly qualified for that kind of operation and the success of the mission depended on my command.

[1]  From the unpublished English translation of Pablo Carballo's *Dios y los Halcones*. Carballo was his flight leader – 'the Captain' – who had to turn back.

The succession of checkpoints forced me to concentrate on the flight. Over Cabo Belgrano [the southern tip of West Falkland] we went through a rainy area for a few seconds. Then we crossed over the southern part of Falkland Sound. The sea was full of gulls floating calmly. We passed another checkpoint at Aquila Island [Speedwell Island] and then met a second area of rain, but we flew on heading straight towards Fitzroy. It poured with rain again for thirty seconds; during that time you can cover a distance of around eight kilometres. I was about to return, because I was afraid that the rain would cover all the islands, but fortunately we managed to see a clearance behind the curtain of water, and this encouraged me to continue with the planned course. As we got nearer to the target I ordered the flight to accelerate to 900 kph and stay right down on the sea.

Forty seconds before the target we saw a Sea Lynx helicopter, so I hid behind a hill to avoid being detected. Twenty seconds later we found a Sea King on the ground; we performed the same manoeuvre and then reached Fitzroy Bay. There was nothing to be seen! I decided to fly on for another thirty seconds, but after that we turned right to start the return flight. Down on the ground we could see many British soldiers, who began shooting at us. A missile crossed behind our flight line from right to left at an angle of about 30 degrees. Just as we were completing the turn, 'Diablo' shouted: 'There are the ships!' Two grey silhouettes could be seen near the coast. I straightened up and banked to the left. Here we go again!

I released my bombs, which scored direct hits on the *Sir Galahad*. Number Two's bombs went long but luckily they hit a vehicle, overturned it and then they exploded. Ensign Carmona also hit the target. The section coming behind us saw that the ship had been hit so they attacked the *Sir Tristram*; 'Chango' and 'Diablo' did not waste their bombs. There was a long pipe on the deck where many life-jackets were tidily placed. Little men – little when seen from the distance – ran towards them, took one each and, one after the other, jumped into the cold sea.

I escaped by hugging the water. I checked to see if we were all there. We were. We looked at each other's damage; the

'Chango' and the 'Diablo' had been hit but not seriously. The enemy had been greatly hurt that day, and I had carried out what my flight leader had asked me to do: 'Take them to glory.'

Cachón and the other four pilots had made one of the best-executed Argentine air attacks of the war. The small amount of defensive fire had enabled them to come in at sufficient height to allow most of their bombs enough time in flight to become live, and the pilots' aim had been good. The three bombs which struck the *Sir Galahad* exploded and started a fierce fire. Forty-eight men died here, and the ship was completely gutted. One of the two bombs which hit the *Sir Tristram* exploded, causing less serious damage and killing two Hong Kong Chinese seamen. This was all a considerable setback to the British preparations for the attack on Stanley and was a clear success for the Argentines.

When the Skyhawks returned to their base and reported the success, it was decided to send out two more formations of four Skyhawks to continue the attacks in an attempt to add to the damage already caused to the British. Four aircraft of the 4th Fighter Group made the first attack, roaring in over the British units deployed around Fitzroy. But this area was well defended, and the units there greeted the Skyhawks with a hail of fire from every type of infantry weapon and from Rapier missile launchers. This attack caused no casualties to the British troops. The four Argentine aircraft were all damaged, and, if the *Sir Galahad* attack was one of the best Argentine air attacks of the war, this was one of the most fortunate for the Argentines because the damaged planes only managed to return to San Julián by the narrowest of margins.

The last Argentine air operation of that memorable day scored a minor success but then ran out of luck. Four Skyhawks of the 5th Fighter Group found a lone British landing craft in the Choiseul Sound. The first two Skyhawks attacked, and a bomb and some cannon fire all but destroyed the small craft, killing six of the men on board. But a pair of Sea Harriers saw the attack and swiftly disposed of three of the four Skyhawks, a Sidewinder missile causing the first one to explode in a fireball, another Sidewinder cutting the second aircraft in half and the third aircraft crashing into the shore, its pilot trying to outrun and evade the Sidewinder chasing it. All three pilots were killed. The very shaken fourth pilot only just made it to a Hercules tanker which helped him home. Some Mirages flying as escort at 35,000 feet were unable to intervene in the action.

The Argentine troops on Mount Harriet observed the attack on the *Sir Galahad* and *Sir Tristram* and saw the smoke from the *Galahad*'s fierce fire. News of the serious British casualties also reached Stanley, and some consideration was given to moving out a force of troops and attempting an attack on the British in the Fitzroy area while they were still unbalanced and recovering from the after-effects of the blow. But to make such an attack would have meant leaving the artillery cover of the prepared defences and moving into an area under direct observation by the British, with all the response from British artillery and air attack which that would entail. It was decided not to make any move.

## 15 · The Defenders of Stanley

The steady approach of the British had brought the two sides to the eve of the war's climax. The bombing of the *Sir Galahad* set back the British plans by forty-eight hours, but on Friday 11 June they stood ready to commence their attacks on the Argentine defences west of Stanley. The political future of a huge area of the South Atlantic was about to be decided on the outcome of a series of battles on hills with the innocuous sounding names given to them by earlier inhabitants of the islands – Mount Longdon, Two Sisters, Mount Harriet, Tumbledown Mountain, Wireless Ridge, Mount William, Sapper Hill. It is a useful time to examine the state of the Argentine force which would have to fight these battles.

The strength of the Argentine units was between 8,500 and 9,000 men, of whom maybe 5,000 could be classed as fighting troops – infantry, artillerymen, armoured car crews and a few commandos. There were six infantry units – five army regiments and a marine infantry battalion – to face the seven infantry units which the British would be able to bring up for the battle. The Argentines had forty-five field guns – three of 155 mm (one more had recently arrived by air) – and forty-two of 105 mm – which were stocked with at least 10,000 rounds of ammunition; the British possessed thirty 105-mm guns and would have to bring all their ammunition forward by helicopter from San Carlos, but the British also had the advantage of naval gunfire support from ships operating each night from just off the coast.

The opposing forces may appear to have been almost even if the survey is confined to ground units, with the Argentines having the advantage of being the defenders in strong positions which they had prepared over many weeks. But the Argentines had lost both air and sea superiority. It is true that there was an area around Stanley town and airfield where Argentine anti-aircraft defences prevented low-level aircraft attack, but the hills where the battles would be fought were not included in that cover. Moreover, the Argentines' own air support had all but evaporated. Only a handful of serviceable Pucará ground-attack aircraft were now available; they would have little influence on the outcome of the coming battles. All of the naval Aeromacchis and Turbo-Mentors were out of action except for one Aeromacchi which was withdrawn to the mainland on 30 May. Similarly, the helicopter force had dwindled almost to nothing. The last two serviceable Chinooks, belonging to the Air Force, also withdrew to the mainland on 9 June. An Argentine 'commando officer' told me that he was on this flight and that the intention was to collect a newly formed commando company together with 10,000 rounds of hollow-charge explosives which had been requisitioned from a French petroleum company in Argentina with the intention of returning to the Falklands and operating in the British rear. But this man refused to give his name, and, whatever the truth of this, the Chinooks never returned to the Falklands, the Air Force probably having refused to commit them to what appeared more and more to be a hopeless cause.

The mainland air units had also become almost irrelevant. No one could deny that the attack units had tried their best to stop or slow down the British progress, but thirty-six aircraft had been lost, and the only remaining sorties flown from the mainland would be a few Canberra night raids and some Dagger and Skyhawk 'hit-and-run' attacks which had little effect. Finally, the Super Étendard unit had used its last Exocet, a fact which was known to the British and which allowed the British ships, particularly the two aircraft-carriers, to come in much closer to the scene of action.

And what of the Argentine Navy, which had started off this Malvinas crusade just ten weeks earlier? I asked Vice-Admiral Lombardo whether a final fleet action was ever considered at this time:

No. We had no more fleet effectively. The *Belgrano* was sunk. The *Veinticinco de Mayo* had no aircraft. The two Type 42 destroyers were out of action; one had hit a rock, and the other was having engine troubles. We had no operational submarines.

Our two old American destroyers were only capable of making 15 knots. Our best tanker – the *Punta Medanos* – was unserviceable and was being brought up from the south under tow. The only good modern ships we had left were the *Drummond*, *Gránville* and *Guerrico*. These were all at sea near Puerto Belgrano, and I asked Admiral Anaya if I could send them to intercept the British supply ships sailing between Ascension Island and the Malvinas. But he said 'no', I was not to expand the conflict.

The Argentine commanders at Stanley realized how isolated and unsupported their positions were. Galtieri was urging them to be 'more aggressive and more mobile', but the whole build-up and disposition of the forces around Stanley had been based on an agreed policy of static defence, forcing the British to come forward and attack. What the soldiers in the Falklands resented was the virtual state of siege in which they now found themselves, without any air or sea support and with no sign that any further help would be coming from the mainland or that any political initiative was being attempted. In short they felt abandoned – the Army left facing potential disaster while the Air Force and Navy stood by on the mainland and did nothing.

It was against this background that what became known as the 'Daher mission' took place. Brigadier-General Américo Daher was Chief-of-Staff to Menéndez. Galtieri ordered Daher's return to Buenos Aires to bring a first-hand report on Menéndez's intentions, and Menéndez used the occasion to demand more help. Daher flew out during the night of 9 June on a naval Fokker F-28 which had brought in supplies and was taking out wounded men. This is Daher's account:

> The meeting with Galtieri was at Army Headquarters at the Libertador Building on 10 June, but it did not take place until the evening because my flight from the south was delayed by bad weather. We all had to sit up late that night.
>
> I proposed a series of operational ideas with the basic intention of gaining time to allow us to make a plan either for eventual success or for a reasonably negotiated settlement. It required a concentration of our resources, using the Navy, risking it all if necessary, also the mainland air units and some

parachute units of IV Brigade at Córdoba. These forces would
all have to be committed to give us a strictly local sea and air
superiority, dropping the parachute troops in the rear of the
British forces near Stanley and bringing across the 5th Regiment from Port Howard to attack San Carlos and the 8th
Regiment from Fox Bay to move into the rear of the British
troops at Goose Green.

But Galtieri said the junta would not risk the fleet and what
remained of the Air Force and that we had enough troops in
the Malvinas to sort it all out ourselves. Our view was that the
junta should have taken the risks involved to save us in the
Malvinas. But it was no good. I was told to tell Menéndez that
he must be prepared to fight to the end, even if we had to die.
We were not to surrender.

I then went on to meet General García and Vice-Admiral
Lombardo with requests for more ammunition, fuel and food.
Hardly anything useful was arriving, although they were finding
room on the supply flights for such things as mail and presents
of chocolate for the troops.

So the mission achieved nothing. Vice-Admiral Lombardo says that
Daher's proposals were considered to be 'illogical' and he pointed
out that the plan to move the two army regiments across Falkland
Sound from West Falkland would require the use of the *Bahía Buen
Suceso*, which was beached and abandoned at Fox Bay.

Daher flew back to Stanley on the night of 13 June. British artillery
was firing on the airfield, so Daher's plane could not land, and he
had to return to the mainland. When I suggested that this saved him
from becoming a prisoner of war, he quickly responded that he did
become a prisoner, confined by his own people in a barracks near
Buenos Aires for two months after the war while his part in the
Falklands defeat was investigated.

Argentine soldiers who served in the Falklands said that there were
three Argentine armies present – the 'army in the town', the 'army
on the coast' and the 'army in the hills'. The men in the town –
Stanley – were mostly in administrative, headquarters or support
units; they had good accommodation, shower facilities and hot food,

and were safe from shelling and air attack because they lived and worked among the Falkland civilians. The 'army on the coast' was the men in units in the coastal sectors around Stanley and at the airport. These men – the infantry of the 3rd, 6th and 25th Regiments, together with most of the artillerymen and the air force men – were not so fortunate as the men in Stanley, though they were not exposed to too severe weather conditions and were often able to visit Stanley. But the third group of men, the 'army in the hills', were having a grim time. They occupied positions on high and exposed ground up to seven miles distant from Stanley and had little or no opportunity to go down to the town. The long delay before the British landed at San Carlos and then the further wait while the British moved forward to Stanley had condemned these men to a debilitating wait of at least six weeks in their hill positions, twice the time that any British troops had spent in the open. The approach of the British from the west would result in these Argentine soldiers having to bear the brunt of the coming fighting. The three Argentine units which would have to face this final ordeal were the 4th and 7th Regiments and the 5th Marine Infantry Battalion. Pure chance gave this doubtful honour to one unit each from III Brigade and X Brigade and one from the Marine Corps.

These men had spent the waiting period in tents, trenches or shelters made of stones and turf. Members of these units will never forget the cold, the wind, waterlogged trenches and their hunger and fatigue during that long wait. The digging of positions had seemed easy where there was a good depth of soil, but the Argentine soldiers soon discovered that the soil consisted of a top layer that allowed rain to pass through quickly, but then there was a lower layer of soil which absorbed and held the water. The bottom of every trench thus became flooded every time it rained. Frostbite and 'trench foot' became prevalent, causing a steady drain of casualties; several men made comparisons with conditions in First World War trenches. Alan Craig, an Anglo-Argentine conscript in the 7th Regiment on Mount Longdon, provided this description of the conditions he and his comrades had to endure:

> In theory we could go back to the town once a week for a shower, in a shed with makeshift shower equipment, but we

were so hungry and weak, and it was such a long walk, that many of us didn't bother to go; I only went twice in two months. We were cold, wet and hungry – really very hungry – and tired. Our equipment was good, but we really didn't get the material to keep it clean; things got very rusty. There was no possibility of washing your clothes – and certainly none of getting them dry afterwards. I had three issue pants and three of my own; I just threw most of them away in the end. I had three pairs of socks; I wore them all at once and never changed them. Our clothes had been the ones issued in La Plata – for the climate of La Plata; the only thing they gave us extra for the cold weather was an Israeli-made anorak. It was good, but I used to be on guard from 1.00 till 3.00 a.m. most nights with a chap who became a good friend of mine, and it was always bloody cold then. We had three thin blankets, a sleeping-bag and a thin mattress each – not enough to keep us warm, but we would lie together with another man and share.

The worst part was the lack of food. Each morning we had *mate cocido* – a type of hot tea but with no milk and only a little sugar. Then there was a hot plate of soup at midday; I say 'hot' – it was usually cold by the time we got it. It was made of dehydrated vegetables and meat – not much meat. We had the same thing again in the evening. There was no bread, occasionally some water biscuits. But there were the sheep. There was a group of our men who used to kill a sheep, cook it and then sell it to us or swap it for a packet of cigarettes. There was a store of food at Moody Brook, and these men came up during the day and sold it to us; the chap who hadn't any money was really out of luck. That was a real racket. Some men went down to that food store to steal; it was guarded, but there was a way in. I didn't go, but one of my friends did; he nearly got caught. The army did give us a plastic pack of food, one per person per week. These contained two packets of sweets, four water biscuits, one tin of cold stew, some fuel tablets and a box of matches. Most of us sat down and ate the food straight away, possibly keeping the tins for the second day, but after that another wait of five days before the next packet. Often the packets were broken open and things were missing. I heard that there were containers of gift food for us down at Port Stanley but I never got any of it, except some chocolate that a soldier sold to me.

Cigarettes! That was a different story. There were two types of cigarette packet, one with an official stamp with the price on a blue seal; those were sent out privately in parcels. My mother told me after the war that she had sent me six parcels with such cigarettes and some biscuits. I found four of them at La Plata when I got back; the other two must have gone to the Malvinas, but I never saw them. The other cigarette packets had different labels and they were donated by the various tobacco companies as free gifts for the soldiers. Men used to come up from the town *selling* the free cigarettes and towards the end they were even selling the blue label cigarettes, which meant that someone in the Post Office at Port Stanley was opening our parcels and selling the contents.

And then there was the tiredness and the difficulty of getting everything up to us. Once we had to go down to Stanley to fetch some ammunition. We arrived back exhausted, and one man collapsed. An officer came up, took out his pistol and said that he had better get moving, but one of the soldiers got his gun out, pointed it at the officer and said he had better leave the man alone. The officer quietened down then and walked away. Then, another time, we had to fetch up a mobile cooker mounted on two wheels. To get this up we cut out a whole section of fence – several timber posts with the connecting strands of wire – and attached it to the cooker. Twenty or thirty of us then took the strain, pushing on the posts. We felt like horses when we dragged it all the way to the foot of Mount Longdon. It took us all afternoon to do that; it kept getting stuck in the mud, and the ground was rough – little streams covered with grass which you suddenly fell into.

Many of the men stood it very well. We had a lot who came from the slums of Buenos Aires, and they were used to rough conditions – mud and water and suchlike; they had never known anything much better. Those who had been away to school and had a good home suffered the worst. We had been accustomed to having a good home and a bed every night. We had two men

in our company who had self-inflicted wounds and another one
in B Company; the sad thing is that they were all chaps from
my type of background. One shot his thumb off and one shot
his heel. I don't know what the other man did; they said it was
an accident. They all got back home.

The 5th Marines, whose peacetime base was at Río Grande in Tierra
del Fuego, were the only one of those three units up in the hills with
proper cold-weather clothing and experience of operating in this
type of country. The 4th Regiment – on Mount Harriet and Two
Sisters – found the biggest contrast with conditions at their base in
Argentina; its men had been recruited and trained in the subtropical
province of Corrientes.

The food supply position improved early in June with the arrival
of the *Bahía Paraíso*, which was now a hospital ship and brought in a
supply of food on 1 June and, after taking its first load of wounded
to the mainland, came in with another load of food on 8 June. The
food problem then became one not of quantity but of distribution.
Every unit had five days' reserve of food at its position, but the
delivery of fresh and cooked food to the forward units was always a
problem, particularly for those units whose cooking equipment never
left Argentina. Brigadier-General Jofre has this comment to make on
the constant complaints about food: 'Young men of eighteen to
twenty have insatiable appetites and are never satisfied with the
amount of food they have. Then there was the cold climate and the
length of time spent out in the open. No wonder they wanted to eat
all the time.' Jofre also strongly refutes the suggestion that officers
had special rations. The diaries of air force men at Stanley airfield
show that they had a different scale of rations from the army units
and lived quite well. The 'air bridge' still continued, but only essential equipment was brought in. The arrival of the *Bahía Paraíso*
meant that the evacuation of the sick and wounded could proceed on
a proper basis, and there was never a build-up of wounded at Stanley;
this was a major contribution to the maintenance of morale. A second
hospital ship, the *Almirante Irizar*, also became available in June.

The approach of the main British force overland from distant San
Carlos caused the Argentine command in Stanley to reconsider its

defensive disposition and policy. The commander directly responsible was Brigadier-General Jofre, but Menéndez, as Commander-in-Chief, would have the last word. Jofre describes the Argentine appreciation:

> On 26 May, when the British were nearly ready to move out from San Carlos, Menéndez told me that he believed the British would move towards Stanley 'on horse'; that is a military term meaning that they would move overland on either side of the ridge of high ground. For that reason, he gave me the 4th Regiment which had been under Brigadier-General Parada until then, and the regiment was ordered to move its position; instead of facing the sea on Mount Challenger and Wall Mountain, they were to swing north and fortify Two Sisters and Mount Harriet. That gave us an extra layer of defence to face the approach on either side of the high ground across the island.

> Then my staff and I tried to decide how the British would attack the defences. We believed they would attack Mount Longdon, Two Sisters and Mount Harriet but that, if they captured those positions, their final push would come in the south, along the main track into Stanley, possibly on the same day. We did not realize that the British had such a strong capability of fighting by night. We knew the Goose Green battle had been partly night and partly day, but not the full scale of their night ability. We also believed that the British still had the ability to make a landing on a new sector, possibly in Berkeley Sound, and attack Stanley from the north.

The result of this appraisal was that there was no major transfer of units except for the realignment of the 4th Regiment. The whole of the Stanley area was to be defended on a 'hedgehog-type' perimeter system, and many troops would remain deployed around the airfield and east of the town while the crucial battles were fought in the west. Only the 4th Regiment changed its location. This was a unit which had come across from Argentina as part of III Brigade, the brigade whose heavy equipment never arrived. At the end of April the regiment had been allocated a coastal defence sector and had prepared defences there and waited; it was the most distant unit from the comforts of Stanley, which was nine miles away. The regimental commander, Lieutenant-Colonel Diego Soria, describes the effect of the recent order to move:

> So, on 28 May, we were given a new task; we had to move and prepare new positions. We were forced to improvise our defences under the pressure of imminent action. We had no barbed wire; we asked for some, but nothing came. We had no timber with which to construct bunkers. The most serious problem was that the men had no individual spades; we only had a few for the whole regiment. But we tried to do the best we could. On 31 May the British started their artillery fire.

The 4th Regiment, with 450 men, was defending two hill features and the intervening low ground. But, as Jofre says, this was an extra layer in the defences, and there were other units behind. To the north, however, the 7th Regiment was thinly spread over Mount Longdon and Wireless Ridge, with its positions facing more to the north than to the west. Because of the Argentine assumption that the British would concentrate their final attack in the south, this over-extended unit would have to face any British attack in the north on its own and with no supporting units in its rear.

Some help was sent from Stanley to strengthen the western defences; in particular, extensive minefields were laid. The British later made the accusation that some of the mines were scattered haphazardly by helicopter and, again, that incomplete records were kept. Jofre stresses that, although mines were brought forward by helicopter, they were never scattered by helicopter. Also, he says, records were properly handed over by his engineer commander after the war, but he does admit that some of the last minefields which were hurriedly laid may not have been properly recorded. Notes in the diary of a mortar officer on Two Sisters illustrate other types of help being provided in those last days – a further 120-mm mortar and ammunition sent on 4 June, four night-sights on 6 June, two machine-guns from a Pucará for anti-aircraft defence on 11 June.[1]

The first clashes took place. The British were patrolling extensively to discover the location of the Argentine defences and they suffered

---

[1]  The diary was found on Two Sisters after the battle there; the name of its author is not known.

# The Defenders of Stanley, 11 June 1982

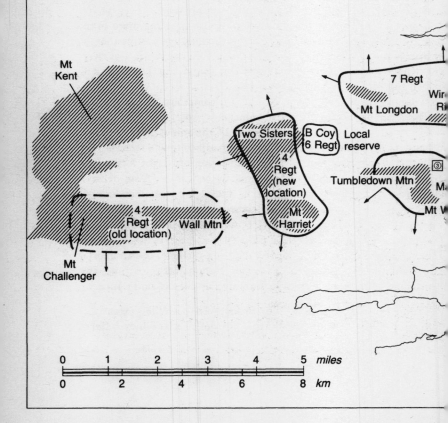

6 Regt

Regimental sectors;
arrows indicate the direction
in which defences faced

⫼ ① ⫼ Artillery units

① 3rd Arty Regt (18 × 105–mm, 3 × 155-mm guns)
② 4th Arty Regt (14 × 105–mm guns)
③ Marine Arty Battery (6 × 105-mm guns)
④ B Battery/101st AA Regt (8 × 30–mm guns)–
  also responsible for ground defence of its sector

Mt
Kent

7 Regt

Wir
Ri

Mt Longdon

Two Sisters

B Coy
6 Regt

Local
reserve

4
Regt
(new
location)

③

Tumbledown Mtn

Ma

4
Regt
(old location)

Wall Mtn

Mt
Harriet

Mt W

Mt
Challenger

| 0 | 1 | 2 | 3 | 4 | 5 | *miles* |

| 0 | 2 | 4 | 6 | 8 | *km* |

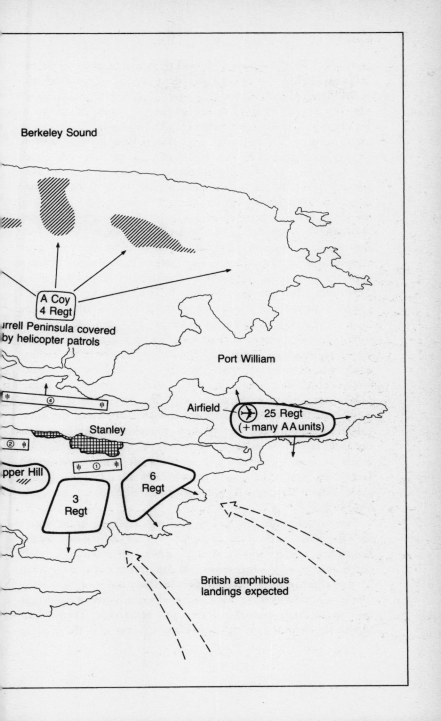

Berkeley Sound

A Coy
4 Regt

urrell Peninsula covered
by helicopter patrols

Port William

Airfield — 25 Regt
(+many AA units)

Stanley

④

②

pper Hill

①

6
Regt

3
Regt

British amphibious
landings expected

several casualties when men stepped on mines or when, as on one occasion, there was a mix-up over the positions of two parts of a Royal Marine patrol and four men were killed by fire from their own side. On another occasion a British patrol (from 3 Para) had to withdraw rapidly and leave items of equipment behind when it came under accurate Argentine fire near Murrel Bridge; five Argentine casualties are claimed by the British unit, but no Argentine record can be found of that. The most reliably recorded clash occurred in the early morning of 6 June when a party of Argentine marine engineers, protected by infantry of the 4th Regiment, came out to lay mines in the southern approaches to Two Sisters. The Argentines believed they would be safe from observation in thick mist and rain. But the party bumped into a British observation patrol (from 45 Commando) which had been laid up there for several hours. A sharp engagement took place in which the British unit later claimed fifteen Argentines killed and three wounded. The actual number of Argentine dead was four – three marines and an infantryman, one of the marines being cut in half by a small missile – and one man was wounded. The Argentines must have put up a good fight because British records show that their patrol had to call on artillery shelling and smoke so that they could withdraw. The only British casualty was the officer in charge of the patrol, who was shot in one finger. (There was a humane sequel to this action. Soon after it, the Argentine marine engineers made contact with a sergeant of the Royal Engineers, who allowed the Argentines to recover the bodies of their dead and take them back to Two Sisters for burial there. The Argentines spoke very well of this sergeant's helpful attitude; they called him 'Uncle Sam'. The Royal Engineers have identified him as Sergeant Halkett, serving at that time with 59 Independent Commando Squadron, RE.)

The Argentines on the hills were always in danger from British shell fire or air attack. There was now constant shelling both by the British field artillery and by warships, which were in action on most nights. The naval gunfire was an old danger and not considered to be very effective by the Argentines, who described it as 'zonal fire'. The British field artillery was considered a much greater danger, at least to the Argentines in the area west of Stanley. The men on Mount Harriet could actually see British helicopters in the distance bringing the British guns forward. The arrival of the British field artillery brought aimed fire by day, so that the hitherto quiet and safety of daylight hours no longer existed. The Harrier attacks – mainly by RAF aircraft at this stage – were frightening but not too frequent. The Argentine units on the hills had all been recently issued with Russian SAM-7 hand-held anti-aircraft missile launchers, but these were not very effective, mainly because of their unfamiliarity. The diary of the mortar officer on Two Sisters shows that on 5 June two Harriers escaped 'by human error' – the missile operator had mislaid the sight – and on 9 June a corporal did fire a missile, but it fell ten metres from a nearby Argentine position, while on 10 June two more Harriers were engaged but 'with no success'. The officer recorded that the sergeant in charge of the missiles was 'under great psychological difficulty which rendered him completely ineffective. I have taken complete charge and I hope the Harriers come back tomorrow and I will try to get a couple. It is noticeable how people's characters change in these circumstances. I hope there will not be great failings when we really have to fight.'

It is difficult to be precise, but it is probable that up to seventeen Argentine soldiers – eight infantry, four artillery and five others – were killed by artillery and Harrier attack during this period, with an unknown number of men being wounded. A man who served in one of the Argentine hospital ships at that time says that wounds by field artillery fire were by far the commonest cause of the casualties evacuated in his ship. Morale in general remained good, the buoyancy of being in the 'Malvinas' still remained, and most of the Argentine soldiers were prepared to do their best when the British attacks came. But there was a naïvety about what would be expected of them when the real fighting began and over-optimism about the outcome, based mostly on ignorance and on the constant lying about events of the war so far. Few men knew what had happened at Goose Green when the 12th Regiment had been outfought and a strong garrison forced to surrender. The Argentines put great faith in their minefields. It was believed that these would force the British to attack by day and that the firepower of infantry weapons and observed artillery fire would hold off attacks in such open country. They believed their equipment and training were good, but theirs was an army based on conscript service and mainly second-hand equipment and which had not fought an external war within living memory. Only a few Argentines realized how superior were the units about to attack them. On 1 June, Brigadier-General Menéndez sent this special message to all his troops:

MY MEN! The hour of the final battle has arrived. All our efforts, the hours of waiting, the cold, the tiredness, the vigilance, have come to an end. The adversary is getting ready to attack Puerto Argentino [Stanley] with the rash and hateful intention of conquering the capital of the Malvinas. Every man must fully understand what his duty is. The enemy will be destroyed by the decisive action of each one at his combat post. If each man with his rifle, his mortar, his machine-gun or artillery piece fights with the valour and heroism which has always characterized us, then victory is certain.

The gaze of all Argentina is on us; our parents, wives, fiancées and children, all our families have total confidence in us. In the supreme hour we have the duty not to betray them.

We have contracted a sacred responsibility to our comrades who have fallen in action to convert their personal sacrifice into a page of glory for Argentina and we cannot allow their heroism to be in vain.

Not only must we beat them, we must do it in such a way that their defeat is so crushing that they will never again have the impertinence to invade our land. TO ARMS! TO BATTLE!

The British were ready to attack by the evening of Friday 11 June. The daylight hours of that day had been deceptively quiet, with just routine shelling and Harrier raids on the Argentine hill positions. Some Pucarás had attempted to attack British artillery positions in the Mount Kent area the previous night and would repeat the operation in the coming evening; there were no casualties on either side. The most unusual action of the day was a British attempt to kill Brigadier-General Menéndez. The British believed that Menéndez held a regular morning conference in the Town Hall/Post Office building on Stanley's waterfront, and a Wessex helicopter, hovering over the high ground more than three miles to the north, fired two AS-12 wire-guided missiles at the building. One missile failed; the second flew on, just missing the intended target and striking the Police Station on the other side of the road. There were no casualties, only some shaken Argentine military policemen. But the attack was based on faulty intelligence. Menéndez did not visit this building regularly; all of his conferences were held in the main Argentine Command Post, which was in Stanley House 600 yards away. It is fortunate that no civilians were killed; a warning intended for the Post Office staff did not reach them.

All was ready for the British attacks. Much thought had been given to the overall plan. A seemingly attractive option of driving through on a narrow front in the south -- which is what the Argentines expected – was not adopted. Such an attack, on Two Sisters and Mount Harriet, with a further drive past Tumbledown Mountain, Mount William and Sapper Hill, would have concentrated the British effort and enabled the Argentine positions on Mount Longdon and Wireless Ridge to be bypassed. But the necessary move forward of the British artillery by helicopter after the first phase of the attacks would have been overlooked by Mount Longdon, so the British were forced into an attack on a broad front of more than four miles. The first phase of this would take place in the coming night and would be handled entirely by Brigadier Thompson's 3rd Commando Brigade. The attacks would develop from north to south, with 3 Para attacking Mount Longdon at one minute past 9.00 p.m., followed by 45 Commando attacking Two Sisters and 42 Commando attacking Mount Harriet. The British infantry would outnumber the Argentine defenders by about two to one.

The importance of the actions about to commence cannot be overemphasized. The British had brought almost all their fighting units up to the Stanley defences, and although not all would be committed on this first night, there were virtually no fresh troops in reserve and no more on the way from distant Britain. The British troops were tiring and suffering from the increasingly cold weather. If the three attacks on what was only the outer ring of the Argentine defences failed, if the British soldiers could not master the techniques of night fighting, if the Argentine soldiers could hold off the attacks, then the British would be in serious trouble. There was a risk that stalemate might follow, and then the future control of the Falklands would be in doubt.

The scene of the first attack was Mount Longdon, a steep-sided hill a mile long and running roughly west to east. The main ridge was 600 feet high in places, about 300 feet higher than the surrounding ground. The hill formed only a small part of the long sector allocated to the 7th Regiment, whose commander was Lieutenant-Colonel Ortiz Giménez. The sector was named *Plata* (Silver) and stretched from Mount Longdon as far eastwards as the northern arm of Stanley Harbour nearly seven miles away. The Argentines were not expecting to be attacked here, hence the large area over which the 7th Regiment was stretched.

Mount Longdon itself was held by only B Company, with three platoons, but reinforced by a platoon of the 10th Engineer Company acting as infantry and a section of between five and eight heavy 12.7-mm machine-guns manned by marines. Contrary to British reports, there were no commandos present. The local commander on the hill was Major Carlos Carrizo Salvadores, second-in-command of the

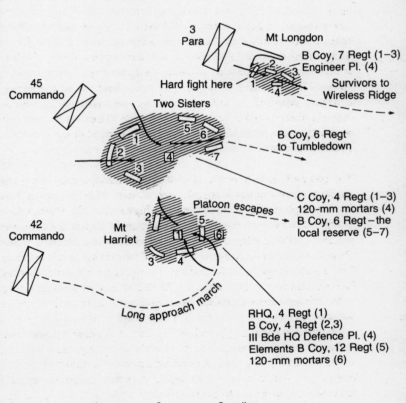

# Night of 11 to 12 June

British units and attacks

Approximate position of Argentine

platoons and heavy mortars – 1, 2, etc.

High ground

3 Para

Mt Longdon

B Coy, 7 Regt (1–3)
Engineer Pl. (4)

Hard fight here

Survivors to
Wireless Ridge

45 Commando

Two Sisters

B Coy, 6 Regt
to Tumbledown

C Coy, 4 Regt (1–3)
120-mm mortars (4)
B Coy, 6 Regt – the
local reserve (5–7)

Platoon escapes

42 Commando

Mt Harriet

Long approach march

RHQ, 4 Regt (1)
B Coy, 4 Regt (2,3)
III Bde HQ Defence Pl. (4)
Elements B Coy, 12 Regt (5)
120-mm mortars (6)

| 0 | 1 | 2 | 3 | miles |

| 0 | 2 | 4 | km |

7th Regiment. Because it was the north-western corner of the Argentine defences around Stanley, the Mount Longdon positions basically faced north and west – two platoons on the northern side, one platoon on the western end and the engineer platoon in reserve. The Argentines had no special name for the hill; some mistakenly called it 'Monte London'.

The British unit attacking the hill was 3 Para, a tough, well-trained battalion which had trekked all the way from San Carlos and was anxious to show that it could repeat the success of its sister battalion at Goose Green. The main difficulty for 3 Para was that its position facing Mount Longdon, on Mount Vernet, was nearly five miles away across open ground which was interspersed with minefields. Long-range daylight observation of Mount Longdon had not revealed the exact location of the Argentine defences, and night patrolling had proved difficult. The plan 3 Para had was to attack with two companies, one to seize a subsidiary hill about 500 yards north of Mount Longdon and to use this as a fire base, while the second company assaulted the hill's western end and attempted to work its way along the main ridge supported by the fire of the company in the northern position. Unfortunately for the British, this plan entailed their troops attacking the most heavily defended parts of the hill.

The paras completed their approach to the jumping-off line, which was on a little stream about half a mile from the foot of the hill, and the two assault companies commenced their final advance a little late, at 9.15 p.m. There was no artillery fire at this stage; the intention was to get right up to the Argentine positions in silence. The advancing men reached more than halfway before being detected. They were aided in this by a serious lapse on the part of the Argentines. There was a Rasit radar set on the hill which on previous nights had successfully detected the approach of British patrols and caused fire to be brought down on them. But an officer ordered that the set be switched off on this night for fear that the British could detect its emissions and shell its location. This was an example of the Argentine assumption that any major British attack would take place in daylight or just before dawn. One Argentine officer says that 'the British would have had to pay a much higher price for Mount Longdon if that radar set had been switched on'.

But the British advantage was lost when one of their men stood on a mine which exploded, badly injuring the soldier. Surprise was now lost. The British rushed forward. Much firing started, and the battle began in earnest. The next stages went badly for the British. The attempt to establish a fire base on the subsidiary hill north of Longdon failed when the British company here (3 Para's A Company) found that the position was overlooked by the Argentine defences on the main hill, and the paras were forced to withdraw after being engaged by small-arms and mortar fire. Meanwhile, the second attacking company (B Company) was pinned down under heavy fire in gulleys in the steep western face of the hill and suffering heavy casualties.

The main battle for Mount Longdon lasted several hours and was fought out on that western end of the hill. The paras worked forward only slowly. They were often held up, particularly by the marine-manned heavy machine-guns, which were well handled. British artillery fire immediately fell on the eastern end of the hill, and the Argentine mortar positions were soon put out of action. At one stage the British pulled back slightly and allowed their own artillery fire to 'creep' back along the hill almost as far as the leading British troops, to soften up the Argentine defence before the British could move forward again. The British mortars were in constant action. Star-shells, machine-gun tracer and explosions flashed back and forth. It was hell. The attacking British company on the western end of the hill suffered 50 per cent casualties before they eventually reached the limit of their objective, the mid-point of the long ridge. The Argentine platoon which had held them up was commanded by Second Lieutenant Juan Baldini, who was killed and was posthumously decorated for his bravery. Also killed was a forward artillery observation officer, Lieutenant Alberto Ramos, whose last message to his battery was that his position was surrounded. At one stage the Argentines mounted what they called a 'counter-attack', by sending forward their reserve, the engineer platoon. But a night counter-attack is an extremely difficult operation; it is likely that the engineer platoon was able to do no more than move forward and stabilize an existing but shaky defence line, forcing a temporary halt to the British advance.

But the British eventually succeeded, and the Argentine defence was broken. A British NCO, Sergeant Ian McKay, was awarded a posthumous Victoria Cross for putting one of the most persistent

Argentine positions out of action; this would be the only Victoria Cross awarded in the fighting around Stanley and is an indication of the ferocity of the action at the western end of Mount Longdon. Now 3 Para's A Company came up and took over the attack. Initially, they too had to fight hard, but the Argentines finally collapsed, and the entire length of the hill was captured just before dawn. Major Carrizo Salvadores had remained in touch with his regimental headquarters, more than two miles away in the rear, and a platoon of the company on Wireless Ridge was sent forward to reinforce the men fighting on Longdon; but, in the words of Major Antonio Pérez Cometto, the regiment's Operations Officer, 'the platoon was destroyed'. Another platoon was then dispatched, but Brigadier-General Jofre, who was following events in his Command Post at Stanley, cancelled its move because he realized that Mount Longdon was as good as lost. The battle had lasted nearly ten hours. The Argentines had fought well. Nineteen British soldiers were killed, and about thirty-five were injured. It would turn out to be the most costly single battle of the war for the British. The exact number of Argentine dead is not known, because the 7th Regiment's records do not differentiate between men killed on this night and in other actions; but twenty-nine bodies were later exhumed from the graves dug after the battle by 3 Para, and, while none of the bodies could be identified, it can be estimated that there were twenty-one from the 7th Regiment, three marine machine-gunners, one artillery officer and possibly one engineer. One further man probably died of wounds after the battle; his body was later found and identified at Teal. Apart from the two officers already mentioned, most of the dead were conscripts. One of these was particularly unfortunate; among the dead was Alfredo Gattoni, a married man who had deferred his call-up for the maximum allowable seven years. There were no conscripts from the youngest class – of 1963; this was a result of X Brigade's ability to replace most of its new conscripts with reservists from the previous year and its policy of keeping the few 1963 men who did reach the Falklands out of the fighting area. About half of the Longdon garrison, including Major Carrizo Salvadores, managed to withdraw from Mount Longdon when the fighting ended, but about fifty Argentines were taken prisoner.

The next Argentine position to be attacked was the two-mile-long feature of Two Sisters, so named because of its two prominent hills; the westerly peak was just over 1,000 feet high, the easterly one only slightly lower. The Argentines called this place Dos Hermanas, a direct translation of 'Two Sisters'. This area had not been included in the original Stanley defence scheme but had been allocated to Lieutenant-Colonel Diego Soria's 4th Regiment after the British landings at San Carlos; the defences were thus not as strong as those on other sectors. The garrison on Two Sisters was made up of two companies, but these were from different regiments. C Company of the 4th Regiment was on the western hill, while the eastern one was occupied by B Company of the 6th Regiment, which was acting as a general reserve for this area. Command was divided. Major Ricardo Cordón, second-in-command of the 4th Regiment, was the senior officer on the western hill, and Major Oscar Jaimet on the eastern one. Cordón was responsible to Lieutenant-Colonel Soria, who was on the neighbouring hill at Mount Harriet; Jaimet was under the direct command of Brigadier-General Jofre in Stanley. Major Cordón's garrison on the western hill, facing the British advance from San Carlos, was stronger, with about 170 men and some mortars. There was also one of the Rasit radar sets here but it had a defect and could not be used. Major Jaimet, on the eastern hill, had approximately 100 to 120 men. A British officer talking with Brigadier-General Jofre at the end of the war said that, given the potential strength of the feature, he would have 'grown to old age on Two Sisters before losing it'.

The British attacking here were the Royal Marines of 45 Commando, who had also marched all the way from San Carlos. The unit planned to attack in three phases, the first an advance by one company carrying some of the unit's heavy weapons directly from the west to capture the western hill, where its support fire could help the subsequent attacks of two other companies from the north, which would strike the saddle between the two hills and then turn and capture the eastern one. But the attack did not develop according to plan. The Royal Marine company (X Company) making the first move was so heavily burdened with the heavy weapons and ammunition that it was two hours late in arriving at its start line, and this and the main attack from the north had to take place simultaneously.

The result of this was that the Argentines on the western hill were struck by attacks from two directions, one directly on the western edge of the hill and one on its rear where the mortars and heavy machine-guns were located. There was also very effective British artillery support. The only serious hold-up experienced by the British was when the northern attack was pinned down for over an hour by small-arms and mortar fire. But a charge (by 45 Commando's Z Company) broke the stalemate, and the defence on the western hill then broke. The commander of the Argentine mortar platoon was killed, and at least one of the rifle platoon commanders was wounded. Despite the mass of small-arms fire exchanged, the Royal Marines suffered no casualties at all from such fire, only from mortars and artillery. The exact number of dead in the Argentine company on this western hill is not known, but it is believed that this vital feature was given up with the loss of five men killed in addition to the mortar officer. Most of the Argentines retreated to the south-east towards Tumbledown Mountain three miles away, where they were collected by Captain López Patterson, who later brought the wounded back to Stanley.

B Company of the 6th Regiment, on the eastern hill, had not been directly attacked by the first British assault. Second Lieutenant Augusto La Madrid, one of the platoon commanders here, describes his night:

I was watching the fighting on Mount Longdon before the attack on Two Sisters. I was perfectly placed. My Lytton night binoculars were very good, and I could see British troops in the Murrell Bridge area firing on Longdon; it was possibly a mortar or a missile detachment. I could even hear their commands. They were about 400 metres away, so I moved one of my machine-guns further to the right, so as not to reveal its main position, and it opened long-range fire on the British.

Then came the attack on Two Sisters. They came in from my rear. The first thing I heard was the 12.7-mm machine-gun with the 4th Regiment firing. It was a heavy machine-gun – a series of thuds, rather than the quick rattle of the 7.62-mm machine-guns. There was a very long exchange of fire. It is difficult to say how long things take in a battle. Some of the fire came our way, but it was only the effect of the fire fight between the Royal Marines and the 4th Regiment. Then I heard orders shouted in English. I thought of trying to make a counter-attack, but that would have been madness because it would have meant going downhill and then up again, so I decided not to – and I had no orders anyway.

Then we were ordered to fall back to 'Cambio' – the alternative position where the reserve ammunition was in the rear of Two Sisters. We got there and prepared to receive an attack or to counter-attack, but not to retreat. But the Royal Marines didn't come any further. They fired on us and mortared us, but they didn't press their attack. I think they did not have the aggression of the paras. We replied to their fire. Then came a second order, to fall back to the supplementary position at Tumbledown. The Argentine artillery was going to bombard Two Sisters whether we were there or not. Subteniente Franco's platoon was left as a rearguard, but he made it back to Tumbledown OK.

It is probable that only three or four men from this company were killed, all by artillery fire.[1]

The effect of the battle for Two Sisters was that the Argentines were driven out of their positions by dawn after a poor defence in which less than ten Argentines died and which only inflicted casualties of four men killed and ten injured on the Royal Marines. Fifty-four Argentines were taken prisoner, including Major Cordón, who was judged after the war to have handled the battle badly and was retired from the army.

The final battle of the night was for the compact, rocky mass of Mount Harriet, a difficult objective for the British because the approach by the attacking unit would have to penetrate several mine-fields. The main garrison on the hill was provided by Headquarters and B Company of the 4th Regiment, supported by the usual heavy weapons. Recent reinforcements were the III Brigade HQ Defence

[1] Private Oscar Poltronieri of this company was awarded the Cruz-La Nación Argentina al Heroico Valor en Combate, the highest Argentine decoration for bravery. The citation gives no dates but refers to actions in the Two Sisters–Tumbledown Mountain area: 'always volunteering for dangerous missions, manning a machine-gun, holding up attacks, always the last man to withdraw, sometimes overrun by the English, twice given up for dead but always returning to his platoon'. Poltronieri, who survived, was the only conscript awarded this medal during the war, and part of the actions for which he was decorated probably took place on this night.

Platoon and the solitary platoon of B Company, 12th Regiment, which had been left behind when the main part of that company had been helicoptered from Mount Kent to Goose Green on the day of the battle there. The total Argentine strength was about 300 men under the direct command of Lieutenant-Colonel Soria. The Argentines called the hill Monte Enriqueta, which was again a direct translation of the English name.

The British unit making the attack was 42 Commando, a unit which had been helicoptered from San Carlos to Mount Kent but had then spent a long, cold spell on that mountain. The Royal Marines had used that time well, carrying out intensive patrolling, and their commander had devised a plan of outstanding ingenuity and daring. Bypassing completely the main Argentine defences on the western side of Mount Harriet, he sent two companies right through the minefield area and then well on south of the hill, so that they could attack from the south and south-east, thus striking at the left flank and rear of the Argentine positions.

The first move was carried out successfully when approximately 250 men marched nearly four miles through the night, avoiding the minefields and reaching their start lines without being detected. Still in silence, the first attack company (K Company) started moving up the hill, and the leading marines were actually among the Argentine trenches and tents on the rear of Mount Harriet before being detected. A single shot started the battle. The ensuing action took place among the positions occupied by the 4th Regiment's mortars and by the infantry of the 12th Regiment platoon occupying what had been considered a deep reserve position until the British attack came in at that point. The infantry battle here lasted about an hour. It is believed that six Argentines were killed, and one Royal Marine died when he entered an Argentine tent and was so close to one of the occupants that he was actually pushing aside the Argentine's rifle when he was shot. The commander of the Argentine mortar platoon was among the wounded, and all four of his 120-mm mortars were put out of action.

When the Argentine defence on the rear of the hill was overcome, the Royal Marines wheeled left and started to advance into the centre of the main position. At the same time, the second attacking company (42 Commando's L Company) was attacking from the south, overrunning the trenches held by the III Brigade HQ Defence Platoon, which lost three men killed. There was much action in the centre of the hill top. First Lieutenant Ignacio Gorriti was the senior officer of the 12th Regiment whose men had been struck by the first attack on the rear of the hill. His account illustrates the fragmented nature of this night action:

We seemed to have been fighting for about an hour; no one else seemed to be in action. I went back to the Command Post and asked Colonel Soria for a platoon from another part of the hill with an officer to help me make a counter-attack on the enemy's flank on my sector. Colonel Soria sent an officer to fetch a platoon, but I never saw him again. I had to go back to my men. I went to the tents where a reserve group were and kicked the side of the tents and told them to come with me. They wouldn't come; they said they couldn't find their boots and rifles, etc. So I took two of my own soldiers to refill the magazines for me; one of them lagged behind, and I found out later that he was killed. He was an Indian soldier and had been very useful because he had always been able to find water for us – and he used to make me coffee. My FLN rifle wasn't working properly; it kept firing three shots at a time; I couldn't make it do single shots – and that was the best of three rifles I tried that night! I was making a little counter-attack on the flank of the British who were attacking my men. My radio wasn't working; the wires were all cut by shelling. Our other radios had no batteries. So I could not pass orders to my men – it was just individual action. I could hear the shouts of the British soldiers but I couldn't understand one word, although I can understand some English.

Then I lost my footing; the rocks were very icy. I fell on my back and lost my rifle. I lay for a second or two then reached out my arm to pick up my rifle. Just as I did so a burst of machine-gun fire passed just near my head and hit the rock behind me, and I was hit in the back by some splinters. I thought I was wounded but I found out later that I had so many clothes on that I was not hurt. I thought I was going to die; that was the first time I was afraid, and I hid in some rocks for a bit. Then I heard some action behind me where the

reserve platoon would not come with me before, but they were
fighting hard now. One of their men, a 4th Regiment man, had
an anti-aircraft machine-gun and took this into action. He did
very well, firing off a belt of ammunition, then dropping back
into a hole, then coming up and firing another belt. He did this
several times. It became quite a famous little incident. I don't
know his name, but he survived.

British accounts of the fighting also mention this machine-gunner.
His name is not known. Another man to fight well here was First
Lieutenant Jorge Echeverría, who was hit five times by British bul-
lets; he too survived. One of his corporals, Roberto Baruzzo, received
Argentina's highest decoration for administering first aid under fire
and saving his officer's life.

The fighting had now lasted for more than four hours, and the
Argentine defence was about to collapse. The Royal Marines were
near Lieutenant-Colonel Soria's Command Post. Soria had been
trying to move troops from the western end of his positions to make
a counter-attack, but the company commander there said that such a
move was 'quite impossible' because British artillery and mortar
fire was completely pinning down the two platoons under his command. Soria was also in touch with Commander Robacio of the 5th
Marine Infantry Battalion on Tumbledown, two and a half miles
away, and Robacio was arranging for the marine battery there to
provide artillery support. When the British troops came nearer, Soria
moved out of his Command Post and went through the shell fire to
the company which had not so far been in action, though it had been
shelled. First Lieutenant Gorriti must have entered the Command
Post just after Soria left. Gorriti says:

I went back to the Command Post, where I met Captain Fox
and an artillery observation officer, but not Colonel Soria; he
had gone off to his B Company but left everything in his
Command Post – all the radio codes, etc. Now the English
were all around us, and Captain Fox and I set fire to everything.
It was incredible; after years of taking care of army equipment,
there I was setting light to an expensive radio. When all seemed
to be lost, I asked Captain Fox, who had a small radio, to ask
the 5th Marines to fire on to our position. A few others and

myself took shelter in a hole. Suddenly, I saw three Englishmen against the sky. I didn't open fire; I didn't think it was a time for killing. I asked the men with me whether we should fight on or surrender. They told me to decide. That was very difficult – we surrendered. The British were on top of us; it made no sense at all to keep on fighting.

(Lieutenant-Colonel Soria says that he gave the order to set fire to the Command Post before he left.)

As on Mount Longdon and Two Sisters, the battle ended as dawn was breaking. A lone rifleman near the centre of the hill held out till the end, injuring a Royal Marine officer and causing other British casualties, but he was eventually killed by an 84-mm missile fired at only a few yards' range. The name of this brave Argentine soldier is also unknown. Lieutenant-Colonel Soria and the commander of B Company discussed the possibility of attempting to break out, but the company commander said that his men were not capable of such a move after being under shell-fire all night. But one platoon, commanded by Second Lieutenant Lantaro Jiménez, did manage to slip away, the only sizeable body of men to escape from Mount Harriet. Lieutenant-Colonel Soria, two other officers and about sixty men then surrendered. They were escorted down to a track at the foot of the hill, where they joined a large number of Argentines captured on other parts of the position. Ignacio Gorriti described the frustrating attempts of a Royal Marine, an Argentine officer and a Gurkha, who attempted to count the prisoners in three languages and kept getting different totals. Finally, after half an hour, the Royal Marine selected one of the totals given to him and said that would have to do.

The British had captured this important position at a cost of only one Royal Marine killed – the one shot in the Argentine tent early in the battle – and ten men injured. The British estimated 'up to twenty-five' Argentines killed and 'about 300 prisoners', but the true numbers are probably ten killed and about 250 prisoners. Only eight Argentine bodies were recovered from the grave on the hill after the war. Lieutenant-Colonel Soria survived the post-war investigation of Mount Harriet's loss without blame and continued his career in the Argentine Army.

*

The attacking British units had been ordered to continue their advance if the Argentine positions fell quickly and if all other circumstances were favourable, but this was an over-optimistic hope. No further British movement took place; there was enough to occupy them in the newly won positions, which soon came under Argentine shell fire. The results of the night's actions were extremely serious for the Argentines. The entire outer ring of hills in the Stanley defences had been lost. Of the approximately 850 Argentine troops who had manned the three hill positions, 50 were dead and about 420 were prisoners of war, leaving only about 380, who retired towards Stanley. British casualties were 24 men killed (if casualties during the following day from shelling are included) and about 65 wounded. The British were now only 5 miles away from that little town whose occupation was so symbolic in this conflict. Lieutenant-Colonel Héctor Arias, commander of one of the Argentine anti-aircraft units, says: 'I realized that the war was as good as lost after that night; I didn't think the rest of our defences would hold. We were being encircled, the ring getting tighter and tighter. The whole strategy of the British would lead to our inevitable defeat.'

Back in the main Command Post at Stanley, Brigadier-General Jofre had attempted to follow the progress of the battles and to help where possible. He was an energetic commander, and many of the officers fighting on the hills mention vigorous radio exchanges with him. Brigadier-General Menéndez was also present but was content to leave matters in the hands of the officer he had appointed as field commander for the Stanley area. For some time it had appeared that the attack on Mount Longdon might be the only action of the night, and Jofre had decided to mount a major counter-attack there. He contacted the headquarters of the 3rd Regiment, which was holding the sector south of Stanley, and ordered one of its companies to be taken by lorry along the road to Moody Brook Barracks and then along the track which ran almost to the foot of Mount Longdon. Major Guillermo Berazay was the officer detailed to carry out this operation; this is his account:[2]

We were in the Command Post when Jofre told Lieutenant-

---

[2] Major Berazay had lost an eye in an accident as a junior officer, but regulations were waived to allow him to continue his career in a front-line unit.

Colonel Comini to prepare A Company for a special mission and that he wanted an officer of at least *jefe* rank to lead it. The Colonel said he could send two such officers; which one was to go? Jofre said to send the Operations Officer – that was me! I called the commander of A Company, which was our reserve company. He and I went to Stanley House where Jofre was. He showed me the map and told me that things were difficult and that he wanted me to take the company and go up to Tumbledown Mountain. A guide from the 5th Marines would then show us exactly where to place the company.

We were ready to move at about 3.00 a.m., but it was a very frosty morning, and a lot of the trucks we needed were soon in difficulties. Some found it hard to start; others were breaking down or had difficulty with the ground in the dark, and it took a long time to organize the convoy. We could hear the firing, away to the west, but could not see anything because it was too misty. The Colonel gave me his jeep, and we started to move out of Stanley on the road towards Moody Brook. But the road out of the town was steep, and the vehicles all started skidding. I told my driver to swing into the fence on the left, otherwise we would be in the sea. I heard the lorries behind us hitting each other. I ordered the men to get out of the lorries and be ready to march, but their boots were slipping as well, and that slowed us down. It was starting to get light by then, and as soon as we passed the last houses the British started shelling us. The men all took cover. That was the first time I had been under fire. After about five minutes the firing stopped, and we met the guide from the 5th Marines. I got the men moving again, and we got into position just north and north-west of Tumbledown.

So, because of the delays on the icy road, this company took about five hours to move four miles and was able to do no more than establish a blocking position near the track north of Tumbledown.

When the attacks on Two Sisters and Mount Harriet developed, Jofre could do little to help the defenders because of the lateness of the night and because of the greater distance to these positions from

Stanley. He might have considered ordering the 5th Marines on Tumbledown to make counter-attacks but did not do so. When Lieutenant-Colonel Soria's position on Mount Harriet was overrun and contact was lost, Jofre ordered the Argentine artillery to fire on the hill, using Soria's burning Command Post as the aiming point. Jofre turned to Brigadier-General Parada, who was only a bystander in these events, and said: 'May God forgive me if any of our men are still fighting there.' When it later became obvious that all three hill positions were lost, the Argentine artillery started a general bombardment of the hills.

There had been other incidents during the night. One of four British warships which were bombarding land positions was trying to hit one of the heavy 155-mm Argentine guns which was located on the western edge of Stanley. Unfortunately, one of the British shells fell on a house in which ten civilians had congregated for mutual support and to take protection in a makeshift shelter. Two of the civilians were killed, and a third died of wounds – the only Falkland civilians to die during the war. Also on this night the RAF carried out the last of the Vulcan raids from Ascension Island, hoping to drop twenty-one 1,000-lb air-burst bombs above Stanley airfield to scatter bomb fragments and put any remaining serviceable aircraft out of action. But this operation did not proceed as smoothly as the earlier Vulcan raids. There was some confusion in the Vulcan over the bomb-release system, and the bombs failed to explode in the air but exploded on hitting the ground. They did hit the airfield area, but no Argentine casualties or serious damage are recorded.

Another action just before dawn brought success for the Argentines. In an ingenious makeshift operation, two Exocet MM38 launching tubes had been flown across from the mainland and fitted on to a lorry trailer at Stanley; five missiles were available. (These Exocets were of the type normally fitted to ships, not the ones used by the Super Étendards.) The intention was to attack one of the bombarding British warships. The first missile had been launched a fortnight earlier, on the night of 27–28 May, but had not scored a hit. The British had been more careful since then. The trailer had been towed out on to the airport road outside Stanley each night and then returned to the concealment of the town during the day. The operation was under the control of a naval officer, Commander Julio Pérez.

One of the bombarding ships that night was the destroyer HMS *Glamorgan*. The Exocet danger was known, so carefully prepared routes to and from the firing positions were used. But on this night *Glamorgan* was asked to remain in action longer than planned, to support the attack on Two Sisters which started late, and the ship had to take a short cut when withdrawing at the end of her bombardment. The Exocet was aimed on a fixed line, and the movements of *Glamorgan* were being followed by radar. This Argentine account tells what happened:[3]

> The moment the people on the island got the Exocet missiles, they became obsessed with the idea of sinking the frigates that bombarded them at night. Several difficulties were encountered in placing the launcher on a suitable flat surface. The launching ramp was fixed, therefore it couldn't aim, so it was only through the radar that they could detect an impudent frigate passing in front of it. The frigates had several times come very near the line of fire but left without crossing it.
>
> That early morning, a group of men, praying in their inner selves, were watching the radar display. 'Come on, just two degrees more. Move. Just a little more, please!' And it happened. The ship crossed the line, and the radar operator shouted – 'Now!' The propellant burnt in the dark night, and the Exocet left in search of its prey.
>
> Hit! Two officers and some other men danced with delight in the reddish glow of the radar display.

The missile struck *Glamorgan*'s stern, causing severe damage and killing thirteen sailors. The ship was put out of action for the remaining short period of the war. No further opportunity occurred for the Argentines to use the remaining three Exocets.

Daylight came. It was freezing, and a mist hung over the battlefields. The British artillery was quiet after its long night of action. British

---

[3] From the unpublished English translation of *Dios y los Halcones*; the narrator is named as 'Major Medina, a Skyhawk pilot'; he may have been serving on the air force ground staff at Stanley at that time.

helicopters were shuttling the wounded of both sides to the rear.
Several Argentine soldiers were still on the move near the captured
hills. Private Alan Craig, near Mount Longdon, describes his morning:

> I could see the British soldiers up above us carrying the bodies
> of our dead further up the mountain and laying them one beside
> the other. There were a couple of chaps dead near me, and we
> gathered those up. We laid all the dead in a line and covered
> them with blankets. They had all been hit by shell or mortar
> fire. One of them was one of my friends. I didn't feel much
> then, but later I couldn't believe it all, that those chaps were
> dead. We were extremely tired; we hadn't eaten or slept. The
> British up on top could see us easily; they were several hundred
> metres away from us. They waved at us to come up but didn't
> trouble us. The Company Sergeant-Major asked four of us if we
> would take a wounded man down to Moody Brook. We put him
> on a wooden board. He had some shrapnel in his groin and was
> crying his head off with the pain. The incredible thing was that
> he had been constipated for a long time and that stuff stopped
> the shrapnel from going further in. It was afternoon when we
> set off, but almost at once the Argentine artillery opened up;
> they should have been firing over us, but the shells fell nearby.
> Our officer radioed back, and the shelling stopped until we were
> clear. A few more men of C Company got back that afternoon,
> and I think others had got away during the previous night.

The mist lifted later in the day, and the newly installed British
observation posts on the captured hills were able to see many targets
all the way to Stanley. Argentine units reported increased casualties
from shell and mortar fire that day and the next. The British had
hoped to launch their next round of attacks the following night (the
night of the 12th–13th), but the necessary preparations could not be
completed, and there would be a delay of twenty-four hours. That
night was mostly quiet, so quiet that Second Lieutenant La Madrid,
who had withdrawn from Two Sisters the previous night, was able
to take five men back to recover some urgently needed radio batteries
and some blankets left near his old position.

Sunday 13 June came – a fine day. It was an exciting one for the Argentines because this was the last day of the Pope's visit to their homeland; he would leave Buenos Aires that night. Few Argentines realized that their hold over the Falklands would end a few hours after that event. The British were working furiously, bringing up ammunition and supplies for the attacks they hoped to resume in the coming night. They received a nasty shock when eleven Skyhawks swept in from the mainland and nearly caught them by surprise. Some bombs narrowly missed a British headquarters near Mount Kent where a briefing of senior officers was taking place; several helicopters here were damaged, but there were no casualties. The British artillery continued to fire on the remaining Argentine hill positions and on targets around Stanley, causing a few more casualties. The British also tried out a new weapon when two RAF Harriers dropped laser-guided bombs. There were hopes that these could achieve pinpoint accuracy, and claims were made of direct hits on an infantry Command Post on Tumbledown and an artillery position near Moody Brook, but I have no Argentine reports on these attacks.

Darkness came early; it was nearly midwinter. The final blockade-running air flights into Stanley were carried out by some brave Argentine pilots who had to risk shell fire on the airfield from British warships and the danger of night-flying Sea Harriers. Two Hercules came in just after midnight, carrying a large 155-mm gun and much ammunition for it. The aircrews' efforts were completely wasted; these loads would soon fall unused into British hands. The Hercules returned with seventy-two passengers, mainly sick and wounded but including ten air force ground personnel. It is not known whether this was part of a routine rotation of air force men which had started a few days earlier or a straightforward evacuation, with the air force believing that the end was near; almost all of the pilots in the Falklands had already been evacuated. There was no evacuation of army personnel other than sick and wounded. Staff Sergeant Pons, one of the air force passengers, describes the return flight:[1]

> We waited at the runway head where a beacon had been lit for the Hercules; we had to walk carefully because of the ice. It was a long wait, and we were beginning to despair when we heard the beautiful sound of the aircraft's engines; it was the nicest sound I had ever heard. We helped to unload everything when it landed. A shell fell on my foot, but I didn't care. We were ordered to board, so I committed myself to God. The engines, which had never been stopped, began to be set to full power, and we linked arms for the take-off. All of a sudden the engines stopped. Through the intercom we were told there was a Red Alert signal. We ran towards the shelters; the Hercules remained alone and helpless on the icy runway. We could see the star-shells fired by the British; they were very near. 'They can't destroy the Hercules now,' I thought desperately.
>
> We were given the departure order when the danger was over. We went into the plane as anxiously as before, took our places and began to pray, to pray fervently, because it was our last opportunity. It began to taxi; I think I said around a hundred Our Fathers, and the Hercules took off under the command of Captain Víctor Borchert and co-pilot Captain Hernán Daguerre; it was 21.33 hours. Nobody said a word. An hour later the interior lights were turned on; that meant the danger had passed. Everything was over. We embraced each other excitedly. When we calmed down, our thoughts went back to those who were left behind. At 23.52 hours we arrived on the mainland. My family were waiting for me.

The very last flight to Stanley was made by a naval Fokker F-28 (call sign 5-T-21) in the early hours of 14 June. This aircraft was carrying some army howitzers and Brigadier-General Daher who was attempting to return to his post from his 'last ditch' mission to Buenos Aires. However, the naval pilot was unable to land because the

[1] From the unpublished English translation of *Dios y los Halcones*.

air force Hercules was standing on the runway and so he had to return to the mainland.

In what would prove to be the last Argentine air attack of the war, two Canberras escorted by two Mirages flew from the mainland during the evening, and the Canberras carried out high-level bombing runs over the Mount Kent area, their bombs causing neither damage nor casualties. The British destroyers *Cardiff* and *Exeter*, on station to the south, plotted the flights by radar and launched several Sea Dart missiles. One of the Canberras was hit by *Exeter* at a near extreme altitude of about 40,000 feet, and one of the Mirages only just escaped a similar fate. The pilot of the Canberra, Captain Roberto Pastrán, managed to eject and was eventually retrieved by British forces after the surrender, but his navigator and crew comrade in six years of flying, Captain Fernando Casado, was trapped in the aircraft and presumably died when it crashed into the sea. He was the last Argentine Air Force man to die for the Malvinas.[2]

The British continued their advance that night, 2 Para attacking Wireless Ridge in the north and the 2nd Scots Guards attacking Tumbledown Mountain in the centre. If Tumbledown could be captured quickly, the 1/7th Gurkhas would follow through and assault the smaller position of Mount William. The Argentines expected attacks but believed that the main British effort would be in the south, against Tumbledown and the track which passed a mile and a half south of that hill and led into Stanley four miles away.

The attack on Tumbledown started first. This rocky ridge, a mile and a half long but very narrow, 750 feet high at its most prominent points, completely dominated a large area of open ground and was certainly the key point in the remaining defences around Stanley. Some Argentine maps name it Cerro Destartelado – a near-literal translation – but very few of the Argentine soldiers who fought there used that name; most used the English name, usually pronouncing it 'Tumblee-down'.

The Argentine defence sector containing Tumbledown and Mount William had been occupied by the 5th Marine Infantry Battalion ever since that unit arrived in the Falklands as Argentine's response

---

[2] The lost Canberra carried the Argentine serial B-108; it had been WH 886 when it served in the RAF with Nos 44, 73 and 207 Squadrons.

# Final Actions, 13 to 14 June

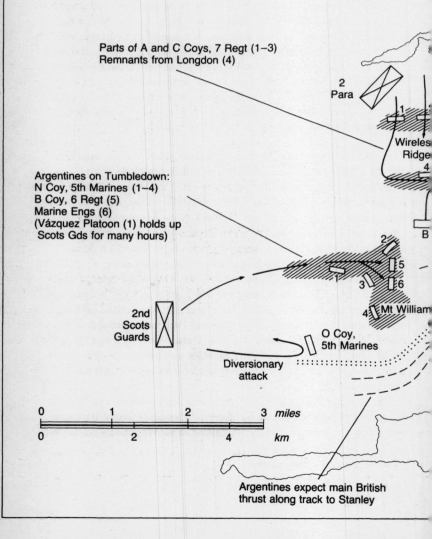

Parts of A and C Coys, 7 Regt (1–3)
Remnants from Longdon (4)

2
Para

Wireless
Ridge

Argentines on Tumbledown:
N Coy, 5th Marines (1–4)
B Coy, 6 Regt (5)
Marine Engs (6)
(Vázquez Platoon (1) holds up
Scots Gds for many hours)

B

Mt William

2nd
Scots
Guards

O Coy,
5th Marines

Diversionary
attack

0        1        2        3  *miles*

0            2            4  *km*

Argentines expect main British
thrust along track to Stanley

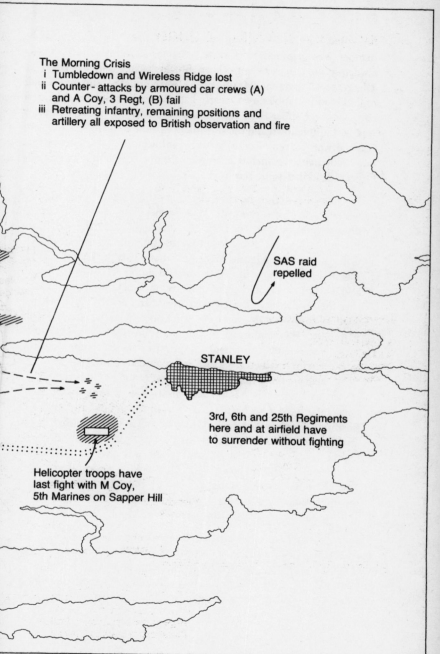

The Morning Crisis
  i Tumbledown and Wireless Ridge lost
 ii Counter-attacks by armoured car crews (A)
    and A Coy, 3 Regt, (B) fail
iii Retreating infantry, remaining positions and
    artillery all exposed to British observation and fire

SAS raid
repelled

STANLEY

3rd, 6th and 25th Regiments
here and at airfield have
to surrender without fighting

Helicopter troops have
last fight with M Coy,
5th Marines on Sapper Hill

to United Nations Resolution 502 in early April. The battalion commander was Commander Carlos Robacio, short in stature, nearly always smiling, an efficient officer. But Robacio's unit was covering a large area. Battalion Headquarters were situated one and a half miles behind Tumbledown, nearly halfway back to Stanley. M Company was on Sapper Hill, even nearer to Stanley. Only N Company was on Tumbledown and the sub-hill of Mount William. O Company – actually only a reinforced platoon – had been the battalion reserve, but Lieutenant-Commander Antonio Pernias, the unit's Operations Officer, describes some recent changes:

> We had been following carefully every move the British made from Goose Green onwards. We assumed they knew the location of most of our positions. In the night after the British attacks on Mount Longdon and the other hills, we sent O Company to near Mount William so that a part of the battalion was in a place where the British would not expect it to be. We also moved most of the 106-mm mortars on the assumption that the British had located their posts. It worked; the British artillery continued to fire on the empty positions but not on the new ones. We reinforced N Company on Tumbledown and formed some new counter-attack groups near Battalion Headquarters with marines and with the Panhard armoured car crews.
>
> We also assumed that the British attacks were being made on a step-by-step basis, taking one position at a time and then consolidating it. Our basic policy was to try to hold any of our positions which were attacked until dawn, in the hope that the British would withdraw if they failed to complete the position's capture. My assessment for this night was that the British would attack Tumbledown first, then mount a second attack from Two Sisters and Mount Harriet up the track to the south, on to Mount William, then through to Sapper Hill. That was the reason we put O Company forward of Mount William.

The Argentine marines considered themselves to be better troops than the army units and they probably were. Their 'rank and file' were still conscripts, but the marine system of taking in new conscripts steadily throughout the year resulted in the unit having a much higher level of training when dispatched to the Falklands, and there were none of the younger 1963 Class recruits present. Other advantages enjoyed by the unit were its better cold-weather clothing and the fact that it had been allowed to remain intact and had not suffered the numerous detachments of men as had many of the army units; it was also supported by its own Marine Artillery Battery. The unit was fully on the alert as night fell, quite expecting to be attacked that night; one officer says: 'We were all pleased; for better or worse we wanted to get it over.' A few army troops were also present; these were men of the 4th, 6th and 12th Regiments who had escaped from Two Sisters and Mount Harriet two nights earlier. When Brigadier-General Jofre visited Tumbledown that day, he had urged these men to fight hard and avenge their earlier defeat.

The first part of the plan devised by the commanding officer of the Scots Guards was that a diversionary attack should take place along the track south of Tumbledown. This was duly carried out by about thirty spare guardsmen, not men from the main rifle companies. The guardsmen were accompanied by some engineers to deal with minefields and were supported by four light Scimitar and Scorpion tanks, the first time these had been used in the Falklands. It was a clear, quiet night, but very cold, and it would snow later. The diversionary force moved along the track and duly engaged the southernmost elements of the marine O Company on the flank of Mount William. There was a brisk exchange of fire and grenades which went in the Argentines' favour. Two guardsmen were killed and seven wounded. The tanks encountered mines, and one was disabled and abandoned. The attacking force turned back, believing that it had accomplished its diversionary role, but it was pursued by artillery and mortar fire and it ran into another minefield in which two more men were wounded, including one who lost a foot. The British later assumed that they had killed about ten Argentines, but the actual Argentine casualties were one killed and an unknown number wounded. This action did not draw in any Argentine reserves but it may have temporarily focused attention in the south while the main Scots Guards attacking force was approaching Tumbledown. Lieutenant-Commander Pernias was still convinced five years later that the diversion along the track had been intended as the main British move and that, if his O Company had not stopped it, the British would have exploited their progress along the track with vehicles,

naval gunfire support and an eventual helicopter lift of troops to
drive right on into Stanley.

The Scots Guards' plans for the main attack was to tackle Tumbledown's long, thin ridge in three phases, working from west to east,
with each of the battalion's three rifle companies capturing in turn
approximately one-third of the objective. The operation began with
a silent approach by the guardsmen of G Company on to the western
end; but there were no Argentines on that part of the ridge, and it
was occupied without difficulty and without the move being detected.
Left Flank Company now passed through but, after covering part of
the objective, came under a hail of Argentine fire. The fighting
which followed between the attacking Scots Guards company and
the defenders on that part of the ridge would largely determine the
outcome of the whole battle for Tumbledown Mountain.

The British thought there were two Argentine companies on
Tumbledown, but Lieutenant Villabraza's N Company was the only
one present. This was, however, a particularly strong company, with
four instead of the normal three marine platoons, plus a marine
engineer platoon and about fifty men from army units. N Company
was also particularly well supported by mortar and heavy machine-
gun detachments. But nearly all of the company was on the eastern
end of the ridge, deployed to dominate the open ground to the north
and the south, particularly to the south down to the track along
which the main British attack was expected. This left just young
Sub-Lieutenant Carlos Vázquez's No. 4 Platoon to face the Scots
Guards in the middle of the ridge. This was not even a regularly
constituted platoon but had been assembled from spare marines
after the main unit arrived in the Falklands. There were twenty-six
marines and a few marine engineers, with sixteen army men under
their young officer, Second Lieutenant Oscar Silva of the 4th Regiment, who had recently fought well on Two Sisters. This composite
platoon was also facing mainly to the south in the expectation that
the British would attack by day. Vázquez says: 'We expected that we
were going to have a good time there on the high ground, overlooking
the poor guys who would have to fight it out below us.' But the
Scots Guards' attack was coming in from the west and by night.

When I was preparing my first Falkland book, I was fortunate in being able to interview two platoon commanders and three NCOs of the Scots Guards company attacking here and was able to describe the long fight they had.[3] When I went to Argentina, I was equally fortunate in meeting Sub-Lieutenant Vázquez. Here is his account; his description of the fighting conforms closely to that of the Scots Guards:

At about 23.00 one of my men was wounded by shelling, and I moved over to help him. I left my rifle and ran to his position. While I was doing that, the artillery stopped, and I heard a Sterling light machine-gun firing, exactly at the mouth of my foxhole; it had a distinctive sound, and I knew that it was the British. When I peered out of the hole I was in, I could see two British soldiers, one of them smoking, a cigarette in his mouth; they were passing one on each side of my position. With my pistol and a hand grenade, I ran back to my Command Post, probably right through the British soldiers. They didn't react quickly enough. They fired at me and I at them, but no one was hit. There was a star-shell at the time. I couldn't reach my position, so I pretended to be hit and fell as though I was dead. The British soldiers stepped over me. When the light went out, I got up and was able to reach my Command Post. The British crossed right on top of my platoon position and finished up surrounding us. Some of them were actually mixed up with our own positions; there were a lot of rocks and some empty fox-holes. So a fight started all round, at distances varying between ten and fifty metres.

As time passed, there seemed to be more British troops, and they were getting closer. The rifle and machine-gun fire was intense, and there were hand grenades; some phosphorus ones were being used by the British. The marines in the foxhole near me were killed. There were also the little hand-held rockets which they were using, but they were not very effective in my area. One missile hit the machine-gun position in a hole in the rocks near me but it did not explode – but the machine-gunner was killed later. He was Suboficial Castillo; he was considered a hero. There were so many explosions at the height of the

---

[3] On pp. 360–4 of *Operation Corporate* (*Task Force* in paperback).

fighting that I couldn't always tell which weapons were being used. I had a FAL rifle firing anti-tank grenades and hand grenades. The hand grenades were difficult to use because we were on a slope and the combat was so close that the grenades landed and rolled on before they exploded. Also the British soldiers were behind rocks, jumping up and running forward to our positions, and there was no time for grenades to be used properly.

During that first attack, the British showed themselves very confidently. For example, one man on his own made a lone attack on one of our foxholes. It was really one-to-one combat. That kind of tactic was only used in the first rush; they didn't do it later – I think it was too costly. I think the British thought it would be easy at first and they were overconfident. If they had been more careful and had used more hand grenades as they came over our holes, they could have cleared us up. They used a lot of hand grenades against empty positions.

About 01.00 most of the British were occupying positions among our own holes and had our positions covered. I realized we could not survive where we were, so I ordered by radio that the 81-mm mortars start firing on our position. The idea was that, even though it might cause us casualties, it would hurt the British more. That surprised the British and caused some disorder; we were able to open fire again. The British withdrew, to their rear and into higher ground. That was how we drove off the first attack. I think we were more surprised than the British were.

There was a pause then. We started shouting at them, things like 'Bravo' and suchlike. There is an English book which states that the Argentine marines were singing, but that is not true; we were just shouting. Our casualties up to then were light – about five dead and some wounded. I reported the situation by radio to the company commander. He asked me if I would like to withdraw, but I answered that, even though I was not in complete control, the British were leaving, and I would stay put. That was the last chance we had to get out.

At 02.00 sharp, the British attacked again. The fight started in the same way as before, but this time the British were in the rocks above and behind us where they had placed some machine-guns about twenty-five metres behind my position and above us. To start with, I thought it was our engineer platoon which had been supporting us from there earlier. I told the company commander to get them to stop firing. That was when I found out that the engineers had been pulled back, but I hadn't been told. That fire was a nuisance, but I don't know how effective it was because we had no inter-platoon radio; we had to shout orders along the line. One machine-gun in the rocks was firing on my position, and that stopped me shouting my orders. I fired two anti-tank grenades back at it, but that machine-gun was knocked out by a machine-gun on my left which was manned by a young conscript. The use of tracer by the British helped us, first to identify who were the British and, second, when the range was over thirty metres, you just had time to get your head down and take cover when it fired.

The battle went on again until between 02.30 and 03.00, when the situation became so serious that it was decided that our mortars and artillery should fire on our position again. But this time there was less effect on the British because many of them were in as good cover as my men. When the artillery stopped, the fight started again. The British changed their tactics now. They started assaulting our positions from several directions at once. This technique caused us a lot of casualties, and they started taking out our positions one by one. Most of our casualties occurred during that period from 03.00 onwards. It was about then that the army officer Second Lieutenant Silva was killed – fighting like a hero. What happened was that a marine machine-gunner on my right was killed, and the marine who relieved him was wounded. Silva carried the wounded man into cover and returned with one of his soldiers to fire the machine-gun. This man was then killed – the main action was taking place there. Second Lieutenant Silva kept encouraging all his men in that section, encouraging them to carry on fighting. That was very dangerous, because the British were right among those positions. Silva was killed by a shot in his chest and another in his arm. One army soldier came all the way along to me to report this – another outstanding act.

Another thing I remember is ordering one of my 60-mm mortar men – Marine Rotela – to set up his mortar vertically and fire off all his ammunition. He did so and fired fifty-four rounds.

By 07.00 there were only two foxholes left – mine and the one next to it. All our machine-guns were out of ammunition, and the rest of our ammunition was also running out. I had many men wounded. Four British then reached the other remaining foxhole and threw a phosphorus grenade into it; both men inside were wounded, and one was shot with a Sterling as he ran out. I spoke with the battalion commander on the radio at 07.00, reported the position and asked for reinforcements. He said that none were available. I looked out at 07.15, and three British soldiers were knelt there, aiming their weapons at me from two metres away. That was the end for me.

Other Argentine officers freely give credit to Sub-Lieutenant Vázquez and his platoon, including the army men present – 'They were the heroes of Tumbledown.' These men had held up the Scots Guards for many hours, killing five guardsmen and wounding between twenty and thirty others. Of the twenty-six marines in Vázquez's platoon, six were killed and four wounded, while the army men are believed to have suffered up to seven fatal casualties, including Second Lieutenant Silva, and several wounded. This combined marine–army platoon thus suffered more than 50 per cent casualties. Three men were later given high awards for bravery: the marine NCO Julio Castillo, Second Lieutenant Silva and an army corporal; but they were all posthumous awards. Sub-Lieutenant Vázquez and at least two of his surviving NCOs were also decorated.

After Sub-Lieutenant Vázquez's position had been overrun, a counter-attack was ordered. The troops to be used were not the three marine platoons still remaining on Tumbledown but the army men of B Company, 6th Regiment, who were present on the eastern end of Tumbledown under Major Oscar Jaimet and a marine engineer platoon. A keen young army platoon commander, Second Lieutenant La Madrid, one day off his twenty-second birthday, describes what happened:

My platoon was sent in first; it was in the best shape and location. It was dark, but the British were firing star-shells. I

moved off with my men. I had practised a night counter-attack
in cadet school a year before and knew the theory. I had also
taken an infantry company tactics book with me to the Malvinas
and had been studying it. Finally, I had a copy of *Soldado
Aislado* [*The Isolated Soldier*], the translation of an American
manual. My men were willing but they had never seen this
sector in daylight. As for me, I had just received a telegram
from my father, a Professor of History, telling me to fight on to
the end – 'Victory or death – your father will bless you.' I
thought, with that blessing, I was ready to die. I preferred to
die with honour than to be a coward. I couldn't tolerate the
idea of going home without doing some actual fighting.

We moved off through a gap in the rocks; I spread my men
out behind the men who were still fighting. My orders were not
to let anyone pass, not even Argentine soldiers. I went forward
to make a reconnaissance and could see that the British had two
machine-guns and a missile launcher in action. I went through
another gap in the rocks and was surprised by three men speaking in English behind and above me and firing over the top of
me. I could see them with my night binoculars; there were
about twelve of them in all. I was anxious to get back to my
platoon. I took a rifle grenade and fired at where I had seen the
first three men. I heard it explode and some shouts and cries of
pain, and the sound of someone falling down the rocks. I ran
back to my position and ordered my men to open fire. We
stopped them, but they thinned out and came round our flanks;
their deployment was very good. They also engaged us with
light mortars and missile launchers. This went on for a long
time, and we suffered heavy casualties; we had eight dead and
ten wounded. We started to run short of ammunition, particularly for the machine-guns. Also, I could see that we were
outflanked, with the British behind us, so we were cut off from
my company. Some of my men had been taken prisoner.

I reorganized and found that I was down to sixteen men. I
started to retire. The British above me were firing machine-
guns, but we passed close to the rocks, actually under the
machine-gun fire. I left six men in a line with one machine-gun
to cover our retreat, but really we were fighting all the time; we

could not break contact. They came on us fast, and we fell back; it was starting to get light. The whole hill had fallen by then, and we were on lower ground, just south of Moody Brook. We eventually got through to Stanley, through what I would like to say was a perfect barrage fired by the Royal Artillery. We had to wait for breaks in the firing, but I still lost a man killed there. I had thirteen men at the end, from the forty-five I started with, but another seven men joined us later.

Second Lieutenant La Madrid was later decorated for bravery. Another officer involved here, Sub-Lieutenant Héctor Mino, was given the highest award when he reorganized his marine engineer platoon after being wounded in the leg and refusing help for himself until all of his wounded men had received medical attention. These actions, by La Madrid's and Mino's platoons, were probably part of the opposition encountered by the third of the attacking Scots Guards companies (Right Flank Company) which captured the final stretch of the ridge at the cost of several men wounded but no deaths.[4]

So the Argentines lost Tumbledown, but only after a stout and prolonged resistance which upset the British timetable and caused the proposed attack by the Gurkhas on Mount William to be postponed, thus saving M Company of the 5th Marines the attentions of some very aggressive Gurkhas who were anxious to get into action before the war ended. The credit for the defence of this important feature should be shared by Sub-Lieutenant Vázquez's marines and the various army men involved. The three other marine platoons of N Company were never closely involved and they withdrew to Sapper Hill. The exact Argentine casualties on Tumbledown (not counting the earlier diversion on the track to the south) are difficult to establish because so many units were involved, but more than twenty Argentines were killed – six or more marine infantry, three marines from the heavy machine-gun company and an officer and about twelve army men; the army men had done at least as much fighting as the marines and suffered accordingly. Only a few Argentines became prisoners. The Scots Guards casualties on Tumble-

---

[4] The severe wounding here of a Scots Guards officer, Lieutenant Robert Laurence, inspired a play, *Tumbledown*, written by Charles Wood and published in book form by Penguin in 1987.

down itself were five killed in the battle and two killed by mortar fire soon afterwards, with about forty men wounded.

Another battle, nearly as fierce as the one on Tumbledown, was meanwhile being waged a mile or so to the north, where 2 Para was attacking the extensive area known as Wireless Ridge, situated north of the long valley through which the Moody Brook stream flowed. There were actually two parallel ridges running east–west; the southern one was the more prominent but this only reached a height of 300 feet in one place, and the whole position did not compare in any way in height or rockiness with Tumbledown or any of the other hills in the Stanley defences. Again some Argentine maps use a direct translation, naming the area Cordón de la Radio, but I never heard that title used in conversation, only 'Wireless Ridge'.

The area was part of the huge sector defended by Lieutenant-Colonel Giménez's 7th Regiment, which had already lost part of its strength on Mount Longdon. The northern ridge was held by two platoons of A Company and one of C Company; these positions all faced north. The southern ridge, although being a stronger natural feature, was treated as a rear position and only had some of the heavy weapons and a mixture of men, none in a properly formed company. Some of the men here were survivors of the Longdon battle and are described by Major Antonio Perez Cometto, the regiment's Operations Officer, as being of little use; most of them had come back from Longdon without the magazines of their rifles. The area had been heavily bombarded during the preceding day and accurately attacked by RAF Harriers; several men had been wounded and laboriously carried down to the track near Moody Brook where they were loaded into ambulances. In short, this was a sector which had never been given high priority, where the natural defences were not strong and which was weakly held by a tired conscript unit.

It was the bad luck of these Argentines on Wireless Ridge to be attacked by 2 Para, a unit benefiting from the experience of its successful battle at Goose Green, employing a sound plan and supported by four light tanks and much artillery. The story of the main battle can be quickly told on this occasion, because the paras successfully captured both the northern and southern ridges, making very good use of field and naval artillery, the fire of the tanks and their own heavy weapons. The northern ridge fell with the loss of only one para dead to Argentine artillery fire and a few injured; thirty-seven Argentines were captured there. The tanks and heavy infantry weapons then lined up on that ridge and 'shot in' the next para attack, which rolled up the southern ridge from its western end as far as a 'stop line' imposed upon the paras because of another British operation which will be described later. Two paras were killed on the southern ridge, one by stray British shell fire and one by Argentine small-arms fire, this last man being the only British soldier to be killed by Argentine infantry weapons on Wireless Ridge!

The paras halted at a position just short of the 7th Regiment's Command Post, only a few hundred yards from the old Royal Marines barracks at Moody Brook and only two miles from the first houses in Stanley. Most of the defenders who were not casualties left their positions. The last weapons in action were three 120-mm mortars near the Command Post. Two of these dug their base plates too far into the soil during their hectic firing; the third ran out of ammunition. 'And so', says Major Pérez Cometto, 'we lost the battle.' The 7th Regiment's casualties for the night were approximately fifteen killed and many wounded.

The more interesting aspect of the Wireless Ridge fighting from the Argentine side is the mounting of the most seriously pressed Argentine counter-attacks of the war. These were ordered by Brigadier-General Jofre. None of the 7th Regiment's men were in fit condition, but there were two other bodies of troops available. These were seventy 'dismounted' armoured car crewmen who attempted an attack from the direction of Stanley under Captain Rodrigo Soloaga, who was later decorated. This attack was beaten off by 2 Para, and up to six of the armoured car men were killed. The second counter-attack was carried out by A Company of the 3rd Regiment which had tried to move forward by lorry over icy roads during the fighting two nights earlier but had only reached Moody Brook valley. Major Guillermo Berazay was in command of this force. His men were on the southern side of the valley. He had watched the progress of the battles on Tumbledown and Wireless Ridge, each less than a mile away on either side of his men; he was actually on higher ground than Wireless Ridge and could see the action there particularly well:

It was like a theatre; I had never seen anything like it before. After the artillery fire came the fire of the infantry action – a lot of tracer. I could actually see the British working their way along the ridge by the light of the star-shells. Between 03.00 and 04.00 I heard Commander Robacio of the marines telling Jofre on the radio that 'Guillermo' – that was my call sign – could be released to help the 7th Regiment. I thanked Robacio for that doubtful honour.

Jofre told me to prepare my men to cross the valley and then, fifteen to twenty minutes later, ordered me to Moody Brook to meet guides from the armoured car men and a company from the 25th Regiment which Jofré was sending. I got to Moody Brook, but there were no guides from the armoured car people – they were already in action – nor anyone from the 25th Regiment. I reported all this to 'Oscar' – Jofre's call sign. 'OK,' he said. 'Just go up the hill and you will meet Colonel Giménez.'

The tracer fire seemed to have died down, so I presumed that the British had taken all of the hill. I placed the company commander and the heavy weapons in a fire support base among the trees around a small house. Nothing happened for a few minutes, so we moved forward with the machine-guns but got no more than a hundred metres when the British opened up. I ordered the officers to take the rifle platoons up – not in column but in line.

Private Horacio Benítez was in one of the rifle platoons:

We were lined up – the whole company in one long line. There were no trees, no rocks, no cover of any kind. It was like a Christmas party; everything was flying – machine-gun tracer crossing between both sides, mortars, rocket launchers. That valley was more than a kilometre wide. We had to go downhill first, across the valley and then up the other side. When we reached the foot of the ridge, the British fired star-shells which turned night into day. We stopped and looked at each other, saying, what do we do now? We could see three British machine-gun posts which opened fire on us. Then we saw that the British came into the open and were firing small hand-held missiles. From below, they were like a ball of fire coming towards us. We had never seen anything like it; we did not have weapons like that in our army. It was so desperate that some of the men rushed back; the British fire followed them. They didn't know which way to run.

The rest of us started to go forward again, but only about twenty men got to the top; I was one of them. Six of us split into two groups. My group stayed while Lieutenant Aristiaga [5] and two men went round to the right. The first of them to be hit was Rinaldi, hit in the knee. Then Lieutenant Aristiaga was hit in the neck, the bullet hitting his rosary beads. While that was happening, we moved up. There was a machine-gun position which I got behind; I was only a few metres away from them but I was able to climb up under the fire because of the slope of the ground. Sergeant Vallejos told me to open fire with my FAP.[6] I fired a magazine of twenty rounds; when I was replacing the magazine, it seemed to me that the British were laughing. I opened fire again. Then the British rushed at us. I fired another magazine and then got into some cover. They started throwing grenades at us. Next to me was another boy called Aumassane. A grenade fell near him, and the force of the explosion blew him up into the air. He was badly hurt; he had six lumps of metal in his back. He walked across to me – he didn't know what he was doing – and told me he was going back. He gave his rifle to one man, his ammunition to another and off he went. Then another grenade came, a phosphorus one, and his clothes were on fire. We told him to get away because he was like a torch. He started to roll over the ground and tear his clothes off. I don't know how he saved himself. We did crazy things – we were so desperate.

The fighting went on. The British were in the rocks in front of us. One of our men, Ricardo Barrios, was also in the rocks not far from the British and was firing anti-tank grenades at them with his rifle. Perhaps the British thought there were many more of us – but we were only a few. On our side, we

---

[5] Diego Aristiaga's name is sometimes misquoted; even Menéndez in his memoirs called him 'Arreseigor'.

[6] FAP – automatic rifle on a bipod.

thought it was only a patrol in front of us, but it was the whole of that Parachute Battalion, and we didn't know it. We had no communication with our headquarters. We were isolated. I was trying to get some ammunition from a dead man. I got a handful but, when I had filled my magazine and was loading my weapon, I looked up and the British were right in front of me; one was pointing his rifle at me and he opened fire. The bullet hit the side of my helmet, entered and ripped my ear and lodged at the back of my head. That finished me off.

Three men from this company were killed and many more injured in this counter-attack. An officer from 2 Para described these counter-attacks as 'quite sporting efforts, but without a sporting chance'.

(The conscripts of the company which carried out this counter-attack were a well-knit group, all having been on the verge of release from their unit when sent to the Falklands. This was the only real fight by their regiment during the war, and the wounded conscripts finished up in the same military hospital in Argentina. Many were youths from poor districts of Buenos Aires and they experienced difficulty in obtaining employment after the war; there was at least one suicide and several mental breakdowns. Horacio Benítez and some of the other wounded in hospital decided to try to keep in touch, with the intention of providing mutual support. The Mayor of Buenos Aires provided them with a disused garage rent free for ten years, and here they set up the 'Veterans of the Malvinas Co-operative' which operates both as a trading and as a social centre. It was still going strong five years after the war but only, as one member says, 'after much work and self-sacrifice'.)

The failure of the counter-attacks on Wireless Ridge represented a crisis for the Argentine command. Its first planning had envisaged an attack on Stanley from a sea-borne landing in the south; and then, after the San Carlos landings, the main threat was seen as coming in from the south-west, along the track south of Tumbledown Mountain. The Argentines had disposed of their forces accordingly. (It should be stated that a steady stream of minor diversionary moves by the British had been intended to strengthen these Argentine misconceptions.) Now the British appeared to have broken through on this weak and unexpected sector. There were no natural defences between 2 Para and Stanley, only open ground dotted with artillery positions.

Brigadier-General Jofre reacted vigorously to the apparent threat. He spoke personally on the inter-unit radio net that was still operating, stating that any man seen giving an order to withdraw that was not confirmed by radio was to be shot on the spot. Major Berazay was ordered to take those of his men who had survived the counter-attack to form a 'blocking position' between Moody Brook and the town. Berazay did this and placed his men just in front of the 105-mm guns of the 4th Mobile Regiment which had been firing all night in support of the Wireless Ridge battle. The artillery unit's commander was Lieutenant-Colonel Carlos Quevedo. Only one of his guns remained in action; of the remainder, some had dug themselves into the peaty ground with the constant firing, and the others' breeches were jammed. Jofré ordered Quevedo to fall back to the town with his men, but the artillery officer asked for permission to remain with the last gun, to help cover Berazay's men. Carlos Quevedo would like it to be known that he was not 'serving the last gun', as legend has stated, but simply remaining with its regular crew. (Lieutenant-Colonel Quevedo and Major Berazay were both decorated after the war. They were just about the only officers of their ranks to receive medals; nearly all officers above the rank of major considered themselves fortunate if they avoided being court-martialled.)

Jofre believed that these recent moves had stopped a British advance on Stanley, at least for the time being. The Argentines did not know that 2 Para had been ordered not to move beyond their present position on Wireless Ridge. The reason for this was that the SAS and some Royal Marines were mounting a raid from the north on Cortley Hill ridge, a long, narrow piece of land running from Moody Brook to form the northern arm of Stanley Harbour. The SAS enjoyed a certain measure of independence, and the operation they mounted was more of a hindrance than a help to the main efforts of the night, forcing 2 Para to halt their advance and requiring artillery support when it ran into trouble.

Cortley Hill ridge was manned by B Battery of the 101st Anti-Aircraft Regiment whose eight Hispano-Suiza 30-mm guns and some

12.7-mm machine-guns formed the northern arc of Stanley's anti-aircraft defences against low-flying aircraft. But Jofre had also ordered that the battery provide the local ground defence and had sent along two mortars which had once belonged to the Royal Marine garrison at Stanley and a marine infantry party. The S A S set off in three raiding craft but had to pass near the moored hospital ship *Almirante Irizar*. A member of the ship's crew was a commando-trained soldier. Without thinking of the rules of the Geneva Convention or asking anyone's permission, he grabbed a radio, called the call sign of the Argentine unit on the ridge and warned them of the raid. Major Jorge Monge, the sector commander, alerted all his positions and ordered them to open fire. The raiding party was driven off, lucky to escape with only three men wounded and some damaged boats. The anti-aircraft battery suffered no casualties in the raid but did have two men killed by some British artillery 'overs' from the Wireless Ridge Battle. Brigadier-General Jofre later sent Major Aldo Rico and his commando company (the 602nd Commando Company) to search the ridge in case any British troops had got ashore there.

# **18** · The End

With the coming of daylight on Monday 14 June, events unfolded with dramatic suddenness. The soldiers of both sides who had endured the weeks of boredom, exposure, fatigue, hunger and danger were now to see a lightning-swift end to their ordeal.

The collapse had started with the loss of Wireless Ridge, which left the British there able to dominate all the open ground to the west of Stanley. (See 'The Morning Crisis' on the map on page 253.) The whole of the Argentine defence system on that side of the town was now outflanked. Large numbers of Argentine soldiers started streaming back from Moody Brook, Tumbledown and Mount William. The British on Wireless Ridge opened fire with every weapon they had; artillery fire was added, and even four Scout helicopters appeared and carried out missile and machine-gun attacks – the first time that helicopters had dared appear over the battlefield in daylight since Carlos Esteban's men had shot down two Gazelles at Port San Carlos on the morning of the British landings. Private Juan Diez was one of the men who had earlier taken part in the counter-attack on Wireless Ridge; now he found himself on the receiving end of a helicopter attack:

We fell back to Moody Brook, handed over our wounded and started making our way back towards Puerto Argentino because of the fire from the ridge. Suddenly a helicopter appeared from behind the ridge. It fired a missile which hit one of our men in the stomach and cut him into two parts – a direct hit. I was thrown over by the blast and also hit in the arm and the heel by the machine-gun fire with which the helicopter was spraying the ground; another bullet grazed my waist. I wanted to live, so

I hopped all the way into Puerto Argentino and eventually reached the kelpers' hospital there. I was looked after by an Argentine doctor and a civilian who gave me a direct blood transfusion. So now I have English blood in me and I should really take a nice cup of tea in the afternoon. The pain set in after a bit; it was terrible until they gave me some morphine.[1]

Brigadier-General Jofre realized that any defence positions in this open ground were now untenable. He gave Major Berazay permission to withdraw his men to the edge of Stanley and also ordered Lieutenant-Colonel Quevedo to abandon his last serviceable gun and bring its crew back to the town.

There remained only one tenable defence position to the west of Stanley – Sapper Hill, a small, grassy eminence 453 feet high, situated a mile to the south-west of Stanley. M Company of the 5th Marine Infantry Battalion was well dug in here and reasonably safe from the mayhem of British fire falling in the open ground. Other marines from Tumbledown and Mount William had also gathered here. The British commanders realized that a swift attack on Sapper Hill might succeed in capturing this last position in front of Stanley. 45 Commando was ordered to push along the track towards the hill as fast as possible, and the Welsh Guards were given some helicopters and ordered to land on the track, outside the range of the weapons on Sapper Hill, to prepare an attack. It should be explained that, after the *Sir Galahad* disaster, two Royal Marine companies were attached to the Welsh Guards from 40 Commando, which had been left in the rear to defend the San Carlos base area. Three Sea King helicopters (from a unit whose main duty before the war was the training of anti-submarine helicopter pilots) picked up the first lift of the Royal Marines attached to the Welsh Guards and brought them, not to a safe distance from Sapper Hill, but to the track right at the foot of the hill. The Argentine marines opened fire, hitting one of the helicopters and wounding one Royal Marine in the arm. The British returned the fire and killed three Argentines. The British

---

[1] Juan Diez, who must have been a typical *chico* conscript, was absolutely fascinated to be visited at the Malvinas Veterans' Co-operative in Buenos Aires by an English writer. He often laughed and joked and was teased by the other members present. My Argentine lady interpreter commented: 'They are still boys, really.' That meeting brought home to me the youth and innocence of so many of the Argentine conscripts who were thrust into a war against units of Britain's professional army.

were still in an exposed position so they radioed for artillery fire to be brought down on to the hill. But the artillery officer at the company headquarters handling the request suddenly shouted: 'Check firing. Check firing. There are white flags in Stanley.' A cease-fire had been agreed. (There were actually no white flags in Stanley; that oft repeated report was a mistake.) The time was between 1.00 and 1.30 p.m.

The last shots of the war had been fired. It is ironical that the final encounter had taken place on, or almost on, the route taken by Pedro Giachino and his Amphibious Commando for their attack on the Royal Marines at Government House on the night of the Argentine invasion ten and a half weeks earlier, and that marines of both sides were now involved in this final clash at Sapper Hill. Conscript Marines Roberto Leyes, Eleodoro Monzón and Sergio Robledo were the last Argentines killed in action in the war. (Some Argentine officers made the complaint to me that their men on Sapper Hill were killed after the cease-fire and that this was the reason why this little fight was not recorded in any British history of the war, but it is quite clear that the cease-fire order reached the British troops after the helicopters landed them too close to the hill and after firing by both sides had taken place.)

Major-General Moore's staff had been trying to contact Brigadier-General Menéndez through the civilian radio station at Stanley since at least 9.00 a.m. Initially, Menéndez did not respond. His long-term plan for this situation was that he would withdraw his forces east of Stanley and fight on from the airfield peninsula. He had always promised the people of Stanley he would not fight in the town. Menéndez's own memoirs [2] show that he spoke by radio telephone to Galtieri that morning; the conversations – there may have been two calls – were inconclusive. Galtieri could not believe that the situation was so desperate and insisted that the Argentine units should be attacking, not falling back. Menéndez was equally insistent that the situation was hopeless and he urged Galtieri to make a statement finally agreeing to accept the United Nations Resolution 502 of early April which called for a voluntary Argentine withdrawal from the islands; this would save Menéndez from the ignominy of

---

[2] Carlos M. Turolo, *Malvinas – Testimonio de su Gobernador* (Sudamericana, 1983), pp. 305–6.

surrender. Menéndez still had nearly three full regiments of infantry which had not yet fired a shot, together with some artillery, the armoured cars and the air force personnel at the airfield. He could evacuate Stanley and hold out a little longer if Galtieri would use the time to make a political move, but Galtieri would not agree to something which would probably lead to his own downfall as President and he refused Menéndez's plea. So Menéndez took his own decision.

Captain Barry Melbourne Hussey was the officer listening at the radio shack to the British suggestions and taking them back to Menéndez at Government House. This is Hussey's description:

Menéndez would not get involved but told me to let the civilian operator keep in touch. Doctor Bleaney, the young lady doctor, was also helping.

The events of the previous night and of that morning are something that you have to live through to understand. The way people were fighting, the casualties and the thunder of the big guns going off all night, the tracer, the star-shells – all this would give any military commander an unmistakable picture of the real situation. Brigadier-General Menéndez was on the spot; he could see everything that was happening, was receiving all the messages. Brigadier-General Jofre was telling him that all his positions had been overrun. The plan to fall back and fight on from the airfield was overtaken by events. All our positions – not the town – were under shell fire.

When Menéndez finished talking to General Galtieri, he told me to go back to the radio and tell the British that he was willing to discuss terms. I spoke myself; I felt it was my responsibility, not that of the civilian radio operator, to tell the British that Menéndez was ready to talk. We arranged a time and a route for their helicopter to come in. I think I was talking to Rod Bell.[3]

Several hours would elapse before the helicopter arrived. The British troops came up to the western end of Stanley but were ordered not to go into the main part of the town; this was a cease-fire, not yet a surrender. Stanley remained full of Argentine troops

[3] Captain R. D. Bell, Royal Marines, a fluent Spanish speaker.

all during that day and the next night. Here are some of their experiences. Major Berazay was the officer who had organized a counter-attack on Wireless Ridge the previous night and then tried to form a blocking position outside Stanley until ordered to withdraw:

> I got back to the edge of the town, and the British stopped firing. I lined my men up and led them into the town. I have to admit that I was in tears. I had not been able to do any fighting myself. I had not even seen a British soldier, but I had lost a lot of men. I would have much preferred to be fighting myself with my own weapon.
>
> I left my men in the town and went to report to Jofre. He embraced me, and I told him what had happened. He told me to report back to my regiment, which was forming a final defence line on the edge of the town. I never completed that task. While I was getting some food for the men, I heard from the radio that all military operations must cease. I felt bad – not for the officers and NCOs – we were professionals – but for the young soldiers, and also for the people back at home. They would perhaps think that we had not fought properly.

Adrián Gómez-Csher was a conscript of the 7th Regiment who had fought on Mount Longdon and was now at a collecting point for men of various units in Stanley:

> They kitted us out with new equipment and clothes, and then there was a quick Mass at which a chaplain gave general absolution and a sermon; he thought that the fighting would continue. I can remember what he said. He started off as though he was talking to some children. Then he changed his tone and said that we had to go back and fight and that we should never surrender. Our cause was just. We had to kill as many British soldiers as possible, to regain the islands that were ours. God would understand and forgive us. I knew by then that a lot of what we were being told was all lies, so I didn't accept what the chaplain said.

Javier Pereda was a radio operator on the hospital ship *Almirante Irizar* which was in Stanley Harbour:

We took our first wounded in on that day. I noticed that most of them only had slight wounds, usually from shell fragments. Many of them were very thin and hungry, and yet there were containers full of food at the edge of the harbour, and we had 500 tons of food in the ship. The army conscripts were talking openly; their view of the war had completely changed. They had a big resentment against their officers; many men told me that they had come to hate their officers more than the British. They had a high regard for the professionalism of the British; it was as though the British were fighting a different war.

I was listening to news on the radio from all sources; I had to pass details of what was happening to the captain. I compared three things: the BBC World Service, our own Argentine News Agency and what I could actually see outside for myself. I was horrified to know the truth of what was happening and to compare that with what the people in Argentina were being told at that time.

Private Mario Prado had come back to Stanley with trench foot:

I could not be treated because there were so many wounded. I was sent with other oddments to man the shoreline in Stanley Harbour. They gave me a rifle. I got to my position, cleaned up the rifle but found that it had no firing pin so I threw it away into the sea. The only thing left for me to do would have been to load the magazines of the other men in my position.

Suddenly everything went quiet, and we were ordered to concentrate in the town, in a large wool store near the Post Office. There was a mass of men there from different units; it was like an anthill. Later in the day an officer opened one of the containers nearby and started handing out food the likes of which had not been seen before, certainly not by the soldiers up in the hills. I got a five kilo cheese and five kilos of a favourite Argentine jam, sweet potato jam. But we didn't feel like eating; we were very nervous. We were all wondering what would happen – would we be left there, sent back home or kept somewhere else as prisoners?

There was a lot of wool in that store, and we covered ourselves with it – and that is how we spent a nice warm night, the first for a long time, and peaceful because it was the first night without any firing.

The commander of the 602nd Commando Company, Major Aldo Rico, is reputed to have spent part of this time on a radio link with the mainland, urging that reinforcements be sent to continue the fight and calling for the court martial of the officers who were considering surrendering. This was the basis for much of his later 'Malvinas hero' reputation and for exaggerated reports in some press articles that he continued active resistance after the surrender.

Major-General Moore and a small negotiating team arrived by helicopter in the late afternoon and met Menéndez and some other Argentine officers in the Secretariat Building; this was the place into which the Argentine civilian administration team had moved ten weeks earlier to establish the new rule over the islands. Major-General Moore would not allow British cameramen to record the ceremony; he did not want to give Menéndez any grounds for objection or delay. Observers who saw the two teams enter an office comment on the contrast between the British officers, in dirty combat dress, straight from service in the field, and the smart uniforms of the Argentine officers who had been able to remain in Stanley. Jeremy Moore brought a simple, typed 'Instrument of Surrender' and invited Menéndez to sign it. Menéndez objected to the word 'unconditionally' before 'surrender', and Moore allowed the word to be struck out. Menéndez then dashed off a scribbled signature, surrendering all his forces. The fantastic episode of a war to decide the sovereignty of the Falkland Islands was over. That place would not, at least in the foreseeable future, become the 'Malvinas'.

# 19 · The Reckoning

The surrender was followed by several days which brought appalling administrative problems to be solved by people who were often quite exhausted by the recent fighting. The main difficulty was to find accommodation in and around Stanley for the soldiers of both sides, most of whom had spent several weeks in the open. Winter had now arrived, and snowfalls were frequent. There was just not enough shelter on the Falklands for the 1,500 local people, the 5,000 or so British troops and double that number of Argentines. On the morning of 15 June, Menéndez, the two other army brigadier-generals and the senior naval and air force officers met Major-General Moore, who informed them that they would be transferred immediately by helicopter to HMS *Fearless* in San Carlos Water and that most of the ordinary Argentine prisoners would have to leave Stanley and go out to the airfield peninsula, which would become a huge prisoner-of-war camp until arrangements could be made to return them to Argentina. Moore hoped that he could return every Argentine prisoner as quickly as possible in order to relieve his problems of accommodation and supply.

And so the Argentines left Stanley that day. It was decided that either Brigadier-General Jofre or Parada would remain at Stanley to co-ordinate the move of the Argentine units and their settlement around the airfield. Jofre volunteered to do this because most of the men involved were from the brigade he had brought from Argentina. Thousands of Argentine soldiers piled their weapons into huge heaps and filed out of Stanley along the airport road under the escort of Royal Marines or paras – a very visible act of defeat. The Argentines did not like the paras, frequently complaining of unduly rough treatment at their hands, but they spoke well of the Royal Marines. Jofre says that the clearance process went much more smoothly when the Royal Marines took over completely from the paras after he complained. His own relations with the British officers he had to deal with he describes as 'courteous, but with cold courtesy'. The ordinary Argentine soldiers were bewildered by the turn of events. One conscript says: 'I know it sounds funny, but until I became a prisoner of war I could not really believe that I was in a war, not in just another military exercise. Also, until that day, I never believed that we could lose.' Another says: 'The concept of prisoner of war was something unimagined by most of the soldiers because Argentina had never been in a war. We could not imagine the state of being a prisoner until it happened.'

The Argentines around the airfield undoubtedly suffered hardship during the next few days, most of them having to exist in tents, corrugated iron shelters, holes in the ground or wooden crates. Conditions were little worse than those experienced earlier in the hill defences, but it was colder now. A massive helicopter lift and transfer by launch soon commenced, and most of the prisoners were transferred directly to the liner *Canberra* and the North Sea ferry *Norland* which would take them home. The British had decided to give priority in the use of these ships for repatriating Argentine prisoners before returning their own men to England.

The men from the Stanley area were not the first Argentine prisoners to go home. The army and air force men captured at Goose Green on 29 May had sailed in the *Norland* a few days earlier and had disembarked at Montevideo in Uruguay on 13 June. The Argentines sent a small merchant ship and a passenger excursion ship to ferry the 1,536 men the short distance across the River Plate to their homeland later that day. The arrival in Argentina of this large number of defeated troops was most embarrassing for the junta, which had not yet prepared the nation for the imminent collapse in the Falklands. Instead of coming to Buenos Aires, the ships were ordered to nearby La Plata and docked at the Río Santiago shipyard, a deliberately isolated location. The Argentine Army sent no one to meet them; the only person of authority to greet these men who had fought for the 'Malvinas' was the local harbour-master! Lieutenant-Colonel Piaggi and the army men were transported quietly to a Non-Commissioned Officer Training School; and, even there,

no one from Army Headquarters met them, only the colonel commanding the school. Two days later, these men were home with
their families just as the news of the general surrender in the Falklands was released to the people of Argentina.

The *Canberra* started the main repatriation when she sailed with a
full load of junior officers, NCOs and conscripts on 18 June. *Norland*, with a smaller load, sailed the following day; the men from the
outlying garrisons at Fox Bay, Port Howard and Pebble Island were
mostly in the *Norland*. These ships could have sailed earlier, but the
authorities in Argentina were reluctant to give permission for their
reception. The country was undergoing an upheaval; a huge psychological shock was being experienced. In the course of one week
the emotions of the people were subjected to the euphoria of the
Pope's visit, the shattering news of the surrender in the Falklands,
the dismissal of their President – for Galtieri was forced to resign on
17 June – and now thousands of defeated troops were about to be
ignominiously transported home in British ships.

The Argentine soldiers spent a quiet two days on that voyage,
apprehensive over what kind of reception would greet them in
Argentina. Private Mario Prado describes the voyage:

> There were some British soldiers guarding us who could speak
> a few Spanish words and they were saying: 'Tierra Argentina
> land, off, off', and making signs that the people at home would
> be cutting off our heads when we reached Argentina. We knew
> that wasn't true of course, but it didn't cheer us up. But they
> did treat us very well in the *Canberra*. The food was good, and
> at lunch and dinner we were given two cigarettes each and then
> allowed out on the deck for ten minutes, because we were not
> allowed to smoke in the cabins.
>
> The cabin had a double bed and a single bed for nine of us,
> but the floors were nicely carpeted, and we all slept on the floor
> so that there wouldn't be any arguments about who had the
> beds. We played cards a lot – *truco* – a favourite Spanish card-
> game. It is a noisy game, and the guards used to come in and
> play a bit as well, also to have a crafty smoke with us.

The *Canberra* docked at the private wharf of a large aluminium
company at Puerto Madryn in the southern province of Chubut.

Ironically it was only a few miles from the Valdés Peninsula where, earlier in the year, the 2nd Marine Infantry Battalion had rehearsed its Falklands landing on ground similar to that near Stanley. Private Alan Craig describes the arrival:

> There was no one there to meet us. We were put into lorries. It is quite a distance from the port to the town, and a lot of people lined the road into town and were throwing biscuits and other gifts to us. They all seemed to be very poor people, so I started to think that what the officers had said about the conscripts being blamed for the defeat was a lie. At the town, all the people were waiting for us, cheering. But we were put into a large shed so that we couldn't talk to them. Then the people we could see across the road started to ask for our phone numbers so that they could phone our families. Some men managed to get out and they gave our numbers to them. Later, when we were being loaded on to the lorries, the people were right up to the fence, and we gave them more numbers. One lady phoned my home and gave the news to my sister, together with news of two more local boys.
>
> Then we were flown to El Palomar at Buenos Aires and all taken to the large army camp at Campo de Mayo where we were housed in the NCO Training School. We were fitted out with *their* uniforms; I think the army did not want to reveal to the public where the conscripts were. We were all fed, attended to like kings in fact; we had never been treated like that before in the army. There were psychological tests, but they were not popular because the doctors tried to tell us that we were speaking untruths about our experiences over there – so we shunned those tests. We were there two days, not allowed to phone home. Our parents at La Plata were getting restive. One boy got out and went home, and a group of parents from La Plata turned up at Campo de Mayo; there was some unrest among the men, and eventually we were released.
>
> We were all awarded Malvinas campaign medals, but I didn't go to get mine. I wasn't interested; I thought it was all balls. I didn't want any medals.

Alan Craig's unit at La Plata was a local one. Those from outlying

cities were soon transferred to their home bases and received raptur-
ous welcomes there. The conscripts of the 1962 Class, like Alan
Craig, were all released immediately; the 1963 Class would have to
complete the remainder of their year of service. The small number
of returning air force men were taken to the NCO School at Ezeiza
Airport; there were no problems about their reception. The reputation of the Argentine Air Force stood very high in public opinion; it
was the Army which was believed to have failed the nation and lost
'the Malvinas'. The Navy, which had started the whole crusade, had
few prisoners returning and was able to avoid the spotlight of public
attention and instant recrimination.

The homecomings were marred for the families of many of the
officers because hardly anyone above the rank of lieutenant was
among the returning prisoners. Major-General Moore had wanted
to return all prisoners to alleviate his administrative problems, but
he had been ordered by London to retain 500 of the most senior
officers 'as a bargaining counter' until Argentina declared that hostilities were ended; there was still the theoretical danger of Argentine
air attack on British ships around the Falklands. So twelve full
colonels, twenty-five lieutenant-colonels and a host of majors and
captains were transferred to the *St Edmund*, a British Rail ferry ship
anchored off San Carlos, where they had a boring, miserable time,
not knowing how long their imprisonment would last. The Argentines called this prison ship 'the pig pen'. Menéndez and the other
more senior officers were still held in HMS *Fearless*. A few technical
NCOs were also kept back for various reasons. One of the senior
officers mentioned earlier in the book avoided this prolonged detention. Lieutenant-Colonel Quevedo, the artillery officer who stayed
with his last serviceable gun on the last day of fighting, was suffering
from a stomach complaint and was urgently in need of a further
operation; he was quickly repatriated on the hospital ship *Almirante
Irizar*.

The wives and families of the officers kept back by the British
became very anxious. Rumours circulated that the prisoners were in
poor condition, and the lists of those held showed some in-
consistencies; it was not known whether some officers were alive or
dead. General Nicolaides, the Army Commander-in-Chief, attended

a series of meetings with wives in the various garrison towns. When he came to Paso de los Libros to meet the wives of the III Brigade units, he was given a particularly hard time by Alicia Gorriti, whose husband Lieutenant Gorriti was the only junior officer of the brigade and the only officer at all of the 12th Regiment not to have returned. (He was the lone officer left behind at Mount Kent when his company was helicoptered into Goose Green on the day of the battle there; all the other officers of the regiment had been captured at Goose Green and returned to Argentina before the end of the war.) Spirited Señora Gorriti demanded that General Nicolaides reveal how many prisoners of war Argentina was holding. The answer was 'one' – Flight Lieutenant Jeffrey Glover, the RAF Harrier pilot shot down at Port Howard on 21 May. This answer was greeted with derision, but it was noticed that those wives who were ambitious for their husbands' careers kept quiet, not wanting to spoil future promotion hopes. But the British failed to persuade Argentina to declare that hostilities were over, and the 500 officers were taken back home in the *St Edmund* a month after the other prisoners. The total number of Argentine servicemen taken prisoner in the Falklands was just over 12,700.

A little-publicized event took place on Cook Island far away in the South Sandwich Islands. The British ships *Endurance* and *Yarmouth* reached that place on 20 June, and some Royal Marines took prisoner, without a fight, the eleven naval personnel manning the scientific and weather station established there by Argentina in 1976. Three British flags were left flying. So ended the Argentine control of the Falklands, South Georgia and that last remaining place in that huge area of the South Atlantic which Argentina claimed and had hoped to retain. I asked Vice-Admiral Lombardo whether Argentine ships had been back to Cook Island since. 'Not to my knowledge,' was his guarded reply.

But 655 men did not come home. These were the Argentine war dead. They were divided among the various services shown in the table on the following page.

('NCOs, etc.' includes all non-commissioned professional men. The two civilians lost in the *General Belgrano* are included in 'Merchant Navy, etc.' Of the 288 conscripts, 224 were from the 1962

Class, 54 from the 1963 Class and 10 from earlier classes who had deferred their service. The fatal British casualties were 255, a figure which includes the three Falkland Islanders killed by shelling.)

| Service | Officers | NCOs, etc. | Conscripts | Total |
|---|---|---|---|---|
| Navy | 9 | 227 | 103 | 339 |
| Army | 16 | 35 | 148 | 199 |
| Air Force | 36 | 13 | 6 | 55 |
| Marines | 1 | 3 | 31 | 35 |
| Merchant Navy, etc. | 2 | 16 | — | 18 |
| Gendarmería Nacional | 2 | 5 | — | 7 |
| Coast Guard | — | 2 | — | 2 |
| Totals | 66 | 301 | 288 | 655 |

Looking at the different services, the heaviest losses of both sides were at sea, with 323 Argentine deaths on the *General Belgrano*, 21 on the *Isla de los Estados*, 8 on the *Alférez Sobral* and one each on the *Narwal* and *Río Iguazú* off the Falklands and on the *Guerrico* and *Santa Fé* in South Georgia – a total of 356. (The British deaths at sea or on ships bombed in Falkland harbours were 197 men.) Other naval deaths were four naval pilots and one seaman from a small naval detachment ashore at Fox Bay who probably died as a result of British naval shelling.

The fatal casualties of the Army, the Marines and the Gendarmería Nacional in land action numbered 239 – one in the initial landing in Stanley, 2 in South Georgia, 228 in the main campaign in the Falklands and 8 in a helicopter which crashed while searching for a suspected British landing party on the mainland. (British fatal casualties on land were 82.) The Argentine deaths in the main land campaign can be subdivided as follows:

| | |
|---|---|
| Infantry | 165 (including marines) |
| Artillery | 18 (11 anti-aircraft, 7 field) |
| Special forces | 12 |
| Engineers | 7 |
| Helicopter crews | 6 |
| Others | 20 |

The heaviest losing units were obviously those directly facing British attacks:

7th Regiment     36 (Mount Longdon and Wireless Ridge)
12th Regiment    35 (Goose Green)
4th Regiment     23 (Two Sisters and Mount Harriet)
5th Marines      17 (Tumbledown and Sapper Hill)

The total number of Argentine pilots and other aircrew killed was 45 – 41 air force men and 4 from the naval air arm. (Four British pilots were killed, one by ground fire at Goose Green and three in accidents. The figures of both sides quoted here do not include casualties in helicopters; the British suffered much heavier casualties in helicopters than did the Argentines.) The Argentine Air Force also had fourteen men killed on the ground in the Falklands, divided, it is believed, between one officer and ten men killed in bombing and shelling incidents and three men killed in the fighting at Goose Green. (Lieutenant Jukic, killed by bombing in his Pucará while trying to take off from Goose Green, is counted as an aircrew casualty.)

The bodies of the dead and of many of the pilots whose planes crashed into the sea were never recovered. The men who died on land in the Falklands remain there. The British traced most of the battlefield graves after the war and offered to return the bodies for burial by families in Argentina, but the Argentine Government refused, stating that the Falklands were Argentine territory and that the bodies should remain there. Pedro Giachino, killed at Government House on 2 April, was the only dead Argentine to be taken home. The British made a cemetery at Darwin and transferred to it the remains of more than 230 bodies. This represents more than 90 per cent of the known Argentine dead. But less than a hundred of the bodies could be identified, the highest number of unidentified being army men who did not have reliable identification tags.

The Argentine material losses were colossal. One cruiser, one submarine, three transport ships and the trawler *Narwal* were all sunk or otherwise lost; three smaller ships were left behind in the Falklands to be captured by the British. Aircraft losses were heavy: 75 fixed-wing aircraft and 25 helicopters. (Total British aircraft losses from all causes were 34: 24 helicopters and 10 Harriers.) Forty-five of the Argentine fixed-wing aircraft were lost while flying in action; 24 of these were shot down by Sea Harriers, the remainder by other means. Of 59 ground-attack aircraft and helicopters taken to the Falklands, only two air force Chinooks and a naval Aeromacchi returned to the mainland.

The material losses of the Argentine Army can be quickly dealt with. Everything taken to the Falklands was lost except for the clothes each man wore when he returned home. The equivalent of three brigades of troops had lost every single weapon and piece of equipment.

The Argentine effort had been a failure, both politically and militarily. The junta had miscalculated the reaction of Britain, of the United States and of much of the remainder of the world. Everyone had been vividly reminded of Argentina's claim to the Falklands, but her use of military force had brought few allies. Apart from her South American neighbours, just about the only country to give active help was Libya – not the most reputable country to have as a friend.

The armed services had tried hard but had clearly been outclassed by the opposing British forces. The Navy, which started the war, gave up any attempt at offensive action as soon as the *General Belgrano* was sunk, and the fleet was then restricted ignominiously to the coastal waters of the mainland. The marine unit with the land force fought well in its one battle at Tumbledown, although most of its fighting was done by a single platoon reinforced with army men. The Aeromacchis and Turbo-Mentors of the naval air arm sent to the Falklands and the handful of old Skyhawks transferred from the aircraft-carrier to a mainland airfield had all been outclassed by the British defences, although the Skyhawk pilots did have one glorious day when they sank HMS *Ardent*, but at a cost that was so crippling that their unit became non-operational during the period when its anti-shipping expertise was most needed. The only unqualified success for the navy was its Super Étendard unit, which made good use of its limited number of Exocets, sinking two ships. The lesson here is that if one wants to wage modern war one needs modern weapons.

The next service to become heavily involved was the Air Force. The courage shown by the Argentine pilots will always be admired, but historical comment should look more carefully at the effectiveness of that courage and the sacrifice of so many pilots' lives.

In reality, the wartime admiration for the Argentine pilots concealed an extensive failure. Let the various types of air operation be examined. The attempt to assert superiority in the air defence role had to be abandoned after the failure of the Mirages and Daggers against the Sea Harriers on 1 May, the first day of real action, and it was never seriously attempted again. This left the fighter-bomber units committed to the dangerous role of ship attack. It was this ship-attack period which attracted so much publicity, but the tactics employed – extreme low-level approach – were not suitable, and too many bombs failed to explode. More than 150 Skyhawk and Dagger sorties were dispatched in anti-shipping bombing attacks. Approximately 100 of these reached the target area. It is believed that 16 aircraft dropped bombs which hit 14 ships (9 warships, 4 landing ships and a landing craft) with 25 bombs; *but only 11 of those 25 bombs were dropped properly and exploded on contact*. The only ship sunk outright by the Air Force was the *Coventry*, although one bomb contributed to the loss of the *Ardent*, and the unexploded bombs in *Antelope* destroyed that ship when British attempts to disarm the bombs went wrong.

In other types of operation, the only 'success' in the high-altitude Canberra bombing operations was the attack on the neutral super-tanker *Hercules*; several Canberra night attacks on British land positions caused hardly any damage or casualties. Similarly, twenty-four Pucarás sent to the Falklands for ground-attack operations lost two pilots and all the aircraft, for the solitary success of shooting down a Scout helicopter during the fighting at Goose Green. The only unqualified success for an Air Force unit can be attributed to the aircraft and crews of the 1st Air Transport Group, particularly to the Hercules aircraft of that unit which performed so steadfastly and effectively in the air-supply and tanker roles, as well as contributing some valuable reconnaissance work. It would be a reasonable Argentine comment, however, that the range from the mainland at which the Air Force was forced to conduct many of its operations was the cause of some of its difficulties, and in general the Air Force was forced to fight a war that it had not sought and for which it was unsuited. Also, if the British task force had not contained the Sea Harriers – the vital aircraft of the Falklands war – the outcome of the air war would have been much different.

But, in the end, the main burden of the war fell on the Army units in the Falklands. One might feel a little sympathy for the commanders and much compassion for the ordinary soldiers left stranded in the islands to face a series of battles which ended in defeat and surrender. Little of the public attention and sympathy from Argentina ever fell upon that far-away army. While warships and aircraft returned to port or home airfields, the cold and hungry soldiers had to stay out on those bleak Falkland hills. The Argentine soldiers never had a chance of beating the British units once the British were established ashore. The Argentines may not have been very well trained or equipped but they conducted themselves with some bravery and honour, and there were no outrages against the civilian population.

Galtieri's junta fell, to be replaced by a new military junta which appointed a retired general, Reynaldo B. Bignone, as President, but this was only a transitional measure; the war would bring an end to military rule in Argentina and the return of democratic government. The armed services were beset by outside criticism and by internal dissension over the shame brought upon the nation by the failure in the war. The Bignone Government decided that scapegoats should be found and penalties applied, so it established what became known as the Rattenbach Commission which, under Lieutenant-General Benjamín Rattenbach, was ordered to determine who was responsible for the failure. The members of the former junta and every senior officer involved in the war, whether on the islands or operating from the mainland, came under investigation. The commission found that all of the junta members, together with Doctor Costa Méndez – their Foreign Minister – Vice-Admiral Lombardo, General García, Brigadier-Generals Menéndez, Jofre and Parada and two full colonels who served in the Falklands were among those who would be charged with various degrees of failure; the only army officer of lesser rank to be charged was Lieutenant-Colonel Piaggi, the commander at Goose Green. A long procession of spasmodic court appearances followed, firstly before the Supreme Council of the Armed Forces and then before the civilian Federal Chamber of Justice. The three junta members who started the war are still (October 1988) in military detention pending appeals of their prison sentences. Brigadier-

General Jofre was absolved of blame but chose to retire in 1983. Lieutenant-Colonel Piaggi was forced to resign his commission and retire. The cases against Vice-Admiral Lombardo and Brigadier-Generals Menéndez and Parada were still progressing sluggishly when I was in Argentina in 1987.

There was one semi-amusing incident. The Argentina civil affairs team who had been in Stanley during the war had an Argentine bank account to pay for the various supplies and services purchased locally and to pay compensation for damage to civilian property. Cheques on this account had been paid to 400 Falkland people or firms and these were later cleared through the normal international banking system. When these cheques reached the Argentine bank after the war the bank workers' union made a public complaint that Colonel Chinni, the team's treasurer, and other officers had paid Argentine money to the enemy. The officers concerned were amazed to find themselves before a court, but it was eventually accepted that they had done no more than their duty and had abided by international law. They were exonerated.

Most of the men who had served in the Falklands resumed their careers or, in the case of the conscripts, returned to civilian life. The conscripts often experienced emotional difficulties settling down again or had difficulty obtaining work. They are bitter at the large employers who appeared on television during the war, promising that no Malvinas veteran – particularly the disabled – would ever want for employment after the war, and the conscripts were also angry at the organizers of the Patriotic Fund to which thousands of ordinary people had donated money and valuable items of jewellery during the war but the proceeds of which did not find their way to the men who suffered most. They compare their treatment with the high esteem shown in Britain for Falkland veterans, the huge welcoming displays to returning ships and units, the grants made by the South Atlantic Fund and the Falkland Victory Parade in London. There was nothing like that for the Argentine soldiers who returned from the war. The volatile public which had demonstrated so jubilantly when Rear-Admiral Büsser's marines seized Stanley in April did little for the defeated army which came home in June.

Argentina still persists with its claim to the Falklands. I dare not forecast the future. On my visit, I found charming, helpful, hospitable people, with not an ounce of hostility, but still with an implacable belief that Argentina should have the islands. I probably spoke with a hundred people; only two of these admitted that the Malvinas claim should be dropped on practical grounds; both were careful to make that statement when no one else was listening. The Malvinas dream is like a national article of faith. It is a highly emotional subject – very like an article of religious faith which must never be challenged; there appears to be no open national discussion on it. I found also an economically distressed country, with inflation running at a rate of 12 per cent *per month*. As I write this last chapter, in 1988, leading British banks are currently writing off large sums of money owed by chronic debtors like Argentina. This means that British people – bank customers and shareholders, and taxpayers who will have to make up the tax shortfall because of the bank write-offs – will be helping to pay for Argentina's side of the Falklands war as well as their own!

I always end my books with comments made by the ordinary people who took part in the events I have been describing.

First Lieutenant Ignacio Gorriti, 12th Regiment:

At the first of several meetings I had with Mr Richard Stevens at Estancia House, I asked him what he thought about us being there. He said he wanted everyone – the English and the Argentines – to leave and for the islanders to be left alone. I told him that we would be staying and making improvements, building roads and suchlike. He replied: 'Look, if I wanted to live in a place with roads, I would go there. But I like it here and I want to be left alone.'

I was very sad to leave Mount Kent because I loved being in the Malvinas and particularly being out in that countryside with just the men of my own company, away from all the regimental surroundings. When I die, I want my ashes to be scattered on Mount Kent.

Major Guillermo Berazay, 3rd Regiment:

I often spoke with a lady whose house we used – a nice woman. When the naval shelling started, she told me that she would not

be talking to me again but that she would like to say this:
'Geographically this may be considered part of Argentina, but
this small boy is the third or fourth generation to be born here.
We feel that the country belongs to us – not to England, not to
Argentina – because we were born here, we live here and also,
as you can see, I am a forty-year-old woman and I look sixty
because life here is very hard, but nobody has ever cared about
us.'

Private Adrián Gómez-Csher, 7th Regiment:

When we first arrived in the Malvinas, the general feeling was
that the war – such as it was – was over; it had been won for
Argentina on 2 April. I only realized I was in a real war long
after I returned home when I started to analyse what had
happened to us. I thought that what we were doing at the time
was right, because our Government had told us that it was
right. But now I realize that so much of what we were told was
rubbish and I think it was all wrong. It was a political mistake
to go to war; they didn't realize who they were going to war
with.

Anonymous senior officer:

When I came back from the war I discovered that the enemy
was not the British, but those who had taken Argentina into
that situation. The relationship we had with the British forces
was completely normal, but our relationship with some of our
own superiors was completely abnormal. We were the victims
of lies and were shunned. The junta and people at other levels
all lied to the country. A lot of my fellow officers would say the
same thing – or at least they would think it.

Sub-Lieutenant Cárlos Vázquez, 5th Marine Infantry Battalion:

I have always admired the British, and it made me very sad that
the only war I ever fought in was against the British.

Second Lieutenant Augusto La Madrid, 6th Regiment:

I think the British fought well; I had a sporting respect for
them, just like opponents after a good rugger match, even if

you have lost. But I have not lost hope that one day I might fight again in the Malvinas with better equipment, better training and settle the debt for those of my men who died there.

# Appendix: Order of Battle of Argentine Units

The purpose of this Appendix is to list all Argentine units actively involved in the South Georgia and Falkland Islands operations between 2 April and 14 June 1982, together with details of their service and of their casualties.

## Argentine Navy (Armada Argentina)

(In listing various operations in which ships took part, 'Task Force 40' was the ships of the amphibious landing force which put troops ashore near Stanley on 2 April 1982, and 'Task Force 20' was the covering naval force at that time; 'Task Force 79' was those ships sent to sea at the end of April and in early May in attempts to engage the approaching British Task Force.)

*Alférez Sobral*   Patrol vessel. On air-sea rescue duty when attacked by Lynx helicopters on the night of 2–3 May. The ship was badly damaged, and the captain and seven men were killed.

*Almirante Irizar*   Polar vessel. Part of Task Force 40, in which its Puma helicopter was damaged in a storm. Became a hospital ship, arriving in the agreed 'Red Cross Box' on 11 June.

*Bahía Buen Suceso*   Fleet transport. Took the Davidoff scrap-metal party to South Georgia in March. Carried supplies to the Falklands, arriving 12 April, then retained for local work. Attacked by Sea Harriers at Fox Bay on 16 May and abandoned; two men were injured. Used by Sea Harriers for target practice after the war and sunk.

*Bahía Paraíso*    Polar vessel. 23–26 March, took small marine party to South Georgia, then assisted in capture of Grytviken on 3 April. Carried out supply runs to the Falklands late in April. Helped in rescue work of *General Belgrano* survivors 3–4 May. Became a hospital ship in late May; carried much-needed food supplies to Stanley and evacuated wounded and sick. Repatriated many men to Argentina after the cease-fire.

*Cabo San Antonio*    Amphibious landing ship. Carried most of the landing force which seized Stanley on 2 April. Transported army and marine equipment to Stanley in further voyages but probably not used after mid-April.

*Comodoro Py* and *Segui*    Destroyers. Both in Task Force 20 and Task Force 79 as aircraft-carrier escorts. From mid-May to the end of the war operated in mainland coastal waters, mainly as radar picket ships.

*Comodoro Somellara* and *Francisco de Gurruchaga*    Patrol vessels used for air-sea rescue duty on air routes to the Falklands; also took part in the search for survivors from the *General Belgrano*.

*Drummond* and *Gránville*    Frigates, though classed as corvettes in the Argentine Navy. Late March, ordered to South Georgia but never proceeded on that task, being retained for Task Force 40. Both ships were in Task Force 79 as a surface-attack group but made no contact with British units. Restricted to mainland coastal waters for the remainder of war.

*General Belgrano*    Cruiser. Her first war cruise was in Task Force 79. Torpedoed and sunk by HMS *Conqueror* on 2 May; 323 crew members were lost.

*Guerrico*    Frigate (corvette). Took part in the capture of Grytviken, South Georgia, on 3 April; damaged by Royal Marines weapons, and one seaman was killed. In Task Force 79 as part of surface-attack group but saw no action.

*Hércules* and *Santísima Trinidad*    Destroyers of British Type 42 design. In Task Force 40, when *Santísima Trinidad* was flagship and landed Amphibious Marines near Stanley. In Task Force 79 as part of aircraft-carrier group; *Hércules* was nearly able to launch a Sea Dart at a Sea Harrier, but eventually neither ship saw action.

*Hipólito Bouchard* and *Piedra Buena*    Exocet-equipped destroyers. In Task Force 20. With *General Belgrano* when the cruiser was sunk in Task Force 79.

*Isla de los Estados*    Naval transport. Part of Task Force 40, carrying stores and food for the first Argentine garrison. Made further supply voyages from the mainland. Sunk by HMS *Alacrity* in Falkland Sound on the night of 10–11 May; 22 men were killed and only 2 survived.

*Punta Medanos*    Fleet tanker. Supported Task Forces 20 and 79 but then suffered a mechanical breakdown which prevented her from being used later in the war.

*San Luis*    Submarine. On war patrol north of Falklands from mid-April to mid-May. Twice fired torpedoes at British ships but without success.

*Santa Fé*    Submarine. In Task Force 40, landing the Buzos Tácticos beach reconnaissance party. Carried a platoon of marines to South Georgia, arriving 23 April, but was attacked by British helicopters while leaving on 25 April and disabled. One seaman was badly injured in the attack and another was accidentally shot and killed by his guard when the submarine was being moved after capture. Scuttled off South Georgia in 1985.

*Veinticinco de Mayo*    Aircraft-carrier. In Task Forces 20 and 79. Her reconnaissance aircraft carried out useful flights on 1 May, detecting British task force ships, but the Skyhawk strike unit could not be launched. Returned to port on 4 May, transferred her aircraft to shore bases and took no further part in the war.

*Falklands Naval Base*    The Argentine Navy established a shore base at Stanley – the Base Islas Malvinas – under the command first of Captain Antonio Mozarelli and then of Vice-Admiral Edgardo Otero. One seaman detached to Fox Bay was killed, probably by British naval gunfire.

## Coast Guard (Prefectura Naval Argentina)

*Islas Malvinas*    Patrol vessel. Sent to Falklands in April for local duties. Captured by the British at the end of the war and used by the Royal Navy as HMS *Tiger Bay*.

*Río Iguazú*    Patrol vessel. Sent to the Falklands in April for local duties. Attacked by Sea Harriers on 22 May while carrying guns and stores to Goose Green; one seaman was killed. Now a wreck at Goose Green.

The Coast Guard also sent two Skyvan transport aircraft and a Puma helicopter to the Falklands. One Skyvan and the Puma were destroyed by naval shelling at Stanley airfield and the second Skyvan by the SAS at Pebble Island. The crews suffered no casualties.

One Coast Guard man was among the dead when the *Isla de los Estados* was sunk.

## Merchant and Other Civil Ships

*Formosa*    ELMA cargo ship. Carried army equipment and food to Stanley in April. Attacked in error by Argentine Skyhawks on 1 May but suffered no casualties. Returned to the mainland.

*Lago Argentino* and *Río Cincel*    ELMA cargo ships. Carried air force stores to Stanley in early April and returned to the mainland.

*Narwal*    Stern fishing trawler. Used for intelligence-gathering. Attacked and damaged by Sea Harriers on 9 May, then captured by Royal Marines. One seaman died of wounds. Sank while under tow the following day.

*Puerto Rosales*    Commercial tanker. Refuelled *General Belgrano* and her escorts in the Task Force 79 operation.

*Río Carcaraña*    ELMA cargo ship. Carried military stores (and television sets) to Stanley in late April; later sent to Falkland Sound, where the ship was attacked by Sea Harriers on 16 May. The ship was damaged and abandoned but remained afloat, attracting various further attacks by the Royal Navy and by Argentine aircraft, being finally sunk on 23 May by missiles fired by a British helicopter.

*Río de la Plata*　ELMA cargo ship. Observed and reported British task force ship movements off Ascension Island until 'warned off' on 24 April.

*Yehuin*　Small oil-rig tender. Sent to the Falklands for minelaying and inter-island supply. Captured at the end of the war and sailed under British control as *Falkland Sound*.

*Forrest* and *Monsunen*　Small coasters owned by the Falkland Islands Company, taken over by the Argentines for inter-island work. *Monsunen* was damaged and ran ashore when attacked by British helicopters on 23 May but was repaired after the war.

### Marines

(The following details will be included where possible for Marine and Army units: Argentine titles of units, names of commanding officers and peacetime bases in Argentina.)

*South Georgia*　The marines who served in South Georgia were a small number of the Buzos Tácticos landed by the *Bahía Paraíso* and commanded by Lieutenant Alfredo I. Astiz, and a reinforced platoon of the 1st Marine Infantry Battalion based at Puerto Belgrano, commanded by Lieutenant Guillermo J. Luna and taken to South Georgia in the submarine *Santa Fé*. Two conscripts of the latter group were killed in the attack on Grytviken on 3 April.

*2nd Marine Infantry Battalion* (Batallón de Infantería de Marina 2)　Commander: Commander Alfredo Weinstabl. Home base: Puerto Belgrano. Captured Stanley on 2 April. One man was slightly wounded.

*Amphibious Commando Company* (Compañía de Comandos Anfibios)　Commander: Lieutenant-Commander Sánchez Sabarots. Home base: Mar del Plata. Attacked Moody Brook Barracks and Government House at Stanley on 2 April. One officer died of wounds in the attack on Government House.

*Tactical Divers* (Buzos Tácticos)　Commander: Lieutenant-Commander Alfredo R. Cufré. Home base: Mar del Plata. Provided the beach reconnaissance party for the 2 April landings. No casualties.

*Marine Field Artillery*   A Battery of the Marine Field Artillery Battalion (Batallón de Artillería de Campana de Marina 1), with six 105-mm guns, was part of the 2 April landing force. Its commander was Lieutenant Mario F. Pérez. There were no casualties, and the battery returned to its home base at Puerto Belgrano.

B Battery, commanded by Sub-Lieutenant Mario R. Abadal, of the same unit arrived in the Falklands later in April and formed part of the Stanley defences. Two conscripts were killed.

*Amphibious Vehicles Battalion* (Batallón de Vehículos Anfibios) Commander: Lieutenant Mario D. Forbice. Home base: Puerto Belgrano. The unit's Amtracs put the main landing force ashore on 2 April and helped capture the airfield and Stanley town. There were no casualties.

*5th Marine Infantry Battalion* (Batallón de Infantería de Marina 5)   Commander: Commander Carlos H. Robacio. Home base: Río Grande. Moved to the Falklands on 8–12 April and manned the Tumbledown Mountain sector of the Stanley defences. Fatal casualties: two NCOs and fifteen conscripts.

*Marine Machine-Gun Company* (Compañía de Ametralladoras 12, 7) An improvised company made up from personnel of the Marine Headquarters Battalion (Batallón Comando) at Puerto Belgrano and commanded by Sub-Lieutenant Sergio A. Dacharry. Equipped with twenty-seven 12.7-mm machine-guns. Intended for the support of the 5th Marines, but some teams were detached to other defence sectors around Stanley. Fatal casualties: seven conscripts.

*Marine Anti-Aircraft Unit*   A detachment of Batallón Antiaéreo de Marina. Commander: Lieutenant-Commander Hector E. Silva. Home base: Puerto Belgrano. Fatal casualties: two conscripts.

*Marine Amphibious Engineer Company* (Compañía de Ingenieros Anfibios de Marina)   Commander: Lieutenant-Commander Luis A. Menghini. Home base: Puerto Belgrano. Operated in the Stanley defence area. Fatal casualties: one NCO and three conscripts.

## Argentine Army (Ejército Argentino)

Overall command of the 'Malvinas Theatre of Operations' was exercised by General Osvaldo J. García, the commander of the V Corps area on the mainland. Two officers, an NCO and five conscripts from the staff of a military school in that area were killed in a helicopter crash on 30 April while searching for a suspected British landing party.

The initial army units sent to the Falklands after the 2 April landings were drawn from IX Brigade, whose commander, Brigadier-General Américo Daher, briefly became the Land Force Commander and later served as Brigadier-General Menéndez's Chief-of-Staff.

*III Brigade*    Commander: Brigadier-General Omar E. Parada. This brigade moved from its peacetime bases in Corrientes Province to the V Corps area to replace units sent to the Falklands and to guard the coastline and the frontier with Chile. The brigade was then ordered to the Falklands with little warning, arriving in the islands between 24 and 29 April, The brigade's units then became dispersed, and Brigadier-General Parada and his headquarters became responsible for Agrupación Litoral, the large area outside the Stanley sector, although Parada's headquarters remained at Stanley.

The major units of III Brigade will be listed elsewhere, but the following minor units suffered fatal casualties: Brigade HQ Defence Platoon – four conscripts (three on Mount Harriet, one at Stanley); 3rd Logistic Battalion – one corporal; 3rd Sanitary Company – one sergeant, one conscript.

*X Brigade*    Commander: Brigadier-General Oscar L. Jofre. This brigade moved from its peacetime locations in Buenos Aires Province to the Falklands in response to the news that the British were dispatching a task force. The brigade's units crossed between 11 and 16 April and were all located around Stanley. Brigadier-General Jofre and his brigade headquarters later took command of all army units in the Stanley area, and he was responsible for the defence of that area.

Fatal casualties suffered by minor brigade units were: Brigade

HQ – two conscripts; 10th Logistic Battalion – two NCOs, one conscript; 10th Signals Company – one conscript.

*3rd Regiment* (Regimiento de Infantería Mecanizado 3) Commander: Lieutenant-Colonel David U. Comini. Home base: La Tablada, X Brigade. Occupied the defence sector south and south-west of Stanley. Suffered five fatal casualties – all conscripts – four of them when A Company took part in the Wireless Ridge battle.

*4th Regiment* (Regimiento de Infantería 4) Commander: Lieutenant-Colonel Diego A. Soria. Home base: Monte Caseros, III Brigade. B and C Companies initially occupied the Mount Challenger–Wall Mountain–Mount Harriet sector facing the coast to the south, but then abandoned Challenger and Wall and took over Two Sisters to form a new layer of defence facing the British advance from San Carlos. A Company, however, was always on detached duty in the Murrell Peninsula north of Stanley, where it saw little action.

B and C Companies fought the battles on Mount Harriet and Two Sisters on the night of 11–12 June, and some men of C Company who escaped from Two Sisters also fought on Tumbledown Mountain two nights later. The regiment suffered twenty-three fatal casualties – two officers, four NCOs and seventeen conscripts.

*5th Regiment* (Regimiento de Infantería 5) Commander: Colonel Juan R. Mabragana. Home base: Paso de los Libros, III Brigade. Stationed at Port Howard, West Falkland, throughout the war and not involved in major action but shelled and bombed at various times. Fatal casualties: eight conscripts, due, it is believed, mostly to naval shell fire, though one man died in Argentina after being evacuated sick.

*6th Regiment* (Regimiento de Infantería Mecanizado 6) Commander: Lieutenant-Colonel Jorge Halperin. Home base: Mercedes, X Brigade. One company of the 1st Regiment was attached to the unit while it was in the Falklands. The main part of the 6th Regiment was allocated to the coastal defence sector south-east of Stanley, where it saw no major action, although it suffered regularly from naval shelling. B Company was detached to the 5th Marines soon after its arrival in the Falklands, was present on Two Sisters when that position was attacked but escaped to Tumbledown where it carried out a counter-attack during the fighting there two nights later. The regiment's fatal casualties were two sergeants and eleven conscripts (one a 1st Regiment man), mostly suffered in the Tumbledown counter-attack.

*7th Regiment* (Regimiento de Infantería Mecanizado 7) Commander: Lieutenant-Colonel Ortiz N. Giménez. Home base: La Plata, X Brigade. Allocated the long sector north-west of Stanley which included Mount Longdon and Wireless Ridge. Suffered fatal casualties of one officer, two NCOs and thirty-three conscripts, mainly in the Longdon and Wireless Ridge battles; these casualties were the highest of any Argentine unit in the Falklands.

*8th Regiment* (Regimiento de Infantería 8) Commander: Lieutenant-Colonel Ernesto A. Repossi. Home base: Comodoro Rivadavia, IX Brigade. Started crossing to the Falklands soon after the United Nations debate of 3 April to demonstrate Argentina's determination to remain in the islands. The main part of the regiment was sent to Fox Bay in West Falkland, where it saw no major action and suffered no fatal casualties. No. 3 Platoon, C Company, was sent to Goose Green later in April to strengthen the defence of the air base there and was involved in the battle at Goose Green in which a corporal and four conscripts of the platoon were killed.

*12th Regiment* (Regimiento de Infantería 12) Commander: Lieutenant-Colonel Italo A. Piaggi. Home base: Mercedes, III Brigade. Crossed to the Falklands on 24 April, one of the last major reinforcements. Most of the regiment was sent to Goose Green, but B Company was detached to the Mount Kent–Mount Challenger area as a protective force for the helicopter park there and as a potential helicopter-borne reserve. The main part of the regiment fought the battle of Goose Green on 28 May. Most of B Company was helicoptered to Goose Green on the evening of that day, but too late for the main action. The regiment surrendered the next morning. A small element of B Company did not reach Goose Green and was involved in the fighting on Mount Harriet on the night of 11–12 June. The regiment's fatal casualties were four corporals and thirty-one conscripts, all or nearly all from A and C Companies at Goose Green.

*25th Regiment* (Regimiento de Infantería 25) Commander: Lieutenant-Colonel Mohamed A. Seineldin. Home base: Sarmiento, IX Brigade. C Company came to the Falklands with the original invasion force, and one platoon landed in an Amtrac and occupied Stanley airfield in the early hours of 2 April. The remainder of the regiment came across by air later in the day. C Company was then sent to Goose Green as the first garrison there, later providing part of Eagle Detachment at Port San Carlos which was in action with Royal Marines on Fanning Head in the early hours of 21 May. C Company later fought in the battle of Goose Green, where an officer, four NCOs and eight conscripts were killed. The main part of the regiment was meanwhile allocated to the defence sector on the Stanley airfield peninsula, where it endured shelling and bombing but, it is believed, suffered no fatal casualties and was not involved in any direct action with British troops.

*3rd Artillery Regiment* (Grupo de Artillería 3) Commander: Lieutenant-Colonel Martín A. Balza. Home base: Paso de los Libros, III Brigade. Transferred to X Brigade when that formation crossed to the Falklands in mid-April. Equipped with 18 105-mm Otto Melara field guns. Four 155-mm guns of the 101st Artillery Regiment were later brought to the Falklands and came under the regiment's control. The unit saw much action in the defence of the Stanley area. Fatal casualties were one officer killed on Mount Longdon in the night battle on 11–12 June and a corporal killed by shell fire at the Regimental Command Post on either 12 or 13 June.

*4th Air Mobile Artillery Regiment* (Grupo de Artillería Aerotransportado 4) Commander: Lieutenant-Colonel Carlos A. Quevedo. Home base: Córdoba, IV (Airborne) Brigade. Transferred to III Brigade for the Falklands campaign. Most of the regiment's 18 105-mm guns were deployed around Stanley, but four guns of A Battery were later sent to Goose Green, where they became involved in the battle, and the guns and crews were forced to surrender. The main part of the regiment took part in the defence of Stanley, in which three conscripts were killed.

*601st Anti-Aircraft Regiment* (Grupo de Artillería Defensa Aerea 601)   Commander: Lieutenant-Colonel Héctor L. Arias. Home base: Mar del Plata. Equipped with twelve twin 35-mm Oerlikon guns with Skyguard radar, three 20-mm Rheinmetall guns, and one Roland and three Tiger Cat missile launchers. Most of the unit was located around Stanley, but No. 3 Section of B Battery was sent to Goose Green with two pairs of Oerlikons. The unit's fatal casualties were an officer, a sergeant and two conscripts killed in the Shrike missile attack carried out by a Vulcan bomber in the early hours of 3 June, and two further conscripts killed in other incidents.

*B Battery, 101st Anti-Aircraft Regiment*   Commander: Major Jorge Monge. Home base: Ciudadela, Buenos Aires Province. Equipped with eight 30-mm Hispano Suiza guns and ten 12.7-mm heavy machine-guns. Located on the Cortley Hill peninsula north of Stanley Harbour, where the unit had little opportunity for action until it helped to repel the SAS raid on the last night of the war. One corporal from the unit was killed in the *Isla de los Estados* and two conscripts by British shelling on the last night of the war.

*601st Combat Aviation Battalion* (Batallón de Aviación de Combate 601)   Commander: Lieutenant-Colonel Juan C. Scarpa. Home base: Campo de Mayo. One Puma was destroyed by Royal Marine fire in the Argentine capture of South Georgia on 3 April. The helicopter force which served in the Falklands consisted of nine Hueys, five Pumas, three Augustas and two Chinooks; all were lost in the Falklands, either being destroyed in action or crashes or being captured by the British at the end of the war. A further Huey crashed on the mainland on 30 April while searching for a suspected British landing party. The unit's fatal casualties were two officers and a sergeant in the mainland crash and an officer and two NCOs in a Puma shot down by a Sea Dart fired by HMS *Coventry* on 9 May.

*9th Engineer Company* (Compañía de Ingenieros de Combate 9) Commander: Major Oscar M. Lima. Part of the original occupation force, arriving in the Falklands on 2 April. Sent to provide the first garrison at Fox Bay, later sent detachments to Port Howard and Goose Green. No fatal casualties.

*10th Engineer Company* (Compañía de Ingenieros Mecanizada 10)

Commander: Major Carlos R. Matalon. Served in the Stanley area; two conscripts were killed.

*601st Engineer Company* (Compañía de Ingenieros de Combate 601)   Commander: Major Jorge L. A. Etienot. Mainly employed in the hill positions west of Stanley; sometimes used as infantry because of a shortage of engineer material. One platoon was involved in the battle on Mount Longdon, where the company's only fatal casualty, a conscript, may have occurred.

*601st Commando Company* (Compañía de Comandos 601)   Commander: Major Mario Castagneto. Arrived in the Falklands in mid-April. Used in small detachments; no fatal casualties.

*602nd Commando Company* (Compañía de Comandos 602)   Commander: Major Aldo Rico. Believed to have arrived at Stanley in late May and to have operated only in East Falkland. Suffered fatal casualties of two officers and three sergeants in various actions with British special forces.

*601st National Guard Special Forces Company* (Compañía de Fuerzas Especiales 601 de Gendarmería Nacional)   Carried out various duties in the Falklands. Two officers, four NCOs and a *gendarme* were killed in a helicopter crash on 30 May.

*10th Armoured Car Squadron* (Escuadrón de Exploración de Caballería Blindada 10)   This unit, under Major Alejandro D. Carullo, came to the Falklands with twelve Panhard armoured cars and was located in and around Stanley. Some of the crews were used in a counter-attack on Wireless Ridge on the last night of the war, and three NCOs and three conscripts were killed either at that time or in other incidents.

*181st Military Police Company* (Compañía de Policía Militar 181)   Commander: Major Roberto Berazay. Carried out provost duties in and around Stanley. No fatal casualties.

The following army units or detachments of units also suffered fatal casualties: Armed Forces Technical Investigation Centre – one officer (in *Isla de los Estados*), one sergeant; Headquarters 1st Armoured Car Brigade – one conscript; 181st Armoured Reconnaissance Detachment – one officer; 181st Signal Battalion HQ – one conscript; 601st Logistic Construction Battalion – one officer; General Roca Military College – two officers, one sergeant, five NCOs (in helicopter crash on the mainland).

## Argentine Air Force (Fuerza Aerea Argentina) [1]

*1st Air Transport Group* (Grupo 1 de Transporte Aéreo)   Home base: El Palomar, Buenos Aires; most operations to the Falklands during the war were from Comodoro Rivadavia, though the tanker aircraft, the Hercules KC-130s, usually operated from Río Gallegos. The unit operated seven Hercules C-130s, two KC-130s and three Boeing 707s, which were heavily used in various transport, reconnaissance, air-refuelling and other duties during the war. One Hercules C-130 was shot down by a Sea Harrier while flying a reconnaissance mission on 1 June; the crew – three officers and four NCOs – were all killed.

*1st Aerial Photographic Group* (Grupo 1 de Aerofotográfico)   Home base: Paraná. The unit contained four Learjets. Clandestine photographic flights of the Stanley area were carried out before the 2 April invasion and then, during the war, more photographic work and some 'pathfinding', when formations of attack aircraft were given navigational help in their approach flights to the Falklands. One Learjet was shot down by a Sea Dart while flying a photographic mission on 7 June; the crew – three officers and two NCOs – were killed.

*2nd Bomber Group* (Grupo 2 de Bombardeo)   Home base: Paraná. Seven Canberra B-62s (ex-RAF aircraft) were deployed to Trelew for war operations under the command of Major J. A. Chevalier. Thirty-five bombing flights – 25 by night, 10 by day – were flown at a cost of two Canberras shot down and three aircrew killed. The only effect of these bombing raids were the hitting of the neutral supertanker *Hercules* on 8 June and the harassment of British ground forces through night raids in the last two weeks of the war.

[1] I would like to acknowledge the excellent research carried out by the team of authors, Rodney A. Burden *et al.*, who wrote *Falklands – The Air War* (Arms & Armour Press, 1986). Because the Argentine Air Force gave me no help when I visited Argentina, most of the factual material in this section comes from the above book, but the interpretations and views expressed are my own.

*3rd Attack Group* (Grupo 3 de Ataque)   Home base: Reconquista. The unit operated Pucará ground-attack aircraft, the only aircraft used in the war which were manufactured in Argentina. Twenty-four aircraft under the command of Major Navarro were deployed to the Falklands, where they flew 186 reconnaissance or ground-attack sorties from Stanley, Goose Green and Pebble Island. A British Scout helicopter shot down during the fighting at Goose Green on 28 May was the only firm success achieved by the unit. Two pilots were killed, one by bombing at Goose Green and one shot down over Goose Green. All twenty-four aircraft were lost, either by bomb or shell damage, SAS raid, shot down or becoming unserviceable and being abandoned at the end of the war. A further Pucará and its pilot were accidently lost on a coastal reconnaissance flight on the mainland; the pilot – Ensign Mario L. Valko – is included in Argentina's official list of war dead.

*4th Fighter Group* (Grupo 4 de Caza)   Home base: Mendoza. 12 to 15 Skyhawk A-4Cs (ex-US Navy aircraft sold to Argentina in 1976) were deployed to San Julián, from where approximately sixty-five predominantly anti-shipping sorties were flown at a cost of seven aircraft shot down by the British defences and two crashed in bad weather; eight pilots were killed and one was taken prisoner by the British. The only successes which may be attributed to the unit were bomb hits on two ships in San Carlos Water on 24 May, but none of the bombs exploded. This was the unit which claimed to have attacked HMS *Invincible* in company with Super Étendards on 30 May.

*5th Fighter Group* (Grupo 5 de Caza)   Home base: Villa Reynolds. Twelve Skyhawk A-4Bs were deployed to Río Gallegos under the group commander, Vicecomodoro Mariel; further aircraft were later deployed to replace losses. More than 100 operational sorties were flown during the war, with considerable success, and the following ships were all hit: *Coventry* (sunk); *Sir Galahad* (burnt out); *Antelope* (sunk after unexploded bomb detonation); *Glasgow, Argonaut, Ardent, Broadsword, Sir Tristram* and Landing Craft Foxtrot 4 (all damaged). Successful bombing of land positions at San Carlos and Ajax Bay also caused damage and casualties to British ground units there. (It should be added that this aggressive unit also attacked

Argentine ships on three occasions: the abandoned *Río Carcaraña* twice and the *Formosa*.) Ten Skyhawks were shot down by the British defences, and nine pilots were killed.

*6th Fighter Group* (Grupo 6 de Caza)   Home base: Tandil. Twelve Daggers (ex-Israeli-built Mirage Vs) were deployed to San Julián under the command of Major Juan Sapolski and twelve more to Río Grande under Major Carlos N. Martínez; the overall deployment was under the control of the unit's commander, Comodoro T. Rodríguez. After early attempts to use the Daggers in the air combat role proved unsuccessful, these aircraft were employed almost exclusively in anti-shipping attacks. Between 150 and 165 operational sorties were flown. Many British warships were attacked, some being damaged by cannon fire or unexploded bombs, but the only bomb which exploded in a ship was the one which hit HMS *Ardent* when that ship was attacked by many aircraft on 21 May. Eleven Daggers were shot down by the British defences, and five pilots were killed; the higher number of pilots surviving than in other units is attributed to their Martin Baker ejection seats, which were more efficient than the seats in other Argentine aircraft.

*8th Fighter Group* (Grupo 8 de Caza)   Home base: Mariano Moreno, Buenos Aires. Approximately 11 Mirage IIIEAs were deployed to Río Gallegos under the group commander Comodoro Carlos Corino. These aircraft proved unsuccessful in early air combat operations, partly because they had no in-flight refuelling equipment, which left them short of flying time over the Falklands. Two aircraft were lost on 1 May, and one pilot was killed. Air combat operations to the Falklands were then suspended. These all-weather fighters, Argentina's only ones, were then redeployed to defend vital mainland targets against British air attack but, when these did not materialize, the Mirages carried out a few more flights to the Falklands in the closing days of the war.

*Helicopters*   Two Chinooks and two Bell 212s were deployed from their home base at Morón, Buenos Aires, to operate in the Falklands. After carrying out many flights, the Chinooks were flown back to the mainland before the end of the war, but the shell-damaged Bells were abandoned at Stanley. There were no personnel casualties.

*Air Transport*   Much valuable air transport work to Stanley was carried out by civil aircraft of the Aerolíneas Argentinas and Austral airlines and by the L A D E semi-military air service. There were no losses or casualties.

*Phoenix Squadron* (Escuadrón Fénix)   Thirty-five modern civil aircraft and their crews were commandeered by the Argentine Air Force during the war to serve in this temporary new unit. Most operations were internal flights, but the squadron carried out some missions in support of offensive operations, such as providing radio relays, navigation assistance on approach flights and decoy operations, though the unit's unarmed aircraft were probably never risked at distances where they would be in danger from British Sea Harriers or ships' missiles.

*Ground Bases in the Falklands*   The Argentine Air Force set up two bases, the Base Aérea Militar Malvinas at Stanley and the Base Aérea Militar Cóndor at Goose Green. Various ground units were dispatched, including an anti-aircraft unit equipped with eight 20-mm Rheinmetall guns. There were fourteen fatal casualties among the ground units – one officer, eight NCOs and five conscripts; seven of these were by bombing at Goose Green on 1 May, two at Stanley on the same day, three in ground fighting at Goose Green on 28 May and two unknown (they were buried at Stanley on 10 and 29 May).

### Naval Air Units

*1st Attack Squadron* (1 Escuadrilla de Ataque)   Home base: Punta Indio. Six Aeromacchi 339As were deployed to the Falklands under the command of Lieutenant-Commander Carlos Molteni and were based at Stanley airfield. Five aircraft were lost through various causes, and two pilots were killed.

*2nd Fighter and Attack Squadron* (2 Escuadrilla de Caza y Ataque) Home base: Bahía Blanca. Commander: Commander Jorge Colombo. Four Super Étendards were deployed to Río Grande from where Exocet attacks were made which resulted in the losses of H M S *Sheffield* and the *Atlantic Conveyor*.

*3rd Fighter and Attack Squadron* (3 Escuadrilla de Caza y Ataque)
Home base: Bahía Blanca. Commander: Lieutenant-Commander
R. A. Castro Fox. The squadron was embarked on the aircraft-carrier
*Veinticinco de Mayo* until early May but carried out no active
operations. Ten Skyhawks A-4Bs were then transferred to Río
Grande and carried out ship attacks, being mainly responsible for
the sinking of HMS *Ardent*. Three Skyhawks were shot down; one
pilot was killed in action and one in a landing accident at Río Grande.

*4th Attack Squadron* (4 Escuadrilla de Ataque)   Home base: Punta
Indio. Four Turbo-Mentor T-34C-1s were deployed to the Falklands under the command of Lieutenant José Pereyra and were
based at Pebble Island. Local reconnaissance flights were carried
out, and there was one brief contact with Sea Harriers on 1 May, but
all four aircraft were put out of action in the SAS raid on the night
of 14 May. The pilots were then used as 'air watchers' on high
ground positions until they were evacuated to Argentina before the
end of the war.

*Anti-Submarine Squadron* (Escuadrilla Antisubmarina)   Home base:
Bahía Blanca. Commander: Lieutenant-Commander Hector Skare.
The unit operated Grumman Tracker S-2Es in various roles, including some valuable reconnaissance flights from the *Veinticinco de Mayo*
which detected the British task force on 1 May. The squadron flew
more than 250 sorties during the war, probably more than any other
Argentine air unit.

*Reconnaissance Squadron* (Escuadrilla de Exploración)   Home base:
Bahía Blanca. Commander: Lieutenant-Commander Julio Pérez
Roca. The unit's four Neptune SP-2Hs carried out various recon-
naissance and anti-submarine operations including the location of
HMS *Sheffield* before that ship was attacked by Super Étendards.
But the unit's aircraft became worn out and were withdrawn from
service before the end of the war.

*1st and 2nd Transport Squadrons* (1 and 2 Escuadrillas de Sostén
Logístico Móvil)   Home base: Ezeiza International Airport, Buenos
Aires. The unit's three F-28 Fellowships and three Electras flew 58

sorties to Stanley, including the last flight of the war on the night of 13 June, as well as many internal flights.

*1st and 2nd Helicopter Squadrons* (1 and 2 Escuadrillas de Helicópteros)   Home base: Bahía Blanca. The Lynx, Alouette and Sea King helicopters of the squadrons carried out many and varied operations during the war. One Alouette was damaged in the fighting at Grytviken, South Georgia, on 3 April, and another was lost when the *General Belgrano* was sunk. A Lynx crashed into the sea while flying from the *Santísima Trinidad* on 2 May. There were no aircrew casualties.

# Acknowledgements

I would like to acknowledge the valuable help given to me by the following members of Argentina's armed forces who all served in the 1982 war and who allowed me to interview them in 1987. The ranks and units shown are those held in 1982. Easily translatable ranks will be shown in English; others will be left in their original form. Conscript soldiers are shown as 'Privates'.

## Army

*Commanders:* Brigadier-General A. Daher, first Land Forces Commander Falklands, then Chief-of-Staff to Brigadier-General Menéndez; Brigadier-General O. L. Jofre, Commander of X Brigade, then Land Forces Commander Falklands, finally Commander 'Puerto Argentino' Army Sector. *3rd Regiment:* Private H. Benítez, Major G. Berazay, Private J. C. Diez, Private A. Fernández, Private L. J. Núñez. *4th Regiment:* Lieutenant-Colonel D. A. Soria. *6th Regiment:* Second Lieutenant A. E. La Madrid. *7th Regiment:* Private A. Craig, Private A. Gómez-Csher, Major A. Pérez Cometto. *12th Regiment:* First Lieutenant I. B. Gorriti, Lieutenant-Colonel I. A. Piaggi, Private M. A. Prado. *25th Regiment:* First Lieutenant C. D. Esteban. *3rd Artillery Regiment:* Major C. A. Bellocchio. *4th Air Mobile Artillery Regiment:* Lieutenant-Colonel C. A. Quevedo. *B Battery, 101st Anti-Aircraft Regiment:* Major J. Monge. *601st Anti-Aircraft Regiment:* Lieutenant-Colonel H. L. Arias.

## Navy

*Commanders and Staffs:* Vice-Admiral J. J. Lombardo, Commander of Naval Operations; Rear-Admiral G. O. Allara, Commander of Task Forces 40 and 79; Commander C. M. Sala, Chief of Submarine Staff. *Alférez*

*Sobral:* Lieutenant S. Bazán. *Almirante Irizar:* Conscript Seaman J. Pereda. *General Belgrano:* Cabo Primero C. Báez, Cabo Principal P. A. Bazán, Captain H. Bonzo, Midshipman G. E. Castillo, Lieutenant J. J. Gómez Meunier, Cabo Primero J. A. Manrique, Suboficial Segundo N. Roldán, Lieutenant-Commander J. F. Schottenheim. *San Luis:* Commander F. M. Azcueta. *Shore Base Staff Stanley:* Cabo Primero M. Escalada, Cabo Principal R. Rodríguez.


## Marines

### 2 April Falklands Landing Force

*Force Commander:* Rear-Admiral C. A. Büsser. *2nd Marine Infantry Battalion:* Lieutenant-Commander H. Santillón, Commander A. Weinstabl. *Amphibious Commando Company:* Lieutenant-Commander G. Sánchez Sábarots. *Amphibious Vehicles Battalion:* Lieutenant M. D. Forbice


### Main Campaign

*5th Marine Infantry Battalion:* Lieutenant-Commander A. Pernias, Cabo Segundo J. C. Sini, Suboficial Segundo M. A. Vaca, Sub-Lieutenant C. D. Vázquez. *Anti-Aircraft Battery:* Lieutenant A. Bafficio, Lieutenant-Commander H. E. Silva. *Amphibious Engineer Company:* Lieutenant-Commander L. A. Menghini.


## Naval Air Command

*Commander Anti-Submarine Task Group* (on mainland): Commander L. C. Vásquez. *2nd Fighter and Attack Squadron:* Sub-Lieutenant A. Mayora. *3rd Fighter and Attack Squadron:* Lieutenant-Commander A. J. Philippi, Lieutenant B. I. Rotolo. *4th Attack Squadron:* Sub-Lieutenant D. G. Manzella. *Anti-Submarine Squadron:* Lieutenant C. E. Cal.


## Merchant Navy

*Bahía Buen Suceso:* Captain O. M. Niella. *Río Carcaraña:* Captain E. A. Dell'Elicine.


## Civil Affairs Team in Stanley

Comodoro C. Bloomer-Reeve (Chief Secretary), Colonel O. R. Chinni

(Treasurer), Colonel M. R. Dorrego (Public Works), Captain B. M. Hussey (Education and Public Health), Comodoro G. Mendiberri (Intelligence).

## Air Force

The Argentine Air Force gave no official help, but Major (in 1982 Captain) Pablo Carballo, who flew wartime missions as a Skyhawk pilot with the 5th Fighter Group, privately gave me an English translation of his book *Dios y los Halcones*, a collection of personal accounts by wartime members of the Air Force. Carballo also gave me unlimited permission to quote from these accounts, a valuable and kindly gesture for which I am most grateful.

## Personal Acknowledgements
### *Argentina*

My interviewing visit to Argentina, a country in which I initially had no relatives or friends and whose language I could not speak, was one of the most difficult tasks of my career; that it was successful is due entirely to the goodwill, co-operation, friendship and hospitality provided by a wide range of helpful people. Virginia Gamba, a historian temporarily resident in London, and Juan E. Fleming, Counsellor in the Argentine Interests Section of the Brazilian Embassy in London, took the time to advise me and help me to obtain a visa and an introduction to Señor Balcarce of the Foreign Ministry in Buenos Aires, which in turn led to official help from the Argentine Army and Navy. The arranging of naval interviews and visits was mostly carried out by Captain Guillermo Montenegro and the army interviews by Brigadier-General Oscar L. Jofre; these two also provided valuable later help by answering many supplementary questions during the writing of the book. The naval interviews were also helped along by Pedro Iturralde (interpreter and companion on the three-day visit to Puerto Belgrano), Captain Eduardo L. Alimonda (commander of the Comandante Espora Naval Air Base) and Otto A. Krapf (adviser to the Naval General Staff).

But this official assistance would probably not have been sufficient to enable me to complete my task properly without the valuable help given to me by private individuals who had no obligation to me in any way, but who gave this help for no other reason but friendship and goodwill. First among these must come the Debenedetti family. Cecilia Debenedetti was a young Argentine woman who happened to be living in my home town when I was contemplating my visit to her country. She gave me much useful advice and arranged with her family to provide me with the enormously helpful use of a room in their flat in central Buenos Aires, together with access to telephones, ferrying by car to distant parts of the city, permission to use their home for a succession of interviews and always a friendly place to relax when 'off duty'. Next to be thanked was a friend of that family, Gladys Halström, who volunteered to be my interpreter and performed this exacting service in about half of all the interviews I carried out during my visit. I shall never forget or be able to thank sufficiently these friendly people. I also wish to thank Cyril and Mary Walmesly for providing valuable contacts and some welcome hospitality, Andrew McLeod for journalistic help and advice, Dr Isidoro Ruiz Moreno for helpful material on Argentine commandos, Guillermo Jasson and Alejandro Stengl for helping to find some ex-conscripts for interview and, finally, Alicia Gorriti, who invited me to her home and persuaded not only a reluctant husband to be interviewed but two other ex-Falkland veterans as well. Unfortunately, Cyril Walmesly died a few weeks after my visit to his home.

## *England*

I also wish to thank the following people who helped me in this country: Michael Gow of Christian Salvesen Plc, Captain D. S. Leggatt RN (a former Naval Attaché in Argentina who gave me some valuable introductions), Brigadier David Chaundler, the Public Relations Departments of the Royal Navy and the Royal Air Force, Anne Bell (my daughter) of the Fleet Air Arm Museum, Yeovilton, Jean Thomas of Boston (for some tricky Spanish translations), Christine Gilmartin, Janet Mountain, Margaret Gardner and Sally-Ann Baxter for typing two drafts of my manuscript, Peter Jay (for help with proofreading) and Neil Kemp of Boston I TeC for his diligent help with much photocopying work. Finally, many thanks to my wife, Mary, for her careful drawing of the preliminary maps and help in compiling the index.

# Bibliography

This bibliography is a limited one because most of my material was drawn from prime sources, but the following books were consulted.

Brown, David, *The Royal Navy and the Falklands War* (London: Leo Cooper, 1987).

Burden, R. A., Draper, M. I., Rough, D. A., Smith, C. R., and Wilton, D. L., *Falklands – The Air War* (London: Arms & Armour Press, 1986).

Carballo, Pablo M. R., *Dios y los Halcones* (Buenos Aires: Editorial Abril, 1983).

Ethell, Jeffrey, and Price, Alfred, *Air War South Atlantic* (London: Sidgwick & Jackson, 1983; published in Argentina as *Guerra aérea sudatlántica*, 1987).

Jofre, Oscar L., and Aguiar, Félix R., *Malvinas – La Defensa de Puerto Argentino* (Buenos Aires: Sudamericana, 1987).

McManners, Hugh, *Falklands Commando* (London: Kimber, 1984; Grafton, 1987).

Middlebrook, Martin, *Operation Corporate* (London: Viking, 1985; revised and reissued in paperback as *Task Force*, Penguin, 1987).

Ruiz Moreno, Isidoro J., *Comandos en acción* (Madrid: Editorial San Martín, 1987).

Turolo, Carlos M., *Malvinas – Testimonio de su Gobernador* (Buenos Aires: Sudamericana, 1983).

# Index